W9-BRO-167

Table of Contents

What's Different About the Moon Sign Book?   5

Weekly Almanac   **7**

   Gardening by the Moon   61

   A Guide to Planting   69

   Companion Planting Guide   73

   Moon Void-of-Course *by Kim Rogers-Gallagher*   75

   Moon Void-of-Course Tables   76

   The Moon's Rhythm   82

      Moon Aspects   83

      Moon Signs   83

      More About Zodiac Signs   90

   Good Timing *by Sharon Leah*   92

      Personalizing Elections   93

      Llewellyn's Astro Almanac   94

      Astro Almanac   95

   Choose the Best Time for Your Activities   107

   How to Use the Moon Tables

      and Lunar Aspectarian   129

      The Five Basic Steps   130

      Using What You've Learned   133

      A Note About Time and Time Zones   134

   January–December Moon Tables, Lunar Aspectarian,

      Favorable & Unfavorable Days   136

   2018 Retrograde Planets   160

   Egg-Setting Dates   161

   Dates to Hunt and Fish   162

   Dates to Destroy Weeds and Pests   163

   Time Zone Map   164

   Time Zone Conversions   165

Weather, Economic & Lunar Forecasts   **166**

Forecasting the Weather *by Kris Brandt Riske*   167

Weather Forecast for 2018 *by Kris Brandt Riske*   171

Economic Forecast for 2018 *by Christeen Skinner*   214

New and Full Moon Forecasts for 2018
  by Sally Cragin   233

2018 Moon Sign Book Articles   **249**

What's the Buzz? Honey and the Use of Backyard
  Apiaries *by Mireille Blacke, MA, RD, CD-N*   250

Man on the Moon: Discovery and Politics
  by Bruce Scofield   262

Simple Meditation for Daily Life
  by Robin Ivy Payton   270

Once in a Blue Moon
  by Charlie Rainbow Wolf   278

The Moon as Autopilot *by Amy Herring*   285

The Nodes of the Moon
  by Dallas Jennifer Cobb   294

2017 © Gorsh25 Image from BigStockPhoto.com

What's Different About the Moon Sign Book?

Readers have asked why *Llewellyn's Moon Sign Book* says that the Moon is in Taurus when some almanacs indicate that the Moon is in the previous sign of Aries on the same date. It's because there are two different zodiac systems in use today: the tropical and the sidereal. *Llewellyn's Moon Sign Book* is based on the tropical zodiac.

The tropical zodiac takes 0 degrees of Aries to be the Spring Equinox in the Northern Hemisphere. This is the time and date when the Sun is directly overhead at noon along the equator, usually about March 20–21. The rest of the signs are positioned at 30-degree intervals from this point.

The sidereal zodiac, which is based on the location of fixed stars, uses the positions of the fixed stars to determine the starting point of 0 degrees of Aries. In the sidereal system, 0 degrees of Aries always begins at the same point. This does create a problem though, because the positions of the fixed stars, as seen from Earth, have changed since the constellations were named. The term "precession of the equinoxes" is used to describe the change.

Precession of the equinoxes describes an astronomical phenomenon brought about by Earth's wobble as it rotates and orbits the Sun. Earth's axis is inclined toward the Sun at an angle of about 23½ degrees, which creates our seasonal weather changes. Although the change is slight, because one complete circle of Earth's axis takes 25,800 years to complete, we can actually see that the positions of the fixed stars seem to shift. The result is that each year, in the tropical system, the Spring Equinox occurs at a slightly different time.

Does Precession Matter?

There is an accumulative difference of about 23 degrees between the Spring Equinox (0 degrees Aries in the tropical zodiac and 0 degrees Aries in the sidereal zodiac) so that 0 degrees Aries at Spring Equinox in the tropical zodiac actually occurs at about 7 degrees Pisces in the sidereal zodiac system. You can readily see that those who use the other almanacs may be planting seeds (in the garden and in their individual lives) based on the belief that it is occurring in a fruitful sign, such as Taurus, when in fact it would be occurring in Gemini, one of the most barren signs of the zodiac. So, if you wish to plant and plan activities by the Moon, it is helpful to follow *Llewellyn's Moon Sign Book*. Before we go on, there are important things to understand about the Moon, her cycles, and their correlation with everyday living. For more information about gardening by the Moon, see page 61.

Weekly Almanac

Your Guide to
Lunar Gardening
& Good Timing for Activities

♑ January

December 31–January 6

The worst sin towards our fellow creatures is not to hate them, but to be indifferent to them: that's the essence of inhumanity.   ∼GEORGE BERNARD SHAW

Date	Qtr.	Sign	Activity
Jan 1, 9:24 pm–Jan 3, 2:23 am	3rd	Cancer	Plant biennials, perennials, bulbs and roots. Prune. Irrigate. Fertilize (organic).
Jan 3, 2:23 am–Jan 5, 3:12 am	3rd	Leo	Cultivate. Destroy weeds and pests. Harvest fruits and root crops for food. Trim to retard growth.
Jan 5, 3:12 am–Jan 7, 7:15 am	3rd	Virgo	Cultivate, especially medicinal plants. Destroy weeds and pests. Trim to retard growth.

Start your year with a clear resolution to become more conscious, be more present, and yet remain at peace with yourself and the world.

_____

_____

_____

_____

○
January 1
9:24 pm EST

JANUARY

S	M	T	W	T	F	S
	1	2	3	4	5	6
7	8	9	10	11	12	13
14	15	16	17	18	19	20
21	22	23	24	25	26	27
28	29	30	31			

2017 © Rabbitti Image from BigStockPhoto.com

January 7–13

Not everything everywhere is for us.   ∿ Stanisław Lem

Date	Qtr.	Sign	Activity
Jan 5, 3:12 am– Jan 7, 7:15 am	3rd	Virgo	Cultivate, especially medicinal plants. Destroy weeds and pests. Trim to retard growth.
Jan 9, 3:05 pm– Jan 12, 2:04 am	4th	Scorpio	Plant biennials, perennials, bulbs and roots. Prune. Irrigate. Fertilize (organic).
Jan 12, 2:04 am– Jan 14, 2:42 pm	4th	Sagittarius	Cultivate. Destroy weeds and pests. Harvest fruits and root crops for food. Trim to retard growth.

Make your own room sprays with essential oils. In a 2-ounce glass bottle, combine distilled water and the essential oils of your choice. Customize blends, including 2 or 3 compatible aromas. Add a few drops of magnesium oil for its healing properties. For a refreshing, relaxing blend, try 15 drops of bergamot with 7 or 8 drops of tangerine or orange essential oil. Leave a bottle in the guest bedroom or bath for friends to enjoy

January 8
5:25 pm EST

JANUARY

S	M	T	W	T	F	S
	1	2	3	4	5	6
7	8	9	10	11	12	13
14	15	16	17	18	19	20
21	22	23	24	25	26	27
28	29	30	31			

2017 © NikiLitov Image from BigStockPhoto.com

January 14–20

The fact that some geniuses were laughed at does not imply that all who are laughed at are geniuses.   ~CARL SAGAN

Date	Qtr.	Sign	Activity
Jan 12, 2:04 am– Jan 14, 2:42 pm	4th	Sagittarius	Cultivate. Destroy weeds and pests. Harvest fruits and root crops for food. Trim to retard growth.
Jan 14, 2:42 pm– Jan 16, 9:17 pm	4th	Capricorn	Plant potatoes and tubers. Trim to retard growth.
Jan 16, 9:17 pm– Jan 17, 3:32 am	1st	Capricorn	Graft or bud plants. Trim to increase growth.
Jan 19, 3:26 pm– Jan 22, 1:27 am	1st	Pisces	Plant grains, leafy annuals. Fertilize (chemical). Graft or bud plants. Irrigate. Trim to increase growth.

Whether you are male or female, commit to reading at least one book this year about a famous individual who is the same gender as you. Let yourself be inspired by how this individual thought, spoke, and acted.

_____

_____

_____

_____

January 16
9:17 pm EST

JANUARY

S	M	T	W	T	F	S
	1	2	3	4	5	6
7	8	9	10	11	12	13
14	15	16	17	18	19	20
21	22	23	24	25	26	27
28	29	30	31			

2017 © marychka Image from BigStockPhoto.com

January 21–27

He who fights with monsters might take care lest he thereby become a monster. And if you gaze for long into an abyss, the abyss gazes also into you.   ~FRIEDRICH NIETZSCHE

Date	Qtr.	Sign	Activity
Jan 19, 3:26 pm– Jan 22, 1:27 am	1st	Pisces	Plant grains, leafy annuals. Fertilize (chemical). Graft or bud plants. Irrigate. Trim to increase growth.
Jan 24, 8:39 am– Jan 24, 5:20 pm	1st	Taurus	Plant annuals for hardiness. Trim to increase growth.
Jan 24, 5:20 pm– Jan 26, 12:40 pm	2nd	Taurus	Plant annuals for hardiness. Trim to increase growth.

From scratch, make a cake, some cookies, or some sort of bread while paying careful attention to what each ingredient does. Make a commitment to understand food in a whole new way this year.

2017 © eskay lim Image from BigStockPhoto.com

January 24
5:20 pm EST

JANUARY

S	M	T	W	T	F	S
	1	2	3	4	5	6
7	8	9	10	11	12	13
14	15	16	17	18	19	20
21	22	23	24	25	26	27
28	29	30	31			

~~~ # February

January 28–February 3

Instruction does much, but encouragement everything.

~JOHANN WOLFGANG VON GOETHE

Date	Qtr.	Sign	Activity
Jan 28, 1:57 pm– Jan 30, 1:53 pm	2nd	Cancer	Plant grains, leafy annuals. Fertilize (chemical). Graft or bud plants. Irrigate. Trim to increase growth.
Jan 31, 8:27 am– Feb 1, 2:13 pm	3rd	Leo	Cultivate. Destroy weeds and pests. Harvest fruits and root crops for food. Trim to retard growth.
Feb 1, 2:13 pm– Feb 3, 4:47 pm	3rd	Virgo	Cultivate, especially medicinal plants. Destroy weeds and pests. Trim to retard growth.

Get a spiral-bound notebook and label it "Clouds." Every day or two go outside, look up at the sky, and notice the clouds. Describe their shape, texture, size, color, direction of movement, and anything else that catches your attention. Draw the clouds that strike you as interesting or take photos and print them and then tape the photos into your notebook. Notice the weather that follows certain kinds of clouds, and learn to be your own weatherman.

○
January 31
8:27 am EST

FEBRUARY

S	M	T	W	T	F	S
				1	2	3
4	5	6	7	8	9	10
11	12	13	14	15	16	17
18	19	20	21	22	23	24
25	26	27	28			

2017 © Felmeeeh Image from BigStockPhoto.com

February 4–February 10 〰️

Trying to define yourself is like trying to bite your own teeth.

~ALAN WATTS

Date	Qtr.	Sign	Activity
Feb 5, 10:56 pm–Feb 7, 10:54 am	3rd	Scorpio	Plant biennials, perennials, bulbs and roots. Prune. Irrigate. Fertilize (organic).
Feb 7, 10:54 am–Feb 8, 8:53 am	4th	Scorpio	Plant biennials, perennials, bulbs and roots. Prune. Irrigate. Fertilize (organic).
Feb 8, 8:53 am–Feb 10, 9:21 pm	4th	Sagittarius	Cultivate. Destroy weeds and pests. Harvest fruits and root crops for food. Trim to retard growth.
Feb 10, 9:21 pm–Feb 13, 10:11 am	4th	Capricorn	Plant potatoes and tubers. Trim to retard growth.

Do you have an aversion to beets? If so, consider that beets are high in vitamin C, fiber, folate, and potassium. Eaten in moderation (a few times a week), beets can decrease blood pressure, boost stamina, fight inflammation, and increase immunity. In addition, beet greens contain more iron than spinach and help to boost the immune system and fight Alzheimer's and osteoporosis!

February 7
10:54 am EST

FEBRUARY

S	M	T	W	T	F	S
				1	2	3
4	5	6	7	8	9	10
11	12	13	14	15	16	17
18	19	20	21	22	23	24
25	26	27	28			

2017 © Svehlik Image from BigStockPhoto.com

∼∼∼ February 11–17

A propensity to hope and joy is real riches: One to fear and sorrow, real poverty.   ∼·DAVID HUME

Date	Qtr.	Sign	Activity
Feb 10, 9:21 pm– Feb 13, 10:11 am	4th	Capricorn	Plant potatoes and tubers. Trim to retard growth.
Feb 13, 10:11 am– Feb 15, 4:05 pm	4th	Aquarius	Cultivate. Destroy weeds and pests. Harvest fruits and root crops for food. Trim to retard growth.
Feb 15, 9:42 pm– Feb 18, 7:05 am	1st	Pisces	Plant grains, leafy annuals. Fertilize (chemical). Graft or bud plants. Irrigate. Trim to increase growth.

Catnip may drive many cats bonkers, but this herb has a practical household use: the active ingredient in catnip (nepetalactone) is a natural, nontoxic repellent for cockroaches. Catnip and nepetalactone are nontoxic to humans and pets. Consider placing small catnip sachets in locations you suspect roaches to be. Make a catnip tea by simmering one teaspoon of catnip leaves in 2 cups of hot water to distill nepetalactone, and spray it where roaches are likely to hide (around baseboards or behind counters). Try another remedy if your cats are overstimulated.

February 15
4:05 pm EST

FEBRUARY

S	M	T	W	T	F	S
				1	2	3
4	5	6	7	8	9	10
11	12	13	14	15	16	17
18	19	20	21	22	23	24
25	26	27	28			

2017 © sorsillo Image from BigStockPhoto.com

February 18–24 ～～～

A great thirst is a great joy when quenched in time.

~Edward Abbey

Date	Qtr.	Sign	Activity
Feb 15, 9:42 pm– Feb 18, 7:05 am	1st	Pisces	Plant grains, leafy annuals. Fertilize (chemical). Graft or bud plants. Irrigate. Trim to increase growth.
Feb 20, 2:12 pm– Feb 22, 7:07 pm	1st	Taurus	Plant annuals for hardiness. Trim to increase growth.
Feb 24, 10:06 pm– Feb 26, 11:42 pm	2nd	Cancer	Plant grains, leafy annuals. Fertilize (chemical). Graft or bud plants. Irrigate. Trim to increase growth.

A lmonds are not only useful for eating. Consider almond products for cleaning and emollient properties. Cleansers derived from almonds will remove excess oil and dirt from your skin, while a handful of almond meal produces an effective facial scrub. Almond butter and oil will moisturize and soften skin: rub almond oil or butter directly into rough areas, such as hands and heels of feet.

2017 © jarafoti Image from BigStockPhoto.com

February 23
3:09 am EST

February

S	M	T	W	T	F	S
				1	2	3
4	5	6	7	8	9	10
11	12	13	14	15	16	17
18	19	20	21	22	23	24
25	26	27	28			

♓ March
February 25–March 3

The only reward of virtue is virtue; the only way to have a friend is to be one.   ～RALPH WALDO EMERSON

Date	Qtr.	Sign	Activity
Feb 24, 10:06 pm– Feb 26, 11:42 pm	2nd	Cancer	Plant grains, leafy annuals. Fertilize (chemical). Graft or bud plants. Irrigate. Trim to increase growth.
Mar 1, 7:51 pm– Mar 3, 3:20 am	3rd	Virgo	Cultivate, especially medicinal plants. Destroy weeds and pests. Trim to retard growth.

Eggshells are extremely rich in calcium, which is a benefit to the human body, but can also be reused in your garden to help plants build cell walls and membranes. Collect your household's used and empty eggshells, grind them into powder, combine this powder with the soil, and provide your flowers and plants with some additional fuel for growth.

○
March 1
7:51 pm EST

MARCH

S	M	T	W	T	F	S
				1	2	3
4	5	6	7	8	9	10
11	12	13	14	15	16	17
18	19	20	21	22	23	24
25	26	27	28	29	30	31

2017 © ThamKC Image from BigStockPhoto.com

March 4–10

I am certainly of opinion that genius can be acquired, or,
in the alternative, that it is an almost universal possession.

~ALEISTER CROWLEY

Date	Qtr.	Sign	Activity
Mar 5, 8:23 am– Mar 7, 5:03 pm	3rd	Scorpio	Plant biennials, perennials, bulbs and roots. Prune. Irrigate. Fertilize (organic).
Mar 7, 5:03 pm– Mar 9, 6:20 am	3rd	Sagittarius	Cultivate. Destroy weeds and pests. Harvest fruits and root crops for food. Trim to retard growth.
Mar 9, 6:20 am– Mar 10, 4:52 am	4th	Sagittarius	Cultivate. Destroy weeds and pests. Harvest fruits and root crops for food. Trim to retard growth.
Mar 10, 4:52 am– Mar 12, 6:44 pm	4th	Capricorn	Plant potatoes and tubers. Trim to retard growth.

Deficiencies of iron (leading to anemia) and calcium (vitamin D deficiency and osteoporosis) may be exacerbated by eating the two minerals together in food or supplement forms. Calcium inhibits absorption of iron; wait at least two hours between taking foods or supplements containing these minerals. In addition, iron absorption is enhanced by vitamin C, so eating foods containing iron and vitamin C at the same time is recommended.

2017 © Felmeeeh Image from BigStockPhoto.com

March 9
6:20 am EST

MARCH

S	M	T	W	T	F	S
				1	2	3
4	5	6	7	8	9	10
11	12	13	14	15	16	17
18	19	20	21	22	23	24
25	26	27	28	29	30	31

March 11–17

All Nature wears one universal grin.   ~HENRY FIELDING

Date	Qtr.	Sign	Activity
Mar 10, 4:52 am– Mar 12, 6:44 pm	4th	Capricorn	Plant potatoes and tubers. Trim to retard growth.
Mar 12, 6:44 pm– Mar 15, 6:12 am	4th	Aquarius	Cultivate. Destroy weeds and pests. Harvest fruits and root crops for food. Trim to retard growth.
Mar 15, 6:12 am– Mar 17, 9:12 am	4th	Pisces	Plant biennials, perennials, bulbs and roots. Prune. Irrigate. Fertilize (organic).
Mar 17, 9:12 am– Mar 17, 2:57 pm	1st	Pisces	Plant grains, leafy annuals. Fertilize (chemical). Graft or bud plants. Irrigate. Trim to increase growth.

Individuals allergic to latex may also show hypersensitivity to certain plant-derived foods, most often occurring with banana, avocado, kiwi, and chestnut. Allergenic cross-reactivity in raw fruits, vegetables, and some tree nuts can cause symptoms including life-threatening anaphylaxis. See *latexallergyresources.org /cross-reactive-food* for more information.

_____

_____

_____

_____

Daylight Saving Time begins March 11, 2:00 am

March 17, 9:12 am EDT

MARCH

S	M	T	W	T	F	S
				1	2	3
4	5	6	7	8	9	10
11	12	13	14	15	16	17
18	19	20	21	22	23	24
25	26	27	28	29	30	31

2017 © Yingko Image from BigStockPhoto.com

March 18–24

Mountains are earth's undecaying monuments.

~Nathaniel Hawthorne

Date	Qtr.	Sign	Activity
Mar 19, 9:07 pm– Mar 22, 1:30 am	1st	Taurus	Plant annuals for hardiness. Trim to increase growth.
Mar 24, 4:53 am– Mar 24, 11:35 am	1st	Cancer	Plant grains, leafy annuals. Fertilize (chemical). Graft or bud plants. Irrigate. Trim to increase growth.
Mar 24, 11:35 am– Mar 26, 7:45 am	2nd	Cancer	Plant grains, leafy annuals. Fertilize (chemical). Graft or bud plants. Irrigate. Trim to increase growth.

When planning your next menu, consider adding one or two meals that don't contain meat. Go meatless and eat dried beans, peas, lentils, and tofu frequently. Compared to animal-based proteins, you're getting less saturated fat, more fiber, more antioxidants, and more phytonutrients. Going meatless at least once a week is a great way to "go lean with protein"—it's also a very economical way to stretch your protein food dollar.

March 24
11:35 am EDT

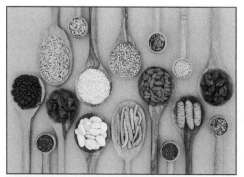

2017 © marilyna Image from BigStockPhoto.com

March

S	M	T	W	T	F	S
				1	2	3
4	5	6	7	8	9	10
11	12	13	14	15	16	17
18	19	20	21	22	23	24
25	26	27	28	29	30	31

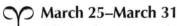 **March 25–March 31**

Tell me, what is it you plan to do with your one wild and precious life?

~MARY OLIVER

Date	Qtr.	Sign	Activity
Mar 24, 11:35 am– Mar 26, 7:45 am	2nd	Cancer	Plant grains, leafy annuals. Fertilize (chemical). Graft or bud plants. Irrigate. Trim to increase growth.
Mar 30, 1:52 pm– Mar 31, 8:37 am	2nd	Libra	Plant annuals for fragrance and beauty. Trim to increase growth.

During the height of the outdoor season, keep some of your flowering perennials in pots of various sizes rather than planting them in the ground. When it's time for an outdoor meal or garden party, collect the various potted flowers and arrange them to liven up your gathering space. As the season begins to shift, plant your flowers in the ground for rebloom next year. Continue this tradition to cultivate a garden full of flowers.

_____

_____

_____

_____

O
March 31
8:37 am EDT

MARCH

S	M	T	W	T	F	S
				1	2	3
4	5	6	7	8	9	10
11	12	13	14	15	16	17
18	19	20	21	22	23	24
25	26	27	28	29	30	31

2017 © Whiteaster Image from BigStockPhoto.com

April ♈

April 1–7

Advice most needed is the least heeded.

~JAPANESE PROVERB

Date	Qtr.	Sign	Activity
Apr 1, 6:57 pm– Apr 4, 2:55 am	3rd	Scorpio	Plant biennials, perennials, bulbs and roots. Prune. Irrigate. Fertilize (organic).
Apr 4, 2:55 am– Apr 6, 2:01 pm	3rd	Sagittarius	Cultivate. Destroy weeds and pests. Harvest fruits and root crops for food. Trim to retard growth.
Apr 6, 2:01 pm– Apr 8, 3:18 am	3rd	Capricorn	Plant potatoes and tubers. Trim to retard growth.

Pick a weekend to clean out your basement, garage, or attic. Make a list of what you have and what you're giving away. Tell people the date and invite them to come over and get what they'd like from the list. Make a cake or some cookies or a healthy smoothie and reward people for coming to get your old stuff. Donate what's left to charities or other organizations.

2017 © monkeybusinessimages Image from BigStockPhoto.com

APRIL

S	M	T	W	T	F	S
						1
2	3	4	5	6	7	8
9	10	11	12	13	14	15
16	17	18	19	20	21	22
23	24	25	26	27	28	29
30						

April 8–14

We are all in the gutter, but some of us are looking at the stars.   ~OSCAR WILDE

Date	Qtr.	Sign	Activity
Apr 6, 2:01 pm– Apr 8, 3:18 am	3rd	Capricorn	Plant potatoes and tubers. Trim to retard growth.
Apr 8, 3:18 am– Apr 9, 2:50 am	4th	Capricorn	Plant potatoes and tubers. Trim to retard growth.
Apr 9, 2:50 am– Apr 11, 2:40 pm	4th	Aquarius	Cultivate. Destroy weeds and pests. Harvest fruits and root crops for food. Trim to retard growth.
Apr 11, 2:40 pm– Apr 13, 11:25 pm	4th	Pisces	Plant biennials, perennials, bulbs and roots. Prune. Irrigate. Fertilize (organic).
Apr 13, 11:25 pm– Apr 15, 9:57 pm	4th	Aries	Cultivate. Destroy weeds and pests. Harvest fruits and root crops for food. Trim to retard growth.

If you do exercise regularly, consider changing your regular routines for some dance routines. Join a dance class for a year, choreograph some new moves in your life, and make a dance costume that brings a little zip into your self-image.

April 8
3:18 am EDT

APRIL

S	M	T	W	T	F	S
1	2	3	4	5	6	7
8	9	10	11	12	13	14
15	16	17	18	19	20	21
22	23	24	25	26	27	28
29	30					

2017 © luckybusiness Image from BigStockPhoto.com

April 15–21 ♈

A woodland in full color is awesome as a forest fire, in
magnitude at least, but a single tree is like a dancing tongue
of flame to warm the heart. ～HAL BORLAND

Date	Qtr.	Sign	Activity
Apr 13, 11:25 pm– Apr 15, 9:57 pm	4th	Aries	Cultivate. Destroy weeds and pests. Harvest fruits and root crops for food. Trim to retard growth.
Apr 16, 4:51 am– Apr 18, 8:02 am	1st	Taurus	Plant annuals for hardiness. Trim to increase growth.
Apr 20, 10:26 am– Apr 22, 1:09 pm	1st	Cancer	Plant grains, leafy annuals. Fertilize (chemical). Graft or bud plants. Irrigate. Trim to increase growth.

If you grow a garden and it produces much more than you can eat, consider donating some of your extra food to a food bank. Even small, rural towns have food collection groups that work to make sure those who need food get it. You will feel good about having fed people, and those who receive the food will be grateful…all of which makes a stronger community.

April 15
9:57 pm EDT

APRIL

S	M	T	W	T	F	S
1	2	3	4	5	6	7
8	9	10	11	12	13	14
15	16	17	18	19	20	21
22	23	24	25	26	27	28
29	30					

2017 © RB design Image from BigStockPhoto.com

April 22–28

The sun, with all those planets revolving around it and dependent on it, can still ripen a bunch of grapes as if it had nothing else in the universe to do.   ~GALILEO GALILEI

Date	Qtr.	Sign	Activity
Apr 20, 10:26 am– Apr 22, 1:09 pm	1st	Cancer	Plant grains, leafy annuals. Fertilize (chemical). Graft or bud plants. Irrigate. Trim to increase growth.
Apr 26, 9:13 pm– Apr 29, 3:11 am	2nd	Libra	Plant annuals for fragrance and beauty. Trim to increase growth.

You can make your own "aqua globe" type watering system with empty bottles. Just rinse out your used wine, beer, or (glass) pop bottles, fill them with water, and then invert them and quickly shove the neck of the bottle deep into the soil. The water will slowly seep down to the plant's root system, where it's needed most.

_____

_____

_____

_____

April 22
5:46 pm EDT

APRIL

S	M	T	W	T	F	S
1	2	3	4	5	6	7
8	9	10	11	12	13	14
15	16	17	18	19	20	21
22	23	24	25	26	27	28
29	30					

2017 © Room76Photography Image from BigStockPhoto.com

May ♉

April 29–May 5

Hitch your wagon to a star.   ∼Ralph Waldo Emerson

Date	Qtr.	Sign	Activity
Apr 26, 9:13 pm– Apr 29, 3:11 am	2nd	Libra	Plant annuals for fragrance and beauty. Trim to increase growth.
Apr 29, 3:11 am– Apr 29, 8:58 pm	2nd	Scorpio	Plant grains, leafy annuals. Fertilize (chemical). Graft or bud plants. Irrigate. Trim to increase growth.
Apr 29, 8:58 pm– May 1, 11:20 am	3rd	Scorpio	Plant biennials, perennials, bulbs and roots. Prune. Irrigate. Fertilize (organic).
May 1, 11:20 am– May 3, 10:06 pm	3rd	Sagittarius	Cultivate. Destroy weeds and pests. Harvest fruits and root crops for food. Trim to retard growth.
May 3, 10:06 pm– May 6, 10:48 am	3rd	Capricorn	Plant potatoes and tubers. Trim to retard growth.

Don't throw away your large plastic pop bottles. Instead, rinse them out, cut off the tops, remove the labels, and place the inverted bottle over tender seedlings. Now you have instant mini greenhouses to help with the hardening-off process, or to protect young plants from late frosts.

○
*April 29
8:58 pm EDT*

May

S	M	T	W	T	F	S
		1	2	3	4	5
6	7	8	9	10	11	12
13	14	15	16	17	18	19
20	21	22	23	24	25	26
27	28	29	30	31		

2017 © Mieszko9 Image from BigStockPhoto.com

May 6–12

When I play with my cat, who knows whether I do not make her more sport than she makes me?

~MICHEL DE MONTAIGNE

Date	Qtr.	Sign	Activity
May 3, 10:06 pm– May 6, 10:48 am	3rd	Capricorn	Plant potatoes and tubers. Trim to retard growth.
May 6, 10:48 am– May 7, 10:09 pm	3rd	Aquarius	Cultivate. Destroy weeds and pests. Harvest fruits and root crops for food. Trim to retard growth.
May 7, 10:09 pm– May 8, 11:11 pm	4th	Aquarius	Cultivate. Destroy weeds and pests. Harvest fruits and root crops for food. Trim to retard growth.
May 8, 11:11 pm– May 11, 8:40 am	4th	Pisces	Plant biennials, perennials, bulbs and roots. Prune. Irrigate. Fertilize (organic).
May 11, 8:40 am– May 13, 2:15 pm	4th	Aries	Cultivate. Destroy weeds and pests. Harvest fruits and root crops for food. Trim to retard growth.

Give your spouse or best friend something different for their birthday this year—a really good astrological reading and chart from an excellent astrologer. Get one done for yourself, then compare the two, discussing similarities and differences while celebrating the uniqueness of each of you.

_____

_____

_____

May 7
10:09 pm EDT

MAY

S	M	T	W	T	F	S
		1	2	3	4	5
6	7	8	9	10	11	12
13	14	15	16	17	18	19
20	21	22	23	24	25	26
27	28	29	30	31		

2017 © Amaviael Image from BigStockPhoto.com

May 13–19

He is a fool who leaves things close at hand to follow what is out of reach.

~Plutarch

Date	Qtr.	Sign	Activity
May 11, 8:40 am– May 13, 2:15 pm	4th	Aries	Cultivate. Destroy weeds and pests. Harvest fruits and root crops for food. Trim to retard growth.
May 13, 2:15 pm– May 15, 7:48 am	4th	Taurus	Plant potatoes and tubers. Trim to retard growth.
May 15, 7:48 am– May 15, 4:43 pm	1st	Taurus	Plant annuals for hardiness. Trim to increase growth.
May 17, 5:47 pm– May 19, 7:11 pm	1st	Cancer	Plant grains, leafy annuals. Fertilize (chemical). Graft or bud plants. Irrigate. Trim to increase growth.

Don't throw away those outdated seeds! They may still be viable. Of course, you don't want to go to the trouble of planting them if they're not going to do anything. An easy way to test them is to put just a few of them between two moist paper towels or damp coffee filters, and place this in a warm spot. If those seeds show signs of sprouting, you should be good to plant!

May 15
7:48 pm EDT

May

S	M	T	W	T	F	S
		1	2	3	4	5
6	7	8	9	10	11	12
13	14	15	16	17	18	19
20	21	22	23	24	25	26
27	28	29	30	31		

2017 © MonaMakela Image from BigStockPhoto.com

May 20–26

Everyone is more or less mad on one point.

~RUDYARD KIPLING

Date	Qtr.	Sign	Activity
May 24, 2:52 am– May 26, 9:39 am	2nd	Libra	Plant annuals for fragrance and beauty. Trim to increase growth.
May 26, 9:39 am– May 28, 6:29 pm	2nd	Scorpio	Plant grains, leafy annuals. Fertilize (chemical). Graft or bud plants. Irrigate. Trim to increase growth.

If you love to garden but have difficulty bending over to weed and pick, consider creating a straw bale garden. Directions and starter cultures can be found and ordered on the Internet, and you can usually find straw bales from local farmers or the hardware store. Arrange the bales the way you want your garden, add the starter, and when the bales are ready—plant! When it's time to weed, pull up a chair and go for it.

_____

_____

_____

May 21
11:49 pm EDT

MAY

S	M	T	W	T	F	S
		1	2	3	4	5
6	7	8	9	10	11	12
13	14	15	16	17	18	19
20	21	22	23	24	25	26
27	28	29	30	31		

2017 © Alison Hancock Image from BigStockPhoto.com

June ♊

May 27–June 2

Life itself is a quotation.   ~JORGE LUIS BORGES

Date	Qtr.	Sign	Activity
May 26, 9:39 am–May 28, 6:29 pm	2nd	Scorpio	Plant grains, leafy annuals. Fertilize (chemical). Graft or bud plants. Irrigate. Trim to increase growth.
May 29, 10:20 am–May 31, 5:27 am	3rd	Sagittarius	Cultivate. Destroy weeds and pests. Harvest fruits and root crops for food. Trim to retard growth.
May 31, 5:27 am–Jun 2, 6:06 pm	3rd	Capricorn	Plant potatoes and tubers. Trim to retard growth.
Jun 2, 6:06 pm–Jun 5, 6:53 am	3rd	Aquarius	Cultivate. Destroy weeds and pests. Harvest fruits and root crops for food. Trim to retard growth.

Get several 3" × 5" index cards and write the following on each one: "I am paying attention to what I do with my attention." Post one in your kitchen, one on your bathroom mirror, one in your bedroom, and one in your car, and over the months become aware of what you are doing with your consciousness.

○
May 29
10:20 am EDT

JUNE

S	M	T	W	T	F	S
					1	2
3	4	5	6	7	8	9
10	11	12	13	14	15	16
17	18	19	20	21	22	23
24	25	26	27	28	29	30

2017 © silver-john Image from BigStockPhoto.com

June 3–June 9

I know faces, because I look through the fabric my own eye
weaves, and behold the reality beneath.   ∼KHALIL GIBRAN

Date	Qtr.	Sign	Activity
Jun 2, 6:06 pm– Jun 5, 6:53 am	3rd	Aquarius	Cultivate. Destroy weeds and pests. Harvest fruits and root crops for food. Trim to retard growth.
Jun 5, 6:53 am– Jun 6, 2:32 pm	3rd	Pisces	Plant biennials, perennials, bulbs and roots. Prune. Irrigate. Fertilize (organic).
Jun 6, 2:32 pm– Jun 7, 5:26 pm	4th	Pisces	Plant biennials, perennials, bulbs and roots. Prune. Irrigate. Fertilize (organic).
Jun 7, 5:26 pm– Jun 10, 12:04 am	4th	Aries	Cultivate. Destroy weeds and pests. Harvest fruits and root crops for food. Trim to retard growth.

You can easily mark out your garden using the handle of one of your gardening implements, such as a hoe or a spade, for example. Put it on the ground next to a yard stick, and with a permanent marker, draw the measurements onto the handle. Presto! You've got a ready-made measuring tool, right in the palm of your hands when you're gardening!

◑

June 6
2:32 am EDT

JUNE

S	M	T	W	T	F	S
					1	2
3	4	5	6	7	8	9
10	11	12	13	14	15	16
17	18	19	20	21	22	23
24	25	26	27	28	29	30

2017 © Serhii Fedoruk Image from BigStockPhoto.com

June 10–16

If you aren't in the moment, you are either looking forward to
uncertainty, or back to pain and regret.   ~JIM CARREY

Date	Qtr.	Sign	Activity
Jun 7, 5:26 pm– Jun 10, 12:04 am	4th	Aries	Cultivate. Destroy weeds and pests. Harvest fruits and root crops for food. Trim to retard growth.
Jun 10, 12:04 am– Jun 12, 2:53 am	4th	Taurus	Plant potatoes and tubers. Trim to retard growth.
Jun 12, 2:53 am– Jun 13, 3:43 pm	4th	Gemini	Cultivate. Destroy weeds and pests. Harvest fruits and root crops for food. Trim to retard growth.
Jun 14, 3:20 am– Jun 16, 3:21 am	1st	Cancer	Plant grains, leafy annuals. Fertilize (chemical). Graft or bud plants. Irrigate. Trim to increase growth.

Create a small, circular flower garden that will have four quadrants. Plant pink blooms in the east quadrant, red blooms in the south, purple in the west, and white blooms in the north. In the center, put a tall, spiky plant surrounded by herbs. The tall spikes represent the high points of life, and the herbs represent the spice of life. Consider it to be a wisdom garden that shows the deepening passions that move us from birth (the pink) through death (the white).

June 13
3:43 pm EDT

JUNE

S	M	T	W	T	F	S
					1	2
3	4	5	6	7	8	9
10	11	12	13	14	15	16
17	18	19	20	21	22	23
24	25	26	27	28	29	30

2017 © alexraths Image from BigStockPhoto.com

June 17–23

I don't want life to imitate art. I want life to be art.

~CARRIE FISHER

Date	Qtr.	Sign	Activity
Jun 20, 8:29 am– Jun 22, 3:11 pm	2nd	Libra	Plant annuals for fragrance and beauty. Trim to increase growth.
Jun 22, 3:11 pm– Jun 25, 12:29 am	2nd	Scorpio	Plant grains, leafy annuals. Fertilize (chemical). Graft or bud plants. Irrigate. Trim to increase growth.

Stock a heart-healthy kitchen with the following cardioprotective foods: Whole grains like oatmeal and barley, sources of vitamins, fiber, and antioxidants, to strengthen your heart and blood vessels. Walnuts, for alpha-linolenic acid, a heart-healthy omega-3 fatty acid. Extra-virgin olive oil lowers LDL cholesterol. Flavonoid-rich fruits (figs, pomegranates, kiwi) contains fiber and vitamins and lowers your risk for heart attacks. Twice a week, eat: legumes (chick peas, lentils) for cardioprotective fiber, vitamin B6, and magnesium; oily fish (salmon, tuna, sardines, mackerel) containing omega-3 fatty acids for increased cardiovascular benefits.

June 20
6:51 am EDT

JUNE

S	M	T	W	T	F	S
					1	2
3	4	5	6	7	8	9
10	11	12	13	14	15	16
17	18	19	20	21	22	23
24	25	26	27	28	29	30

2017 © myviewpoint Image from BigStockPhoto.com

June 24–30

We have too many high sounding words, and too few actions
that correspond with them. ~ABIGAIL ADAMS

Date	Qtr.	Sign	Activity
Jun 22, 3:11 pm– Jun 25, 12:29 am	2nd	Scorpio	Plant grains, leafy annuals. Fertilize (chemical). Graft or bud plants. Irrigate. Trim to increase growth.
Jun 27, 11:52 am– Jun 28, 12:53 am	2nd	Capricorn	Graft or bud plants. Trim to increase growth.
Jun 28, 12:53 am– Jun 30, 12:37 am	3rd	Capricorn	Plant potatoes and tubers. Trim to retard growth.
Jun 30, 12:37 am– Jul 2, 1:31 pm	3rd	Aquarius	Cultivate. Destroy weeds and pests. Harvest fruits and root crops for food. Trim to retard growth.

Put strings of tiny, white Christmas lights around the windows of your living room in June, and put them on a timer so they come on and go off every night. It adds a touch of fairy magic to midsummer nights!

○
June 28
12:53 am EDT

JUNE

S	M	T	W	T	F	S
					1	2
3	4	5	6	7	8	9
10	11	12	13	14	15	16
17	18	19	20	21	22	23
24	25	26	27	28	29	30

2017 © ronstik Image from BigStockPhoto.com

♋ July

July 1–July 7

The big lesson in life, baby, is never be scared of
anyone or anything.
                                    ~Frank Sinatra

Date	Qtr.	Sign	Activity
Jun 30, 12:37 am– Jul 2, 1:31 pm	3rd	Aquarius	Cultivate. Destroy weeds and pests. Harvest fruits and root crops for food. Trim to retard growth.
Jul 2, 1:31 pm– Jul 5, 12:50 am	3rd	Pisces	Plant biennials, perennials, bulbs and roots. Prune. Irrigate. Fertilize (organic).
Jul 5, 12:50 am– Jul 6, 3:51 am	3rd	Aries	Cultivate. Destroy weeds and pests. Harvest fruits and root crops for food. Trim to retard growth.
Jul 6, 3:51 am– Jul 7, 8:51 am	4th	Aries	Cultivate. Destroy weeds and pests. Harvest fruits and root crops for food. Trim to retard growth.
Jul 7, 8:51 am– Jul 9, 12:58 pm	4th	Taurus	Plant potatoes and tubers. Trim to retard growth.

Do you have trouble reading your rain gauge? Put a drop or three of bright food coloring in the bottom of it. The next time it rains, the colorant will mix with the water that your gauge collects, and you'll be able to read it against the measurements much easier.

◐
July 6
3:51 am EDT

July

S	M	T	W	T	F	S
1	2	3	4	5	6	7
8	9	10	11	12	13	14
15	16	17	18	19	20	21
22	23	24	25	26	27	28
29	30	31				

2017 © Fireflyphoto Image from BigStockPhoto.com

July 8–14

A rising tide lifts all boats.   ~ENGLISH PROVERB

Date	Qtr.	Sign	Activity
Jul 7, 8:51 am– Jul 9, 12:58 pm	4th	Taurus	Plant potatoes and tubers. Trim to retard growth.
Jul 9, 12:58 pm– Jul 11, 1:59 pm	4th	Gemini	Cultivate. Destroy weeds and pests. Harvest fruits and root crops for food. Trim to retard growth.
Jul 11, 1:59 pm– Jul 12, 10:48 pm	4th	Cancer	Plant biennials, perennials, bulbs and roots. Prune. Irrigate. Fertilize (organic).
Jul 12, 10:48 pm– Jul 13, 1:31 pm	1st	Cancer	Plant grains, leafy annuals. Fertilize (chemical). Graft or bud plants. Irrigate. Trim to increase growth.

Host a dinner for as many neighbors as you can fit in your backyard. Make it an annual potluck event. Make up fun "predictions" that forecast all sorts of good things for your neighborhood and put them in a bowl rolled up like small scrolls and tied with a pretty ribbon. Let guests pick one from the bowl. It builds a sense of community, gives people something to talk about, and plants the seeds of goodwill among neighbors.

July 12
10:48 pm EDT

JULY

S	M	T	W	T	F	S
1	2	3	4	5	6	7
8	9	10	11	12	13	14
15	16	17	18	19	20	21
22	23	24	25	26	27	28
29	30	31				

2017 © monkeybusinessimages Image from BigStockPhoto.com

♋ July 15–21

Maybe the poets are right. Maybe love is the only answer.

~WOODY ALLEN

Date	Qtr.	Sign	Activity
Jul 17, 3:42 pm– Jul 19, 3:52 pm	1st	Libra	Plant annuals for fragrance and beauty. Trim to increase growth.
Jul 19, 3:52 pm– Jul 19, 9:13 pm	2nd	Libra	Plant annuals for fragrance and beauty. Trim to increase growth.
Jul 19, 9:13 pm– Jul 22, 6:12 am	2nd	Scorpio	Plant grains, leafy annuals. Fertilize (chemical). Graft or bud plants. Irrigate. Trim to increase growth.

Fruit is always in season for a reason. Fruits contain lots of water loaded with nutrients. June strawberries, mulberries, and cherries are followed by July raspberries, blackberries, and blueberries, then August's peaches, plums, and nectarines. Fall brings apples, grapes, and pumpkins, followed by oranges, grapefruit, lemons, and limes—all loaded with vitamin C. Eating organic fruit is one of the best ways to hydrate!

_____

_____

_____

◗

July 19
3:52 pm EDT

	JULY					
S	M	T	W	T	F	S
1	2	3	4	5	6	7
8	9	10	11	12	13	14
15	16	17	18	19	20	21
22	23	24	25	26	27	28
29	30	31				

2017 © ch_ch Image from BigStockPhoto.com

July 22–28

Love is the only thing that we can carry with us when we go,
and it makes the end so easy.   ~Louisa May Alcott

Date	Qtr.	Sign	Activity
Jul 19, 9:13 pm– Jul 22, 6:12 am	2nd	Scorpio	Plant grains, leafy annuals. Fertilize (chemical). Graft or bud plants. Irrigate. Trim to increase growth.
Jul 24, 5:49 pm– Jul 27, 6:41 am	2nd	Capricorn	Graft or bud plants. Trim to increase growth.
Jul 27, 4:20 pm– Jul 29, 7:28 pm	3rd	Aquarius	Cultivate. Destroy weeds and pests. Harvest fruits and root crops for food. Trim to retard growth.

Magnesium oil improves digestion and sleep. This blend of magnesium chloride suspended in a water may also relieve anxiety and reduce inflammation. Put a few drops in your evening bath or mix them with body lotion and rub into your shins or feet. Undiluted magnesium oil rubbed directly into the skin might sting, so add drops to your bath or to body lotion and massage into your shins, feet, or other areas of the skin.

○
July 27
4:20 pm EDT

July

S	M	T	W	T	F	S
1	2	3	4	5	6	7
8	9	10	11	12	13	14
15	16	17	18	19	20	21
22	23	24	25	26	27	28
29	30	31				

2017 © Subbotina Anna Image from BigStockPhoto.com

♌ **August**

July 29–August 4

Get your facts first, and then you can distort them as much as you please.   ~MARK TWAIN

Date	Qtr.	Sign	Activity
Jul 27, 4:20 pm– Jul 29, 7:28 pm	3rd	Aquarius	Cultivate. Destroy weeds and pests. Harvest fruits and root crops for food. Trim to retard growth.
Jul 29, 7:28 pm– Aug 1, 6:54 am	3rd	Pisces	Plant biennials, perennials, bulbs and roots. Prune. Irrigate. Fertilize (organic).
Aug 1, 6:54 am– Aug 3, 3:51 pm	3rd	Aries	Cultivate. Destroy weeds and pests. Harvest fruits and root crops for food. Trim to retard growth.
Aug 3, 3:51 pm– Aug 4, 2:18 pm	3rd	Taurus	Plant potatoes and tubers. Trim to retard growth.
Aug 4, 2:18 pm– Aug 5, 9:32 pm	4th	Taurus	Plant potatoes and tubers. Trim to retard growth.

Every week, lounge in a tubful of warm water as a way of renewing and rebirthing yourself. Use different things in the water depending on the season: salt and soda in winter, oils in spring, herbs like lavender and sage in summer, and something citrusy and bubbly in autumn.

August 4
2:18 pm EDT

AUGUST

S	M	T	W	T	F	S
			1	2	3	4
5	6	7	8	9	10	11
12	13	14	15	16	17	18
19	20	21	22	23	24	25
26	27	28	29	30	31	

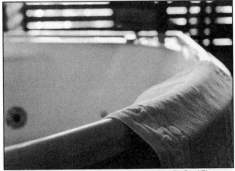

2017 © nito Image from BigStockPhoto.com

August 5–11 ♌

The fact that everybody in the world dreams every night ties
all mankind together.
~JACK KEROUAC

Date	Qtr.	Sign	Activity
Aug 4, 2:18 pm– Aug 5, 9:32 pm	4th	Taurus	Plant potatoes and tubers. Trim to retard growth.
Aug 5, 9:32 pm– Aug 8, 12:01 am	4th	Gemini	Cultivate. Destroy weeds and pests. Harvest fruits and root crops for food. Trim to retard growth.
Aug 8, 12:01 am– Aug 10, 12:18 am	4th	Cancer	Plant biennials, perennials, bulbs and roots. Prune. Irrigate. Fertilize (organic).
Aug 10, 12:18 am– Aug 11, 5:58 am	4th	Leo	Cultivate. Destroy weeds and pests. Harvest fruits and root crops for food. Trim to retard growth.

Are you like me and forever laying down or propping up a garden tool, only to forget where you left it? Paint the top of the handles a bright color (neon orange is a favorite around here). The contrast will make the tools easier to spot so they can be tidied away in their proper place until the next time you need to use them.

August 11
5:58 am EDT

AUGUST

S	M	T	W	T	F	S
			1	2	3	4
5	6	7	8	9	10	11
12	13	14	15	16	17	18
19	20	21	22	23	24	25
26	27	28	29	30	31	

2017 © essa667 Image from BigStockPhoto.com

August 12–18

How strange that Nature does not knock, and yet does not intrude!

~Emily Dickinson

Date	Qtr.	Sign	Activity
Aug 14, 12:57 am–Aug 16, 4:54 am	1st	Libra	Plant annuals for fragrance and beauty. Trim to increase growth.
Aug 16, 4:54 am–Aug 18, 3:49 am	1st	Scorpio	Plant grains, leafy annuals. Fertilize (chemical). Graft or bud plants. Irrigate. Trim to increase growth.
Aug 18, 3:49 am–Aug 18, 12:45 pm	2nd	Scorpio	Plant grains, leafy annuals. Fertilize (chemical). Graft or bud plants. Irrigate. Trim to increase growth.

You don't need a dehydrator to dry your herbs. Place a sheet of paper on the parcel shelf—or even the seat—of your car, and lay out the herbs you wish to dry. Choose a warm and clear day, roll up the windows, and let the heat of the sun do the rest. Your herbs will dry nicely, and your car will smell great!

August 18
3:49 am EDT

August

S	M	T	W	T	F	S
			1	2	3	4
5	6	7	8	9	10	11
12	13	14	15	16	17	18
19	20	21	22	23	24	25
26	27	28	29	30	31	

2017 © svrid79 Image from BigStockPhoto.com

August 19–25

To me, there is no greater calling… If I can inspire young
people to dedicate themselves to the good of mankind, I've
accomplished something. 　　　　　　　~JOHN GLENN

Date	Qtr.	Sign	Activity
Aug 21, 12:00 am– Aug 23, 12:56 pm	2nd	Capricorn	Graft or bud plants. Trim to increase growth.

Plan a vacation. Make it exotic, secluded, educational, or whatever appeals to you. Plan as if money is not an obstacle. Deeply research the location you want to visit, different ways of traveling to get there, and things to do once you arrive. Check out restaurants that serve the kinds of food you might eat when you get there. Whether you go or not is irrelevant because you will have learned almost as much as if you actually went there, and sometimes there is as much fun in the planning as in the travel!

_____

_____

_____

_____

2017 © vclements Image from BigStockPhoto.com

			AUGUST			
S	M	T	W	T	F	S
			1	2	3	4
5	6	7	8	9	10	11
12	13	14	15	16	17	18
19	20	21	22	23	24	25
26	27	28	29	30	31	

♍ September

August 26–September 1

You must learn to be still in the midst of activity and to be
vibrantly alive in repose. ~INDIRA GANDHI

Date	Qtr.	Sign	Activity
Aug 26, 1:32 am– Aug 26, 7:56 am	2nd	Pisces	Plant grains, leafy annuals. Fertilize (chemical). Graft or bud plants. Irrigate. Trim to increase growth.
Aug 26, 7:56 am– Aug 28, 12:35 pm	3rd	Pisces	Plant biennials, perennials, bulbs and roots. Prune. Irrigate. Fertilize (organic).
Aug 28, 12:35 pm– Aug 30, 9:30 pm	3rd	Aries	Cultivate. Destroy weeds and pests. Harvest fruits and root crops for food. Trim to retard growth.
Aug 30, 9:30 pm– Sep 2, 4:02 am	3rd	Taurus	Plant potatoes and tubers. Trim to retard growth.

Empty toilet-roll holders make great seed starters, and everyone has toilet paper! Simply make four 1" cuts around the bottom so you can fold the pieces into a crosshatch pattern. Fill with soil and add your seeds. When you're ready to plant them, there's no need to remove the cardboard—just uncross the bottom and let mother nature do the rest.

○
August 26
7:56 am EDT

SEPTEMBER

S	M	T	W	T	F	S
						1
2	3	4	5	6	7	8
9	10	11	12	13	14	15
16	17	18	19	20	21	22
23	24	25	26	27	28	29
30						

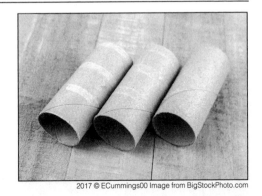

2017 © ECummings00 Image from BigStockPhoto.com

September 2–8 ♍

Books are good enough in their own way, but they are a
mighty bloodless substitute for life.

~Robert Louis Stevenson

Date	Qtr.	Sign	Activity
Aug 30, 9:30 pm– Sep 2, 4:02 am	3rd	Taurus	Plant potatoes and tubers. Trim to retard growth.
Sep 2, 4:02 am– Sep 2, 10:37 pm	3rd	Gemini	Cultivate. Destroy weeds and pests. Harvest fruits and root crops for food. Trim to retard growth.
Sep 2, 10:37 pm– Sep 4, 8:03 am	4th	Gemini	Cultivate. Destroy weeds and pests. Harvest fruits and root crops for food. Trim to retard growth.
Sep 4, 8:03 am– Sep 6, 9:54 am	4th	Cancer	Plant biennials, perennials, bulbs and roots. Prune. Irrigate. Fertilize (organic).
Sep 6, 9:54 am– Sep 8, 10:29 am	4th	Leo	Cultivate. Destroy weeds and pests. Harvest fruits and root crops for food. Trim to retard growth.
Sep 8, 10:29 am– Sep 9, 2:01 pm	4th	Virgo	Cultivate, especially medicinal plants. Destroy weeds and pests. Trim to retard growth.

Intuition is "knowing from within." Make a promise to yourself to practice listening to that still, small voice within. Honor what it tells you, even if this feels awkward at first, and you will find your intuition becoming stronger and more clear.

2017 © Kasia Bialasiewicz Image from BigStockPhoto.com

September 2
10:37 pm EDT

September

S	M	T	W	T	F	S
						1
2	3	4	5	6	7	8
9	10	11	12	13	14	15
16	17	18	19	20	21	22
23	24	25	26	27	28	29
30						

♍ September 9–15

The moment disbelief arises, the spell is broken; the magic, or rather art, has failed. ∼J. R. R. TOLKIEN

Date	Qtr.	Sign	Activity
Sep 8, 10:29 am– Sep 9, 2:01 pm	4th	Virgo	Cultivate, especially medicinal plants. Destroy weeds and pests. Trim to retard growth.
Sep 10, 11:20 am– Sep 12, 2:15 pm	1st	Libra	Plant annuals for fragrance and beauty. Trim to increase growth.
Sep 12, 2:15 pm– Sep 14, 8:45 pm	1st	Scorpio	Plant grains, leafy annuals. Fertilize (chemical). Graft or bud plants. Irrigate. Trim to increase growth.

Seaweed nourishes garden soil. If you live near the shore, harvest seaweed and spread it as a layer under soil or compost. Seaweed balances the soil composition, speeds up the process of composting, and may help repel garden pests. You can use wet or dry seaweed, though the dry variety takes longer to break down. Seaweed can also be used on top of the garden, around trees, and in the hole you dig before planting shrubs or vegetables. The nutrients, minerals, and disease-preventative properties of seaweed contribute to a healthy garden.

September 9
2:01 pm EDT

SEPTEMBER

S	M	T	W	T	F	S
						1
2	3	4	5	6	7	8
9	10	11	12	13	14	15
16	17	18	19	20	21	22
23	24	25	26	27	28	29
30						

2017 © Ruud Morijn Image from BigStockPhoto.com

September 16–22 ♍

Without courage we cannot practice any other virtue with consistency. We can't be kind, true, merciful, generous, or honest.

~MAYA ANGELOU

Date	Qtr.	Sign	Activity
Sep 17, 7:07 am– Sep 19, 7:52 pm	2nd	Capricorn	Graft or bud plants. Trim to increase growth.
Sep 22, 8:27 am– Sep 24, 7:04 pm	2nd	Pisces	Plant grains, leafy annuals. Fertilize (chemical). Graft or bud plants. Irrigate. Trim to increase growth.

Turn an abundance of cucumbers into pickles quickly. Cut cukes lengthwise and short enough to sit about a half inch below the rim of your jar. Pack them in tightly. Create a salty brine with organic apple cider (or an alternate), vinegar, water, sea salt, and spices of your choice, like dill, garlic, mustard, or red pepper. Mix 3 parts water to 1 part vinegar with spices to taste. Heat to boiling. Cover the jarred cukes completely with the boiling brine and refrigerate for an hour before consuming. This is short-term pickling, so eat them within a week.

September 16
7:15 pm EDT

2017 © superivana Image from BigStockPhoto.com

SEPTEMBER

S	M	T	W	T	F	S
						1
2	3	4	5	6	7	8
9	10	11	12	13	14	15
16	17	18	19	20	21	22
23	24	25	26	27	28	29
30						

♎ September 23–29

My favorite animal is the mule. He has more sense than a horse. He knows when to stop eating—and when to stop working.   ~HARRY S. TRUMAN.

Date	Qtr.	Sign	Activity
Sep 22, 8:27 am– Sep 24, 7:04 pm	2nd	Pisces	Plant grains, leafy annuals. Fertilize (chemical). Graft or bud plants. Irrigate. Trim to increase growth.
Sep 24, 10:52 pm– Sep 27, 3:16 am	3rd	Aries	Cultivate. Destroy weeds and pests. Harvest fruits and root crops for food. Trim to retard growth.
Sep 27, 3:16 am– Sep 29, 9:26 am	3rd	Taurus	Plant potatoes and tubers. Trim to retard growth.
Sep 29, 9:26 am– Oct 1, 2:00 pm	3rd	Gemini	Cultivate. Destroy weeds and pests. Harvest fruits and root crops for food. Trim to retard growth.

Planting a couple of trees on the east side of your house helps slow the heat buildup that begins at sunrise and increases as the day warms. Planting two trees on the west side of your house helps reduce the heat load of the afternoon and starts the temperature dropping a little earlier than without trees. Fruit trees provide a bonus—shade, and something to eat.

○

September 24
10:52 pm EDT

SEPTEMBER

S	M	T	W	T	F	S
						1
2	3	4	5	6	7	8
9	10	11	12	13	14	15
16	17	18	19	20	21	22
23	24	25	26	27	28	29
30						

2017 © onepony Image from BigStockPhoto.com

October ♎

September 30–October 6

Books permit us to voyage through time, to tap the wisdom of our ancestors. ~Carl Sagan

Date	Qtr.	Sign	Activity
Sep 29, 9:26 am–Oct 1, 2:00 pm	3rd	Gemini	Cultivate. Destroy weeds and pests. Harvest fruits and root crops for food. Trim to retard growth.
Oct 1, 2:00 pm–Oct 2, 5:45 am	3rd	Cancer	Plant biennials, perennials, bulbs and roots. Prune. Irrigate. Fertilize (organic).
Oct 2, 5:45 am–Oct 3, 5:12 pm	4th	Cancer	Plant biennials, perennials, bulbs and roots. Prune. Irrigate. Fertilize (organic).
Oct 3, 5:12 pm–Oct 5, 7:19 pm	4th	Leo	Cultivate. Destroy weeds and pests. Harvest fruits and root crops for food. Trim to retard growth.
Oct 5, 7:19 pm–Oct 7, 9:10 pm	4th	Virgo	Cultivate, especially medicinal plants. Destroy weeds and pests. Trim to retard growth.

If you don't make broth with the stock from cooking vegetables, let your garden have it! There are valuable nutrients in the vegetable water, and it seems a shame to waste them. Let the liquid cool, and use it when you water your garden or even your potted plants. Your foliaged friends will thank you for it!

2017 © ungvar Image from BigStockPhoto.com

◑

October 2
5:45 am EDT

October

S	M	T	W	T	F	S
	1	2	3	4	5	6
7	8	9	10	11	12	13
14	15	16	17	18	19	20
21	22	23	24	25	26	27
28	29	30	31			

♎ October 7–13

Between every two pine trees there is a door leading to a new way of life.   ~JOHN MUIR

Date	Qtr.	Sign	Activity
Oct 5, 7:19 pm– Oct 7, 9:10 pm	4th	Virgo	Cultivate, especially medicinal plants. Destroy weeds and pests. Trim to retard growth.
Oct 8, 11:47 pm– Oct 10, 12:09 am	1st	Libra	Plant annuals for fragrance and beauty. Trim to increase growth.
Oct 10, 12:09 am– Oct 12, 5:53 am	1st	Scorpio	Plant grains, leafy annuals. Fertilize (chemical). Graft or bud plants. Irrigate. Trim to increase growth.

Introduce bentonite clay into your life! Our ancestors would roll it into small balls and let them dry in the sun. They were carried in small pouches and swallowed to prevent worms, cure diarrhea, correct indigestion, or increase mineral intake. They could be re-wet and used as a paste for burns, bug bites, or snakebite, and even helped reduce the odor of bowel movements, something very important when moving through the wild.

_____

_____

_____

_____

October 8
11:47 pm EDT

OCTOBER

S	M	T	W	T	F	S
	1	2	3	4	5	6
7	8	9	10	11	12	13
14	15	16	17	18	19	20
21	22	23	24	25	26	27
28	29	30	31			

2017 © Coprid Image from BigStockPhoto.com

October 14–20

If food is poetry, is not poetry also food?

~Joyce Carol Oates

Date	Qtr.	Sign	Activity
Oct 14, 3:17 pm– Oct 16, 2:02 pm	1st	Capricorn	Graft or bud plants. Trim to increase growth.
Oct 16, 2:02 pm– Oct 17, 3:36 am	2nd	Capricorn	Graft or bud plants. Trim to increase growth.
Oct 19, 4:20 pm– Oct 22, 2:58 am	2nd	Pisces	Plant grains, leafy annuals. Fertilize (chemical). Graft or bud plants. Irrigate. Trim to increase growth.

Turn off the television for 1 hour once or twice a week and turn on a piece of music that doesn't have words. A symphony that will play for at least 20 minutes is a good choice. Sit down, relax, and let yourself drift with the music. When you go to bed later that night, you will sleep deeply, dream more coherently, and be better able to remember those dreams!

_____

_____

_____

_____

October 16
2:02 pm EDT

OCTOBER

S	M	T	W	T	F	S
	1	2	3	4	5	6
7	8	9	10	11	12	13
14	15	16	17	18	19	20
21	22	23	24	25	26	27
28	29	30	31			

2017 © AntonioGuillem Image from BigStockPhoto.com

♎ October 21–27

Nature does not make any leaps. All plants show an affinity
with those around them, according to their geographical location.
~Carl Linnaeus

Date	Qtr.	Sign	Activity
Oct 19, 4:20 pm– Oct 22, 2:58 am	2nd	Pisces	Plant grains, leafy annuals. Fertilize (chemical). Graft or bud plants. Irrigate. Trim to increase growth.
Oct 24, 10:33 am– Oct 24, 12:45 pm	2nd	Taurus	Plant annuals for hardiness. Trim to increase growth.
Oct 24, 12:45 pm– Oct 26, 3:41 pm	3rd	Taurus	Plant potatoes and tubers. Trim to retard growth.
Oct 26, 3:41 pm– Oct 28, 7:27 pm	3rd	Gemini	Cultivate. Destroy weeds and pests. Harvest fruits and root crops for food. Trim to retard growth.

Make a birdbath out of any bowl by placing a rock in the center. Birds feel secure perching on a rock surrounded by water rather than on the edge of a ceramic or metal bowl. You can place the bowl on top of a planter of similar size or on a tree stump to elevate it, but many birds will make use of a bird bath at ground level too.

_____

_____

_____

○
October 24
12:45 pm EDT

OCTOBER

S	M	T	W	T	F	S
	1	2	3	4	5	6
7	8	9	10	11	12	13
14	15	16	17	18	19	20
21	22	23	24	25	26	27
28	29	30	31			

2017 © Steve Byland Image from BigStockPhoto.com

November ♏

October 28–November 3

Truth is generally the best vindication against slander.

∼ ABRAHAM LINCOLN

Date	Qtr.	Sign	Activity
Oct 26, 3:41 pm– Oct 28, 7:27 pm	3rd	Gemini	Cultivate. Destroy weeds and pests. Harvest fruits and root crops for food. Trim to retard growth.
Oct 28, 7:27 pm– Oct 30, 10:42 pm	3rd	Cancer	Plant biennials, perennials, bulbs and roots. Prune. Irrigate. Fertilize (organic).
Oct 30, 10:42 pm– Oct 31, 12:40 pm	3rd	Leo	Cultivate. Destroy weeds and pests. Harvest fruits and root crops for food. Trim to retard growth.
Oct 31, 12:40 pm– Nov 2, 1:48 am	4th	Leo	Cultivate. Destroy weeds and pests. Harvest fruits and root crops for food. Trim to retard growth.
Nov 2, 1:48 am– Nov 4, 4:01 am	4th	Virgo	Cultivate, especially medicinal plants. Destroy weeds and pests. Trim to retard growth.

Learn a new skill that's really an old skill. For instance, buy a quart of heavy cream and learn to make butter. Mix a batch of cement and make a small piece of sidewalk somewhere. Learn to make paper from scratch, a broom from straw, or a bowl from clay.

2017 © HandmadePictures Image from BigStockPhoto.com

October 31
12:40 pm EDT

NOVEMBER

S	M	T	W	T	F	S
					1	2	3
4	5	6	7	8	9	10
11	12	13	14	15	16	17
18	19	20	21	22	23	24
25	26	27	28	29	30	

♏ November 4–10

Study nature, love nature, stay close to nature. It will never fail you...   ∼FRANK LLOYD WRIGHT

Date	Qtr.	Sign	Activity
Nov 2, 1:48 am–Nov 4, 4:01 am	4th	Virgo	Cultivate, especially medicinal plants. Destroy weeds and pests. Trim to retard growth.
Nov 6, 8:02 am–Nov 7, 11:02 am	4th	Scorpio	Plant biennials, perennials, bulbs and roots. Prune. Irrigate. Fertilize (organic).
Nov 7, 11:02 am–Nov 8, 1:59 pm	1st	Scorpio	Plant grains, leafy annuals. Fertilize (chemical). Graft or bud plants. Irrigate. Trim to increase growth.
Nov 10, 10:55 pm–Nov 13, 10:45 am	1st	Capricorn	Graft or bud plants. Trim to increase growth.

Change up the look of your brimmed hats with colorful adornments. A simple straw or felt hat can be wrapped with a stretchy headband or tied in decorative ribbon. This way you can match an outfit or your mood simply and inexpensively. Jazz up the hats more with feathers attached to the ribbons. Strings of beads can also be slipped over a hat for adornment.

Daylight Saving Time ends November 4, 2:00 am

November 7, 11:02 am EST

NOVEMBER

S	M	T	W	T	F	S
				1	2	3
4	5	6	7	8	9	10
11	12	13	14	15	16	17
18	19	20	21	22	23	24
25	26	27	28	29	30	

2017 © joephotostudio Image from BigStockPhoto.com

November 11–17 ♏♐

I care to live only to entice people to look at Nature's
loveliness.

                                  ~JOHN MUIR

Date	Qtr.	Sign	Activity
Nov 10, 10:55 pm– Nov 13, 10:45 am	1st	Capricorn	Graft or bud plants. Trim to increase growth.
Nov 15, 11:41 pm– Nov 18, 10:56 am	2nd	Pisces	Plant grains, leafy annuals. Fertilize (chemical). Graft or bud plants. Irrigate. Trim to increase growth.

Once a month, find a new recipe with unfamiliar ingredients and make something totally new and different. At the end of the year, you'll have a collection of new dishes that you know how to make. If you're like most people, about half of the dishes will become regular meals for your family, and two or three of them will be family favorites.

_____

_____

_____

_____

November 15
9:54 am EST

NOVEMBER

S	M	T	W	T	F	S
				1	2	3
4	5	6	7	8	9	10
11	12	13	14	15	16	17
18	19	20	21	22	23	24
25	26	27	28	29	30	

2017 © Robyn Mackenzie Image from BigStockPhoto.com

♏ November 18–24

Above all, avoid falsehood, every kind of falsehood, especially falseness to yourself. Watch over your own deceitfulness and look into it every hour, every minute.   ~FYODOR DOSTOYEVSKY

Date	Qtr.	Sign	Activity
Nov 15, 11:41 pm– Nov 18, 10:56 am	2nd	Pisces	Plant grains, leafy annuals. Fertilize (chemical). Graft or bud plants. Irrigate. Trim to increase growth.
Nov 20, 6:43 pm– Nov 22, 11:10 pm	2nd	Taurus	Plant annuals for hardiness. Trim to increase growth.
Nov 23, 12:39 am– Nov 25, 1:38 am	3rd	Gemini	Cultivate. Destroy weeds and pests. Harvest fruits and root crops for food. Trim to retard growth.

Soothe an itchy dog by treating its paws. Itchy skin is sometimes caused by yeast or toxins in the paws that spreads when your dog scratches. Make a paw soak by adding one cup of apple cider vinegar and one cup of hydrogen peroxide to a gallon of water. Juice a lemon as an optional addition with antibacterial, detoxifying benefits. Soak dog's paws for a full half minute and then dry them well.

○
November 23
12:39 am EST

NOVEMBER

S	M	T	W	T	F	S
				1	2	3
4	5	6	7	8	9	10
11	12	13	14	15	16	17
18	19	20	21	22	23	24
25	26	27	28	29	30	

2017 © Yulia Image from BigStockPhoto.com

December

November 25–December 1

Everybody is friends when things are bad enough.

~ERNEST HEMINGWAY

Date	Qtr.	Sign	Activity
Nov 23, 12:39 am– Nov 25, 1:38 am	3rd	Gemini	Cultivate. Destroy weeds and pests. Harvest fruits and root crops for food. Trim to retard growth.
Nov 25, 1:38 am– Nov 27, 3:35 am	3rd	Cancer	Plant biennials, perennials, bulbs and roots. Prune. Irrigate. Fertilize (organic).
Nov 27, 3:35 am– Nov 29, 6:08 am	3rd	Leo	Cultivate. Destroy weeds and pests. Harvest fruits and root crops for food. Trim to retard growth.
Nov 29, 6:08 am– Nov 29, 7:19 pm	3rd	Virgo	Cultivate, especially medicinal plants. Destroy weeds and pests. Trim to retard growth.
Nov 29, 7:19 pm– Dec 1, 9:49 am	4th	Virgo	Cultivate, especially medicinal plants. Destroy weeds and pests. Trim to retard growth.

Tired of having grubby fingernails after being in the garden? Before you work the soil, drag your nails across a bar of soap. The dirt won't be able to get under them as easily, and the soap will already be there when it's time to clean up.

2017 © schoolgirl Image from BigStockPhoto.com

November 29
7:19 pm EST

DECEMBER

S	M	T	W	T	F	S
						1
2	3	4	5	6	7	8
9	10	11	12	13	14	15
16	17	18	19	20	21	22
23	24	25	26	27	28	29
30	31					

December 2–8

I did not know that.   ~JOHNNY CARSON

Date	Qtr.	Sign	Activity
Dec 3, 2:55 pm– Dec 5, 9:49 pm	4th	Scorpio	Plant biennials, perennials, bulbs and roots. Prune. Irrigate. Fertilize (organic).
Dec 5, 9:49 pm– Dec 7, 2:20 am	4th	Sagittarius	Cultivate. Destroy weeds and pests. Harvest fruits and root crops for food. Trim to retard growth.
Dec 8, 7:01 am– Dec 10, 6:39 pm	1st	Capricorn	Graft or bud plants. Trim to increase growth.

Start a love affair with your feet. As we get older, feet often become decrepit. Don't let this happen. Soak your feet for 30 minutes once a week in a pan of warm water with 1 tablespoon of dry mustard and 1 teaspoon of cayenne in it. This greatly increases circulation in feet and legs and pulls toxins out through your feet. It even relieves headache, backache, and cramps. You'll be walking on air!

_____

_____

_____

_____

December 7
2:20 am EST

DECEMBER

S	M	T	W	T	F	S
						1
2	3	4	5	6	7	8
9	10	11	12	13	14	15
16	17	18	19	20	21	22
23	24	25	26	27	28	29
30	31					

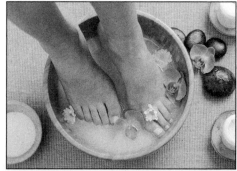
2017 © Rido81 Image from BigStockPhoto.com

December 9–15

An ounce of sauce covers a multitude of sins.

~ANTHONY BOURDAIN

Date	Qtr.	Sign	Activity
Dec 8, 7:01 am– Dec 10, 6:39 pm	1st	Capricorn	Graft or bud plants. Trim to increase growth.
Dec 13, 7:40 am– Dec 15, 6:49 am	1st	Pisces	Plant grains, leafy annuals. Fertilize (chemical). Graft or bud plants. Irrigate. Trim to increase growth.
Dec 15, 6:49 am– Dec 15, 7:44 pm	2nd	Pisces	Plant grains, leafy annuals. Fertilize (chemical). Graft or bud plants. Irrigate. Trim to increase growth.

Get a few CDs or download songs that you loved in high school and that you enjoyed singing along with. Put the music in your car and sing your heart out when you're driving somewhere. It not only exercises your vocal cords and keeps you feeling younger, but you will arrive at your destination in a great mood.

December 15
6:49 am EST

DECEMBER

S	M	T	W	T	F	S
						1
2	3	4	5	6	7	8
9	10	11	12	13	14	15
16	17	18	19	20	21	22
23	24	25	26	27	28	29
30	31					

2017 © chokmoso Image from BigStockPhoto.com

December 16–22

Carry out a random act of kindness with no expectation of reward, safe in the knowledge that one day someone might do the same for you.   ~DIANA, PRINCESS OF WALES

Date	Qtr.	Sign	Activity
Dec 18, 4:37 am–Dec 20, 9:34 am	2nd	Taurus	Plant annuals for hardiness. Trim to increase growth.
Dec 22, 11:28 am–Dec 22, 12:49 pm	2nd	Cancer	Plant grains, leafy annuals. Fertilize (chemical). Graft or bud plants. Irrigate. Trim to increase growth.
Dec 22, 12:49 pm–Dec 24, 11:59 am	3rd	Cancer	Plant biennials, perennials, bulbs and roots. Prune. Irrigate. Fertilize (organic).

Is okra too slimy for you? Okra is a well-known main ingredient in gumbo, where its sliminess is a good thing. Considering that okra is a good source of vitamin C, fiber, B vitamins, vitamins A and K, and folate, try eating okra pods raw, steamed, or cooked into other stewed dishes. One hundred grams of okra provide just 30 calories, 0 grams of saturated fat, and no cholesterol.

_____

_____

_____

_____

○
December 22
12:49 pm EST

DECEMBER

S	M	T	W	T	F	S
						1
2	3	4	5	6	7	8
9	10	11	12	13	14	15
16	17	18	19	20	21	22
23	24	25	26	27	28	29
30	31					

2017 © Naltik Image from BigStockPhoto.com

December 23–29

To make honey, young bee need young flower, not old prune.
~MR. MIYAGI, *THE KARATE KID*

Date	Qtr.	Sign	Activity
Dec 22, 12:49 pm–Dec 24, 11:59 am	3rd	Cancer	Plant biennials, perennials, bulbs and roots. Prune. Irrigate. Fertilize (organic).
Dec 24, 11:59 am–Dec 26, 12:50 pm	3rd	Leo	Cultivate. Destroy weeds and pests. Harvest fruits and root crops for food. Trim to retard growth.
Dec 26, 12:50 pm–Dec 28, 3:23 pm	3rd	Virgo	Cultivate, especially medicinal plants. Destroy weeds and pests. Trim to retard growth.

Make your own shaving lotion with essential oils. Lavender, geranium, and rose have skin-soothing properties, though you can choose and blend based on scent alone. Use equal parts coconut oil and shea butter (⅔ cup each), ¼ cup of olive oil, 2 teaspoons baking soda, and about 20 drops of essential oil. Melt the first two ingredients in a double boiler, remove from heat, mix in olive and essential oils, and refrigerate until solid. Then add the baking soda and use a hand mixer to whip it to desired consistency. Store in a cool, dry place.

December 29
4:34 am EST

DECEMBER

S	M	T	W	T	F	S
						1
2	3	4	5	6	7	8
9	10	11	12	13	14	15
16	17	18	19	20	21	22
23	24	25	26	27	28	29
30	31					

2017 © Svehlik Image from BigStockPhoto.com

December 30–January 5, 2019

I urge you to please notice when you are happy, and exclaim or murmur or think at some point, "If this isn't nice, I don't know what is."

~KURT VONNEGUT

Date	Qtr.	Sign	Activity
Jan 5, 8:28 pm–Jan 7, 1:46 am	1st	Capricorn	Graft or bud plants. Trim to increase growth.

Ask friends, neighbors, family, and colleagues what they need or wish they had in their life…and keep your ears open for something you could easily do or would love to do for one of them. For instance, maybe Susie wants desperately to go visit her ailing mother but can't afford the plane ticket. You could take up a collection from among those who know and love Susie, simply by asking people to contribute to the ticket cost. If they can't afford a contribution of money, maybe they could feed Susie's cat while she's away.

●

January 5
8:28 pm EST

DECEMBER

S	M	T	W	T	F	S
						1
2	3	4	5	6	7	8
9	10	11	12	13	14	15
16	17	18	19	20	21	22
23	24	25	26	27	28	29
30	31					

2017 © Rawpixel.com Image from BigStockPhoto.com

2017 © LisaTuray Image from BigStockPhoto.com

Gardening by the Moon

Today, people often reject the notion of gardening according to the Moon's phase and sign. The usual nonbeliever is not a scientist but the city dweller who has never had any real contact with nature and little experience of natural rhythms.

Camille Flammarion, the French astronomer, testifies to the success of Moon planting, though:

"Cucumbers increase at Full Moon, as well as radishes, turnips, leeks, lilies, horseradish, and saffron; onions, on the contrary, are much larger and better nourished during the decline and old age of the Moon than at its increase, during its youth and fullness, which is the reason the Egyptians abstained from onions, on account of their antipathy to the Moon. Herbs gathered while the Moon increases are of great efficiency. If the vines are trimmed at night when the Moon is in the sign of the Lion, Sagittarius, the Scorpion, or the Bull, it will save them from field rats, moles, snails, flies, and other animals."

Dr. Clark Timmins is one of the few modern scientists to have conducted tests in Moon planting. Following is a summary of his experiments:

Beets: When sown with the Moon in Scorpio, the germination rate was 71 percent; when sown in Sagittarius, the germination rate was 58 percent.

Scotch marigold: When sown with the Moon in Cancer, the germination rate was 90 percent; when sown in Leo, the rate was 32 percent.

Carrots: When sown with the Moon in Scorpio, the germination rate was 64 percent; when sown with the Moon in Sagittarius, the germination rate was 47 percent.

Tomatoes: When sown with the Moon in Cancer, the germination rate was 90 percent; but when sown with the Moon in Leo, the germination rate was 58 percent.

Two things should be emphasized. First, remember that this is only a summary of the results of the experiments; the experiments themselves were conducted in a scientific manner to eliminate any variation in soil, temperature, moisture, and so on, so that only the Moon sign is varied. Second, note that these astonishing results were obtained without regard to the phase of the Moon—the other factor we use in Moon planting, and which presumably would have increased the differential in germination rates.

Dr. Timmins also tried transplanting Cancer- and Leo-planted tomato seedlings while the Cancer Moon was waxing. The result was 100 percent survival. When transplanting was done with the waning Sagittarius Moon, there was 0 percent survival. Dr. Timmins's tests show that the Cancer-planted tomatoes had blossoms twelve days earlier than those planted under Leo; the Cancer-planted tomatoes had an average height of twenty inches at that time compared to fifteen inches for the Leo-planted; the first ripe tomatoes were gathered from the Cancer plantings eleven days ahead of the Leo plantings; and a count of the hanging fruit and its size and weight shows an advantage to the Cancer plants over the Leo plants of 45 percent.

Dr. Timmins also observed that there have been similar tests that did not indicate results favorable to the Moon planting theory. As a scientist, he asked why one set of experiments indicated a positive verification of Moon planting, and others did not. He checked these other tests and found that the experimenters had not followed the geocentric system for determining the Moon sign positions, but the heliocentric. When the times used in these other tests were converted to the geocentric system, the dates chosen often were found to be in barren, rather than fertile, signs. Without going into a technical explanation, it is sufficient to point out that geocentric and heliocentric positions often vary by as much as four days. This is a large enough differential to place the Moon in Cancer, for example, in the heliocentric system, and at the same time in Leo by the geocentric system.

Most almanacs and calendars show the Moon's signs heliocentrically—and thus incorrectly for Moon planting—while the *Moon Sign Book* is calculated correctly for planting purposes, using the geocentric system. Some readers are confused because the *Moon Sign Book* talks about first, second, third, and fourth quarters, while other almanacs refer to these same divisions as New Moon, first quarter, Full Moon, and fourth quarter. Thus the almanacs say first quarter when the *Moon Sign Book* says second quarter.

There is nothing complicated about using astrology in agriculture and horticulture in order to increase both pleasure and profit, but there is one very important rule that is often neglected—use common sense! Of course this is one rule that should be remembered in every activity we undertake, but in the case of gardening and farming by the Moon, if it is not possible to use the best dates for planting or harvesting, we must select the next best and just try to do the best we can.

This brings up the matter of the other factors to consider in your gardening work. The dates we give as best for a certain activity apply to the entire country (with slight time correction), but in your section of the country you may be buried under three feet of snow on a date we say is good to plant your flowers. So we have factors of weather, season, temperature, and moisture variations, soil conditions, your own available time and opportunity, and so forth. Some astrologers like to think it is all a matter of science, but gardening is also an art. In art, you develop an instinctive identification with your work and influence it with your feelings and wishes.

The *Moon Sign Book* gives you the place of the Moon for every day of the year so that you can select the best times once you have become familiar with the rules and practices of lunar agriculture. We give you specific, easy-to-follow directions so that you can get right down to work.

We give you the best dates for planting, and also for various related activities, including cultivation, fertilizing, harvesting, irrigation, and getting rid of weeds and pests. But we cannot tell you exactly when it's good to plant. Many of these rules were learned by observation and experience; as the body of experience grew, we could see various patterns emerging that allowed us to make judgments about new things. That's what you should do, too. After you have worked with lunar agriculture for a while and have gained a working knowledge, you will probably begin to try new things—and we hope you will share your experiments and findings with us. That's how the science grows.

Here's an example of what we mean. Years ago Llewellyn George suggested we try to combine our bits of knowledge about what to expect in planting under each of the Moon signs in order to benefit from several lunar factors in one plant. From this came our rule for developing "thoroughbred seed." To develop thoroughbred seed, save the seed for three successive years from plants grown by the correct Moon sign and phase. You can plant in the first quarter phase and in the sign of Cancer for fruitfulness; the second year, plant seeds from the first year plants in Libra for beauty; and in the third year, plant the seeds from the second year plants in Taurus to produce hardiness. In a similar manner you can combine the fruitfulness of Cancer, the good root growth of Pisces, and the sturdiness and good vine growth of Scorpio. And don't forget the characteristics of Capricorn: hardy like Taurus, but drier and perhaps more resistant to drought and disease.

Unlike common almanacs, we consider both the Moon's phase and the Moon's sign in making our calculations for the proper timing of our work. It is perhaps a little easier to understand this if we remind you that we are all living in the center of a vast electromagnetic field that is Earth and its environment in space. Everything that occurs within this electromagnetic field has an effect on everything else within the field. The Moon and the Sun are the most important of the factors affecting the life of Earth, and it is their relative positions to Earth that we project for each day of the year.

Many people claim that not only do they achieve larger crops gardening by the Moon, but that their fruits and vegetables are much tastier. A number of organic gardeners have also become lunar gardeners using the natural rhythm of life forces that we experience through the relative movements of the Sun and Moon. We provide a few basic rules and then give you day-by-day guidance for your gardening work. You will be able to choose the best dates to meet your own needs and opportunities.

Planting by the Moon's Phases

During the increasing or waxing light—from New Moon to Full Moon—plant annuals that produce their yield above the ground. An annual is a plant that completes its entire life cycle within one growing season and has to be seeded each year. During the decreasing or waning light—from Full Moon to New Moon—plant biennials, perennials, and bulb and root plants. Biennials include crops that are planted one season to winter over and produce crops the next, such as winter wheat. Perennials and bulb and root plants include all plants that grow from the same root each year.

A simpler, less-accurate rule is to plant crops that produce above the ground during the waxing Moon, and to plant crops that produce below the ground during the waning Moon. Thus the old adage, "Plant potatoes during the dark of the Moon." Llewellyn George's system divided the lunar month into quarters. The first two from New Moon to Full Moon are the first and second quarters, and the last two from Full Moon to New Moon the third and fourth quarters. Using these divisions, we can increase our accuracy in timing our efforts to coincide with natural forces.

First Quarter

Plant annuals producing their yield above the ground, which are generally of the leafy kind that produce their seed outside the fruit. Some examples are asparagus, broccoli, brussels sprouts, cabbage, cauliflower, celery, cress, endive, kohlrabi, lettuce, parsley, and spinach. Cucumbers are an exception, as they do best in the first quarter rather than the second, even though the seeds are inside the fruit. Also plant cereals and grains.

Second Quarter

Plant annuals producing their yield above the ground, which are generally of the viney kind that produce their seed inside the fruit. Some examples include beans, eggplant, melons, peas, peppers, pumpkins, squash, tomatoes, etc. These are not hard-and-fast divisions. If you can't plant during the first quarter, plant during the second, and vice versa. There are many plants that seem to do equally well planted in either quarter, such as watermelon, hay, and cereals and grains.

Third Quarter
Plant biennials, perennials, bulbs, root plants, trees, shrubs, berries, grapes, strawberries, beets, carrots, onions, parsnips, rutabagas, potatoes, radishes, peanuts, rhubarb, turnips, winter wheat, etc.

Fourth Quarter
This is the best time to cultivate, turn sod, pull weeds, and destroy pests of all kinds, especially when the Moon is in Aries, Leo, Virgo, Gemini, Aquarius, and Sagittarius.

The Moon in the Signs

Moon in Aries
Barren, dry, fiery, and masculine. Use for destroying noxious weeds.

Moon in Taurus
Productive, moist, earthy, and feminine. Use for planting many crops when hardiness is important, particularly root crops. Also used for lettuce, cabbage, and similar leafy vegetables.

Moon in Gemini
Barren and dry, airy and masculine. Use for destroying noxious growths, weeds, and pests, and for cultivation.

Moon in Cancer
Fruitful, moist, feminine. Use for planting and irrigation.

Moon in Leo
Barren, dry, fiery, masculine. Use for killing weeds or cultivation.

Moon in Virgo
Barren, dry, earthy, and feminine. Use for cultivation and destroying weeds and pests.

Moon in Libra

Semi-fruitful, moist, and airy. Use for planting crops that need good pulp growth. A very good sign for flowers and vines. Also used for seeding hay, corn fodder, and the like.

Moon in Scorpio

Very fruitful and moist, watery and feminine. Nearly as productive as Cancer; use for the same purposes. Especially good for vine growth and sturdiness.

Moon in Sagittarius

Barren and dry, fiery and masculine. Use for planting onions, seeding hay, and for cultivation.

Moon in Capricorn

Productive and dry, earthy and feminine. Use for planting potatoes and other tubers.

Moon in Aquarius

Barren, dry, airy, and masculine. Use for cultivation and destroying noxious growths and pests.

Moon in Pisces

Very fruitful, moist, watery, and feminine. Especially good for root growth.

A Guide to Planting

Plant	Quarter	Sign
Annuals	1st or 2nd	
Apple tree	2nd or 3rd	Cancer, Pisces, Virgo
Artichoke	1st	Cancer, Pisces
Asparagus	1st	Cancer, Scorpio, Pisces
Aster	1st or 2nd	Virgo, Libra
Barley	1st or 2nd	Cancer, Pisces, Libra, Capricorn, Virgo
Beans (bush & pole)	2nd	Cancer, Taurus, Pisces, Libra
Beans (kidney, white & navy)	1st or 2nd	Cancer, Pisces
Beech tree	2nd or 3rd	Virgo, Taurus
Beets	3rd	Cancer, Capricorn, Pisces, Libra
Biennials	3rd or 4th	
Broccoli	1st	Cancer, Scorpio, Pisces, Libra
Brussels sprouts	1st	Cancer, Scorpio, Pisces, Libra
Buckwheat	1st or 2nd	Capricorn
Bulbs	3rd	Cancer, Scorpio, Pisces
Bulbs for seed	2nd or 3rd	
Cabbage	1st	Cancer, Scorpio, Pisces, Taurus, Libra
Canes (raspberry, blackberry & gooseberry)	2nd	Cancer, Scorpio, Pisces
Cantaloupe	1st or 2nd	Cancer, Scorpio, Pisces, Taurus, Libra
Carrots	3rd	Cancer, Scorpio, Pisces, Taurus, Libra
Cauliflower	1st	Cancer, Scorpio, Pisces, Libra
Celeriac	3rd	Cancer, Scorpio, Pisces
Celery	1st	Cancer, Scorpio, Pisces
Cereals	1st or 2nd	Cancer, Scorpio, Pisces, Libra
Chard	1st or 2nd	Cancer, Scorpio, Pisces
Chicory	2nd or 3rd	Cancer, Scorpio, Pisces
Chrysanthemum	1st or 2nd	Virgo
Clover	1st or 2nd	Cancer, Scorpio, Pisces

Plant	Quarter	Sign
Coreopsis	2nd or 3rd	Libra
Corn	1st	Cancer, Scorpio, Pisces
Corn for fodder	1st or 2nd	Libra
Cosmos	2nd or 3rd	Libra
Cress	1st	Cancer, Scorpio, Pisces
Crocus	1st or 2nd	Virgo
Cucumber	1st	Cancer, Scorpio, Pisces
Daffodil	1st or 2nd	Libra, Virgo
Dahlia	1st or 2nd	Libra, Virgo
Deciduous trees	2nd or 3rd	Cancer, Scorpio, Pisces, Virgo, Libra
Eggplant	2nd	Cancer, Scorpio, Pisces, Libra
Endive	1st	Cancer, Scorpio, Pisces, Libra
Flowers	1st	Cancer, Scorpio, Pisces, Libra, Taurus, Virgo
Garlic	3rd	Libra, Taurus, Pisces
Gladiola	1st or 2nd	Libra, Virgo
Gourds	1st or 2nd	Cancer, Scorpio, Pisces, Libra
Grapes	2nd or 3rd	Cancer, Scorpio, Pisces, Virgo
Hay	1st or 2nd	Cancer, Scorpio, Pisces, Libra, Taurus
Herbs	1st or 2nd	Cancer, Scorpio, Pisces
Honeysuckle	1st or 2nd	Scorpio, Virgo
Hops	1st or 2nd	Scorpio, Libra
Horseradish	1st or 2nd	Cancer, Scorpio, Pisces
Houseplants	1st	Cancer, Scorpio, Pisces, Libra
Hyacinth	3rd	Cancer, Scorpio, Pisces
Iris	1st or 2nd	Cancer, Virgo
Kohlrabi	1st or 2nd	Cancer, Scorpio, Pisces, Libra
Leek	2nd or 3rd	Sagittarius
Lettuce	1st	Cancer, Scorpio, Pisces, Libra, Taurus
Lily	1st or 2nd	Cancer, Scorpio, Pisces
Maple tree	2nd or 3rd	Taurus, Virgo, Cancer, Pisces
Melon	2nd	Cancer, Scorpio, Pisces
Moon vine	1st or 2nd	Virgo

Plant	Quarter	Sign
Morning glory	1st or 2nd	Cancer, Scorpio, Pisces, Virgo
Oak tree	2nd or 3rd	Taurus, Virgo, Cancer, Pisces
Oats	1st or 2nd	Cancer, Scorpio, Pisces, Libra
Okra	1st or 2nd	Cancer, Scorpio, Pisces, Libra
Onion seed	2nd	Cancer, Scorpio, Sagittarius
Onion set	3rd or 4th	Cancer, Pisces, Taurus, Libra
Pansies	1st or 2nd	Cancer, Scorpio, Pisces
Parsley	1st	Cancer, Scorpio, Pisces, Libra
Parsnip	3rd	Cancer, Scorpio, Taurus, Capricorn
Peach tree	2nd or 3rd	Cancer, Taurus, Virgo, Libra
Peanuts	3rd	Cancer, Scorpio, Pisces
Pear tree	2nd or 3rd	Cancer, Scorpio, Pisces, Libra
Peas	2nd	Cancer, Scorpio, Pisces, Libra
Peony	1st or 2nd	Virgo
Peppers	2nd	Cancer, Scorpio, Pisces
Perennials	3rd	
Petunia	1st or 2nd	Libra, Virgo
Plum tree	2nd or 3rd	Cancer, Pisces, Taurus, Virgo
Poppies	1st or 2nd	Virgo
Portulaca	1st or 2nd	Virgo
Potatoes	3rd	Cancer, Scorpio, Libra, Taurus, Capricorn
Privet	1st or 2nd	Taurus, Libra
Pumpkin	2nd	Cancer, Scorpio, Pisces, Libra
Quince	1st or 2nd	Capricorn
Radishes	3rd	Cancer, Scorpio, Pisces, Libra, Capricorn
Rhubarb	3rd	Cancer, Pisces
Rice	1st or 2nd	Scorpio
Roses	1st or 2nd	Cancer, Virgo
Rutabaga	3rd	Cancer, Scorpio, Pisces, Taurus
Saffron	1st or 2nd	Cancer, Scorpio, Pisces
Sage	3rd	Cancer, Scorpio, Pisces

Plant	Quarter	Sign
Salsify	1st	Cancer, Scorpio, Pisces
Shallot	2nd	Scorpio
Spinach	1st	Cancer, Scorpio, Pisces
Squash	2nd	Cancer, Scorpio, Pisces, Libra
Strawberries	3rd	Cancer, Scorpio, Pisces
String beans	1st or 2nd	Taurus
Sunflowers	1st or 2nd	Libra, Cancer
Sweet peas	1st or 2nd	Any
Tomatoes	2nd	Cancer, Scorpio, Pisces, Capricorn
Trees, shade	3rd	Taurus, Capricorn
Trees, ornamental	2nd	Libra, Taurus
Trumpet vine	1st or 2nd	Cancer, Scorpio, Pisces
Tubers for seed	3rd	Cancer, Scorpio, Pisces, Libra
Tulips	1st or 2nd	Libra, Virgo
Turnips	3rd	Cancer, Scorpio, Pisces, Taurus, Capricorn, Libra
Valerian	1st or 2nd	Virgo, Gemini
Watermelon	1st or 2nd	Cancer, Scorpio, Pisces, Libra
Wheat	1st or 2nd	Cancer, Scorpio, Pisces, Libra

Companion Planting Guide

Plant	Companions	Hindered by
Asparagus	Tomatoes, parsley, basil	None known
Beans	Tomatoes, carrots, cucumbers, garlic, cabbage, beets, corn	Onions, gladiolas
Beets	Onions, cabbage, lettuce, mint, catnip	Pole beans
Broccoli	Beans, celery, potatoes, onions	Tomatoes
Cabbage	Peppermint, sage, thyme, tomatoes	Strawberries, grapes
Carrots	Peas, lettuce, chives, radishes, leeks, onions, sage	Dill, anise
Citrus trees	Guava, live oak, rubber trees, peppers	None known
Corn	Potatoes, beans, peas, melon, squash, pumpkin, sunflowers, soybeans	Quack grass, wheat, straw, mulch
Cucumbers	Beans, cabbage, radishes, sunflowers, lettuce, broccoli, squash	Aromatic herbs
Eggplant	Green beans, lettuce, kale	None known
Grapes	Peas, beans, blackberries	Cabbage, radishes
Melons	Corn, peas	Potatoes, gourds
Onions, leeks	Beets, chamomile, carrots, lettuce	Peas, beans, sage
Parsnip	Peas	None known
Peas	Radishes, carrots, corn, cucumbers, beans, tomatoes, spinach, turnips	Onion, garlic
Potatoes	Beans, corn, peas, cabbage, hemp, cucumbers, eggplant, catnip	Raspberries, pumpkins, tomatoes, sunflowers
Radishes	Peas, lettuce, nasturtiums, cucumbers	Hyssop
Spinach	Strawberries	None known
Squash/Pumpkin	Nasturtiums, corn, mint, catnip	Potatoes
Tomatoes	Asparagus, parsley, chives, onions, carrots, marigolds, nasturtiums, dill	Black walnut roots, fennel, potatoes
Turnips	Peas, beans, brussels sprouts	Potatoes

Plant	Companions	Uses
Anise	Coriander	Flavor candy, pastry, cheeses, cookies
Basil	Tomatoes	Dislikes rue; repels flies and mosquitoes
Borage	Tomatoes, squash	Use in teas
Buttercup	Clover	Hinders delphinium, peonies, monkshood, columbine
Catnip		Repels flea beetles
Chamomile	Peppermint, wheat, onions, cabbage	Roman chamomile may control damping-off disease; use in herbal sprays
Chervil	Radishes	Good in soups and other dishes
Chives	Carrots	Use in spray to deter black spot on roses
Coriander	Plant anywhere	Hinders seed formation in fennel
Cosmos		Repels corn earworms
Dill	Cabbage	Hinders carrots and tomatoes
Fennel	Plant in borders	Disliked by all garden plants
Horseradish		Repels potato bugs
Horsetail		Makes fungicide spray
Hyssop		Attracts cabbage flies; harmful to radishes
Lavender	Plant anywhere	Use in spray to control insects on cotton, repels clothes moths
Lovage		Lures horn worms away from tomatoes
Marigolds		Pest repellent; use against Mexican bean beetles and nematodes
Mint	Cabbage, tomatoes	Repels ants, flea beetles, cabbage worm butterflies
Morning glory	Corn	Helps melon germination
Nasturtium	Cabbage, cucumbers	Deters aphids, squash bugs, pumpkin beetles
Okra	Eggplant	Attracts leafhopper (lure insects from other plants)
Parsley	Tomatoes, asparagus	Freeze chopped-up leaves to flavor foods
Purslane		Good ground cover
Rosemary		Repels cabbage moths, bean beetles, carrot flies
Savory		Plant with onions for added sweetness
Tansy		Deters Japanese beetles, striped cucumber beetles, squash bugs
Thyme		Repels cabbage worms
Yarrow		Increases essential oils of neighbors

Moon Void-of-Course

By Kim Rogers-Gallagher

The Moon circles the Earth in about twenty-eight days, moving through each zodiac sign in two-and-a-half days. As she passes through the thirty degrees of each sign, she "visits" with the planets in numerical order, forming aspects with them. Because she moves one degree in just two to two and a half hours, her influence on each planet lasts only a few hours. She eventually reaches the planet that's in the highest degree of any sign and forms what will be her final aspect before leaving the sign. From this point until she enters the next sign, she is referred to as void-of-course.

Think of it this way: the Moon is the emotional "tone" of the day, carrying feelings with her particular to the sign she's "wearing" at the moment. After she has contacted each of the planets, she symbolically "rests" before changing her costume, so her instinct is temporarily on hold. It's during this time that many people feel "fuzzy" or "vague." Plans or decisions made now often do not pan out. Without the instinctual "knowing" the Moon provides as she touches each planet, we tend to be unrealistic or exercise poor judgment. The traditional definition of the void Moon is that "nothing will come of this." Actions initiated under a void Moon are often wasted, irrelevant, or incorrect—usually because information is hidden, missing, or has been overlooked.

Although it's not a good time to initiate plans, routine tasks seem to go along just fine. This period is ideal for reflection. On the lighter side, remember there are good uses for the void Moon. It is the period when the universe seems to be most open to loopholes. It's a great time to make plans you don't want to fulfill or schedule things you don't want to do. See the tables on pages 76–81 for a schedule of the Moon's void-of-course times.

Last Aspect   **Moon Enters New Sign**

		January		
2	5:46 pm	3	Leo	2:23 am
4	6:10 pm	5	Virgo	3:12 am
6	9:51 pm	7	Libra	7:15 am
9	11:13 am	9	Scorpio	3:05 pm
11	9:53 am	12	Sagittarius	2:04 am
14	3:48 am	14	Capricorn	2:42 pm
17	1:30 am	17	Aquarius	3:32 am
19	6:52 am	19	Pisces	3:26 pm
21	8:13 pm	22	Aries	1:27 am
23	11:16 pm	24	Taurus	8:39 am
25	10:17 pm	26	Gemini	12:40 pm
28	5:39 am	28	Cancer	1:57 pm
30	11:40 am	30	Leo	1:53 pm
		February		
1	5:59 am	1	Virgo	2:13 pm
3	2:07 am	3	Libra	4:47 pm
5	1:46 pm	5	Scorpio	10:56 pm
8	2:16 am	8	Sagittarius	8:53 am
10	11:38 am	10	Capricorn	9:21 pm
13	12:43 am	13	Aquarius	10:11 am
15	4:05 pm	15	Pisces	9:42 pm
17	5:14 pm	18	Aries	7:05 am
20	6:11 am	20	Taurus	2:12 pm
22	6:46 am	22	Gemini	7:07 pm
24	2:58 pm	24	Cancer	10:06 pm
26	4:51 pm	26	Leo	11:42 pm
28	6:13 pm	3/1	Virgo	12:57 am

Last Aspect   Moon Enters New Sign

			March	
2	6:50 pm	3	Libra	3:20 am
5	1:19 am	5	Scorpio	8:23 am
7	3:55 am	7	Sagittarius	5:03 pm
9	9:27 pm	10	Capricorn	4:52 am
12	11:36 am	12	Aquarius	6:44 pm
15	3:32 am	15	Pisces	6:12 am
17	9:12 am	17	Aries	2:57 pm
19	3:29 pm	19	Taurus	9:07 pm
21	1:21 pm	22	Gemini	1:30 am
23	11:52 pm	24	Cancer	4:53 am
26	2:58 am	26	Leo	7:45 am
28	5:54 am	28	Virgo	10:30 am
30	12:59 am	30	Libra	1:52 pm
			April	
1	2:29 pm	1	Scorpio	6:57 pm
3	12:06 pm	4	Sagittarius	2:55 am
6	9:36 am	6	Capricorn	2:01 pm
8	10:40 pm	9	Aquarius	2:50 am
11	10:55 am	11	Pisces	2:40 pm
13	7:27 am	13	Aries	11:25 pm
16	1:59 am	16	Taurus	4:51 am
17	6:05 pm	18	Gemini	8:02 am
20	8:05 am	20	Cancer	10:26 am
22	10:58 am	22	Leo	1:09 pm
24	2:40 pm	24	Virgo	4:40 pm
26	5:49 am	26	Libra	9:13 pm
29	1:32 am	29	Scorpio	3:11 am
30	10:56 pm	5/1	Sagittarius	11:20 am

Last Aspect   **Moon Enters New Sign**

		May			
3	8:50 pm	3		Capricorn	10:06 pm
6	9:48 am	6		Aquarius	10:48 am
8	10:29 pm	8		Pisces	11:11 pm
11	5:02 am	11		Aries	8:40 am
13	2:05 pm	13		Taurus	2:15 pm
15	4:30 pm	15		Gemini	4:43 pm
17	2:18 pm	17		Cancer	5:47 pm
19	5:14 pm	19		Leo	7:11 pm
20	11:30 pm	21		Virgo	10:03 pm
23	10:55 am	24		Libra	2:52 am
25	5:04 pm	26		Scorpio	9:39 am
28	1:25 pm	28		Sagittarius	6:29 pm
30	2:26 am	31		Capricorn	5:27 am
		June			
1	11:37 pm	2		Aquarius	6:06 pm
4	1:10 am	5		Pisces	6:53 am
7	2:35 am	7		Aries	5:26 pm
9	3:37 pm	10		Taurus	12:04 am
11	11:29 pm	12		Gemini	2:53 am
13	3:43 pm	14		Cancer	3:20 am
15	12:18 pm	16		Leo	3:21 am
17	11:26 pm	18		Virgo	4:41 am
20	6:51 am	20		Libra	8:29 am
21	9:34 pm	22		Scorpio	3:11 pm
24	10:00 am	25		Sagittarius	12:29 am
26	8:53 am	27		Capricorn	11:52 am
29	4:58 am	30		Aquarius	12:37 am

Last Aspect		Moon Enters New Sign			
		July			
1	6:56 pm	2		Pisces	1:31 pm
4	5:47 am	5		Aries	12:50 am
7	3:09 am	7		Taurus	8:51 am
9	12:09 pm	9		Gemini	12:58 pm
10	4:00 pm	11		Cancer	1:59 pm
12	10:48 pm	13		Leo	1:31 pm
14	7:12 pm	15		Virgo	1:31 pm
17	6:50 am	17		Libra	3:42 pm
19	3:52 pm	19		Scorpio	9:13 pm
22	5:18 am	22		Sagittarius	6:12 am
24	4:22 am	24		Capricorn	5:49 pm
26	9:41 am	27		Aquarius	6:41 am
29	5:25 am	29		Pisces	7:28 pm
31	6:42 pm	8/1		Aries	6:54 am
		August			
2	10:52 pm	3		Taurus	3:51 pm
5	7:46 pm	5		Gemini	9:32 pm
7	3:54 am	8		Cancer	12:01 am
9	7:21 am	10		Leo	12:18 am
11	5:58 am	11		Virgo	11:59 pm
14	12:37 am	14		Libra	12:57 am
16	3:56 am	16		Scorpio	4:54 am
18	11:07 am	18		Sagittarius	12:45 pm
20	7:47 pm	21		Capricorn	12:00 am
23	10:19 am	23		Aquarius	12:56 pm
25	12:39 am	26		Pisces	1:32 am
28	9:54 am	28		Aries	12:35 pm
30	7:04 pm	30		Taurus	9:30 pm

Last Aspect   Moon Enters New Sign

		September			
2	1:56 am	2	Gemini	4:02 am
4	2:37 am	4	Cancer	8:03 am
6	8:43 am	6	Leo	9:54 am
8	9:31 am	8	Virgo	10:29 am
10	11:12 am	10	Libra	11:20 am
11	6:58 pm	12	Scorpio	2:15 pm
14	4:54 am	14	Sagittarius	8:45 pm
16	7:15 pm	17	Capricorn	7:07 am
19	1:10 pm	19	Aquarius	7:52 pm
21	1:13 pm	22	Pisces	8:27 am
24	1:26 am	24	Aries	7:04 pm
26	6:28 am	27	Taurus	3:16 am
28	6:36 pm	29	Gemini	9:26 am
30	11:38 am	10/1	Cancer	2:00 pm
		October			
3	4:33 am	3	Leo	5:12 pm
5	7:34 am	5	Virgo	7:19 pm
7	10:03 am	7	Libra	9:10 pm
9	4:50 am	10	Scorpio	12:09 am
11	7:12 pm	12	Sagittarius	5:53 am
13	8:58 pm	14	Capricorn	3:17 pm
16	5:49 pm	17	Aquarius	3:36 am
19	8:27 am	19	Pisces	4:20 pm
21	7:47 pm	22	Aries	2:58 am
23	2:18 pm	24	Taurus	10:33 am
26	10:49 am	26	Gemini	3:41 pm
28	12:37 am	28	Cancer	7:27 pm
30	10:31 pm	30	Leo	10:42 pm

Last Aspect		**Moon Enters New Sign**		
		November		
2	12:32 am	2	Virgo	1:48 am
4	2:26 am	4	Libra	4:01 am
6	3:19 am	6	Scorpio	8:02 am
8	5:42 am	8	Sagittarius	1:59 pm
10	10:35 pm	10	Capricorn	10:55 pm
13	10:13 am	13	Aquarius	10:45 am
15	10:58 pm	15	Pisces	11:41 pm
18	3:04 am	18	Aries	10:56 am
20	5:46 pm	20	Taurus	6:43 pm
22	4:59 am	22	Gemini	11:10 pm
25	12:31 am	25	Cancer	1:38 am
27	2:22 am	27	Leo	3:35 am
29	4:47 am	29	Virgo	6:08 am
		December		
1	9:34 am	1	Libra	9:49 am
3	1:16 pm	3	Scorpio	2:55 pm
5	4:53 pm	5	Sagittarius	9:49 pm
8	5:00 am	8	Capricorn	7:01 am
10	4:27 pm	10	Aquarius	6:39 pm
13	5:20 am	13	Pisces	7:40 am
15	6:49 am	15	Aries	7:44 pm
18	2:21 am	18	Taurus	4:37 am
19	7:42 pm	20	Gemini	9:34 am
22	9:21 am	22	Cancer	11:28 am
24	9:50 am	24	Leo	11:59 am
26	10:37 am	26	Virgo	12:50 pm
28	11:27 am	28	Libra	3:23 pm
30	5:53 pm	30	Scorpio	8:23 pm

2017 © Joeygil Image from BigStockPhoto.com

The Moon's Rhythm

The Moon journeys around Earth in an elliptical orbit that takes about 27.33 days, which is known as a sidereal month (period of revolution of one body about another). She can move up to 15 degrees or as few as 11 degrees in a day, with the fastest motion occurring when the Moon is at perigee (closest approach to Earth). The Moon is never retrograde, but when her motion is slow, the effect is similar to a retrograde period.

Astrologers have observed that people born on a day when the Moon is fast will process information differently from those who are born when the Moon is slow in motion. People born when the Moon is fast process information quickly and tend to react quickly, while those born during a slow Moon will be more deliberate.

The time from New Moon to New Moon is called the synodic month (involving a conjunction), and the average time span between this Sun-Moon alignment is 29.53 days. Since 29.53

won't divide into 365 evenly, we can have a month with two Full Moons or two New Moons.

Moon Aspects

The aspects the Moon will make during the times you are considering are also important. A trine or sextile, and sometimes a conjunction, are considered favorable aspects. A trine or sextile between the Sun and Moon is an excellent foundation for success. Whether or not a conjunction is considered favorable depends upon the planet the Moon is making a conjunction to. If it's joining the Sun, Venus, Mercury, Jupiter, or even Saturn, the aspect is favorable. If the Moon joins Pluto or Mars, however, that would not be considered favorable. There may be exceptions, but it would depend on what you are electing to do. For example, a trine to Pluto might hasten the end of a relationship you want to be free of.

It is important to avoid times when the Moon makes an aspect to or is conjoining any retrograde planet, unless, of course, you want the thing started to end in failure.

After the Moon has completed an aspect to a planet, that planetary energy has passed. For example, if the Moon squares Saturn at 10:00 am, you can disregard Saturn's influence on your activity if it will occur after that time. You should always look ahead at aspects the Moon will make on the day in question, though, because if the Moon opposes Mars at 11:30 pm on that day, you can expect events that stretch into the evening to be affected by the Moon-Mars aspect. A testy conversation might lead to an argument, or more.

Moon Signs

Much agricultural work is ruled by earth signs—Virgo, Capricorn, and Taurus. The air signs—Gemini, Aquarius, and Libra—rule flying and intellectual pursuits.

Each planet has one or two signs in which its characteristics are enhanced or "dignified," and the planet is said to "rule" that sign. The Sun rules Leo and the Moon rules Cancer, for example. The ruling planet for each sign is listed below. These should not be considered complete lists. We recommend that you purchase a book of planetary rulerships for more complete information.

Aries Moon

The energy of an Aries Moon is masculine, dry, barren, and fiery. Aries provides great start-up energy, but things started at this time may be the result of impulsive action that lacks research or necessary support. Aries lacks staying power.

Use this assertive, outgoing Moon sign to initiate change, but have a plan in place for someone to pick up the reins when you're impatient to move on to the next thing. Work that requires skillful but not necessarily patient use of tools—cutting down trees, hammering, etc.—is appropriate in Aries. Expect things to occur rapidly but to also quickly pass. If you are prone to injury or accidents, exercise caution and good judgment in Aries-related activities.

RULER: Mars

IMPULSE: Action

RULES: Head and face

Taurus Moon

A Taurus Moon's energy is feminine, semi-fruitful, and earthy. The Moon is exalted—very strong—in Taurus. Taurus is known as the farmer's sign because of its associations with farmland and precipitation that is the typical day-long "soaker" variety. Taurus energy is good to incorporate into your plans when patience, practicality, and perseverance are needed. Be aware, though, that you may also experience stubbornness in this sign.

Things started in Taurus tend to be long lasting and to increase in value. This can be very supportive energy in a marriage election. On the downside, the fixed energy of this sign resists change or the letting go of even the most difficult situations. A divorce following a marriage that occurred during a Taurus Moon may be difficult and costly to end. Things begun now tend to become habitual and hard to alter. If you want to make changes in something you started, it would be better to wait for Gemini. This is a good time to get a loan, but expect the people in charge of money to be cautious and slow to make decisions.

RULER: Venus

IMPULSE: Stability

RULES: Neck, throat, and voice

Gemini Moon

A Gemini Moon's energy is masculine, dry, barren, and airy. People are more changeable than usual and may prefer to follow intellectual pursuits and play mental games rather than apply themselves to practical concerns.

This sign is not favored for agricultural matters, but it is an excellent time to prepare for activities, to run errands, and write letters. Plan to use a Gemini Moon to exchange ideas, meet people, go on vacations that include walking or biking, or be in situations that require versatility and quick thinking on your feet.

RULER: Mercury

IMPULSE: Versatility

RULES: Shoulders, hands, arms, lungs, and nervous system

Cancer Moon

A Cancer Moon's energy is feminine, fruitful, moist, and very strong. Use this sign when you want to grow things—flowers, fruits, vegetables, commodities, stocks, or collections—for example. This sensitive sign stimulates rapport between people. Considered the most fertile of the signs, it is often associated with mothering. You can use this moontime to build personal friendships that support mutual growth.

Cancer is associated with emotions and feelings. Prominent Cancer energy promotes growth, but it can also turn people pouty and prone to withdrawing into their shells.

RULER: The Moon

IMPULSE: Tenacity

RULES: Chest area, breasts, and stomach

Leo Moon

A Leo Moon's energy is masculine, hot, dry, fiery, and barren. Use it whenever you need to put on a show, make a presentation, or entertain colleagues or guests. This is a proud yet playful energy that exudes self-confidence and is often associated with romance.

This is an excellent time for fundraisers and ceremonies or to be straightforward, frank, and honest about something. It is advisable not to put yourself in a position of needing public approval or where you might have to cope with underhandedness, as trouble in these areas can bring out the worst Leo traits. There is a tendency in this sign to become arrogant or self-centered.

RULER: The Sun

IMPULSE: I am

RULES: Heart and upper back

Virgo Moon

A Virgo Moon is feminine, dry, barren, earthy energy. It is favorable for anything that needs painstaking attention—especially those things where exactness rather than innovation is preferred.

Use this sign for activities when you must analyze information or when you must determine the value of something. Virgo is the sign of bargain hunting. It's friendly toward agricultural matters with an emphasis on animals and harvesting vegetables. It is an excellent time to care for animals, especially training them and veterinary work.

This sign is most beneficial when decisions have already been made and now need to be carried out. The inclination here is to see details rather than the bigger picture.

There is a tendency in this sign to overdo. Precautions should be taken to avoid becoming too dull from all work and no play. Build a little relaxation and pleasure into your routine from the beginning.

RULER: Mercury

IMPULSE: Discriminating

RULES: Abdomen and intestines

Libra Moon

A Libra Moon's energy is masculine, semi-fruitful, and airy. This energy will benefit any attempt to bring beauty to a place or thing. Libra is considered good energy for starting things of an intellectual nature. Libra is the sign of partnership and unions, which makes it an excellent time to form partnerships of any kind, to make agreements, and to negotiate. Even though this sign is good for initiating things, it is crucial to work with a partner who will provide incentive and encouragement, however. A Libra Moon accentuates teamwork (particularly teams of two) and artistic work (especially work that involves color). Make use of this sign when you are decorating your home or shopping for better-quality clothing.

RULER: Venus

IMPULSE: Balance

RULES: Lower back, kidneys, and buttocks

Scorpio Moon

The Scorpio Moon is feminine, fruitful, cold, and moist. It is useful when intensity (that sometimes borders on obsession) is needed. Scorpio is considered a very psychic sign. Use this Moon sign when you must back up something you strongly believe in, such as union or employer relations. There is strong group loyalty here, but a Scorpio Moon is also a good time to end connections thoroughly. This is also a good time to conduct research.

The desire nature is so strong here that there is a tendency to manipulate situations to get what one wants or to not see one's responsibility in an act.

RULER: Pluto, Mars (traditional)

IMPULSE: Transformation

RULES: Reproductive organs, genitals, groin, and pelvis

Sagittarius Moon

The Moon's energy is masculine, dry, barren, and fiery in Sagittarius, encouraging flights of imagination and confidence in the flow of life. Sagittarius is the most philosophical sign. Candor and honesty are enhanced when the Moon is here. This is an excellent time to "get things off your chest" and to deal with institutions of higher learning, publishing companies, and the law. It's also a good time for sport and adventure.

Sagittarians are the crusaders of this world. This is a good time to tackle things that need improvement, but don't try to be the diplomat while influenced by this energy. Opinions can run strong, and the tendency to proselytize is increased.

RULER: Jupiter

IMPULSE: Expansion

RULES: Thighs and hips

Capricorn Moon

In Capricorn the Moon's energy is feminine, semi-fruitful, and earthy. Because Cancer and Capricorn are polar opposites, the Moon's energy is thought to be weakened here. This energy encourages the need for structure, discipline, and organization. This is a good time to set goals and plan for the future, tend to family business, and to take care of details requiring patience or a businesslike manner. Institutional activities are favored. This sign should be avoided if you're seeking favors, as those in authority can be insensitive under this influence.

RULER: Saturn

IMPULSE: Ambitious

RULES: Bones, skin, and knees

Aquarius Moon

An Aquarius Moon's energy is masculine, barren, dry, and airy. Activities that are unique, individualistic, concerned with humanitarian issues, society as a whole, and making improvements are favored under this Moon. It is this quality of making improvements that has caused this sign to be associated with inventors and new inventions.

An Aquarius Moon promotes the gathering of social groups for friendly exchanges. People tend to react and speak from an intellectual rather than emotional viewpoint when the Moon is in this sign.

RULER: Uranus and Saturn

IMPULSE: Reformer

RULES: Calves and ankles

Pisces Moon

A Pisces Moon is feminine, fruitful, cool, and moist. This is an excellent time to retreat, meditate, sleep, pray, or make that dreamed-of escape into a fantasy vacation. However, things are not always what they seem to be with the Moon in Pisces. Personal boundaries tend to be fuzzy, and you may not be seeing things clearly. People tend to be idealistic under this sign, which can prevent them from seeing reality.

There is a live-and-let-live philosophy attached to this sign, which in the idealistic world may work well enough, but chaos is frequently the result. That's why this sign is also associated with alcohol and drug abuse, drug trafficking, and counterfeiting. On the lighter side, many musicians and artists are ruled by Pisces. It's only when they move too far away from reality that the dark side of substance abuse, suicide, or crime takes away life.

RULER: Jupiter and Neptune

IMPULSE: Empathetic

RULES: Feet

More About Zodiac Signs

Element (Triplicity)

Each of the zodiac signs is classified as belonging to an element; these are the four basic elements:

Fire Signs

Aries, Sagittarius, and Leo are action-oriented, outgoing, energetic, and spontaneous.

Earth Signs

Taurus, Capricorn, and Virgo are stable, conservative, practical, and oriented to the physical and material realm.

Air Signs

Gemini, Aquarius, and Libra are sociable and critical, and they tend to represent intellectual responses rather than feelings.

Water Signs

Cancer, Scorpio, and Pisces are emotional, receptive, intuitive, and can be very sensitive.

Quality (Quadruplicity)

Each zodiac sign is further classified as being cardinal, mutable, or fixed. There are four signs in each quadruplicity, one sign from each element.

Cardinal Signs

Aries, Cancer, Libra, and Capricorn represent beginnings and newly initiated action. They initiate each new season in the cycle of the year.

Fixed Signs

Taurus, Leo, Scorpio, and Aquarius want to maintain the status quo through stubbornness and persistence; they represent that "between" time. For example, Leo is the month when summer really feels like summer.

Mutable Signs

Pisces, Gemini, Virgo, and Sagittarius adapt to change and tolerate situations. They represent the last month of each season, when things are changing in preparation for the coming season.

Nature and Fertility

In addition to a sign's element and quality, each sign is further classified as either fruitful, semi-fruitful, or barren. This classification is the most important for readers who use the gardening information in the *Moon Sign Book* because the timing of most events depends on the fertility of the sign occupied by the Moon. The water signs of Cancer, Scorpio, and Pisces are the most fruitful. The semi-fruitful signs are the earth signs Taurus and Capricorn, and the air sign Libra. The barren signs correspond to fire-signs Aries, Leo, and Sagittarius; air-signs Gemini and Aquarius; and earth-sign Virgo.

2017 © World Image Image from BigStockPhoto.com

Good Timing

By Sharon Leah

Electional astrology is the art of electing times to begin any undertaking. Say, for example, you want to start a business. That business will experience ups and downs, as well as reach its potential, according to the promise held in the universe at the time the business was started—its birth time. The horoscope (birth chart) set for the date, time, and place that a business starts would indicate the outcome—its potential to succeed.

So, you might ask yourself the question: If the horoscope for a business start can show success or failure, why not begin at a time that is more favorable to the venture? Well, you can.

While no time is perfect, there are better times and better days to undertake specific activities. There are thousands of examples that prove electional astrology is not only practical, but that it can make a difference in our lives. There are rules for electing times to begin various activities—even shopping. You'll find detailed instructions about how to make elections beginning on page 107.

Personalizing Elections

The election rules in this almanac are based upon the planetary positions at the time for which the election is made. They do not depend on any type of birth chart. However, a birth chart based upon the time, date, and birthplace of an event has advantages. No election is effective for every person. For example, you may leave home to begin a trip at the same time as a friend, but each of you will have a different experience according to whether or not your birth chart favors the trip.

Not all elections require a birth chart, but the timing of very important events—business starts, marriages, etc.—would benefit from the additional accuracy a birth chart provides. To order a birth chart for yourself or a planned event, visit our Web site at www .llewellyn.com.

Some Things to Consider

You've probably experienced good timing in your life. Maybe you were at the right place at the right time to meet a friend whom you hadn't seen in years. Frequently, when something like that happens, it is the result of following an intuitive impulse—that "gut instinct." Consider for a moment that you were actually responding to planetary energies. Electional astrology is a tool that can help you to align with energies, present and future, that are available to us through planetary placements.

Significators

Decide upon the important significators (planet, sign, and house ruling the matter) for which the election is being made. The Moon is the most important significator in any election, so the Moon should always be fortified (strong by sign and making favorable aspects to other planets). The Moon's aspects to other planets are more important than the sign the Moon is in.

Other important considerations are the significators of the Ascendant and Midheaven—the house ruling the election matter and the ruler of the sign on that house cusp. Finally, any planet or sign that has a general rulership over the matter in question should be taken into consideration.

Nature and Fertility

Determine the general nature of the sign that is appropriate for your election. For example, much agricultural work is ruled by the earth signs of Virgo, Capricorn, and Taurus; while the air signs—Gemini, Aquarius, and Libra—rule intellectual pursuits.

One Final Comment

Use common sense. If you must do something, like plant your garden or take an airplane trip on a day that doesn't have the best aspects, proceed anyway, but try to minimize problems. For example, leave early for the airport to avoid being left behind due to delays in the security lanes. When you have no other choice, do the best that you can under the circumstances at the time.

If you want to personalize your elections, please turn to page 107 for more information. If you want a quick and easy answer, you can refer to Llewellyn's Astro Almanac on the following pages.

Llewellyn's Astro Almanac

The Astro Almanac tables, beginning on the next page, can help you find the dates best suited to particular activities. The dates provided are determined from the Moon's sign, phase, and aspects to other planets. Please note that the Astro Almanac does not take personal factors, such as your Sun and Moon sign, into account. The dates are general, and they will apply for everyone. Some activities will not have ideal dates during a particular month.

Activity	January
Animals (Neuter or spay)	12–16
Animals (Sell or buy)	21, 22, 27, 29
Automobile (Buy)	5, 14, 15, 28
Brewing	10
Build (Start foundation)	24
Business (Conducting for self and others)	6, 11, 22, 27
Business (Start new)	24, 25
Can Fruits and Vegetables	10
Can Preserves	10
Concrete (Pour)	3, 4
Construction (Begin new)	2, 6, 16, 22, 27, 29
Consultants (Begin work with)	2, 4, 6, 9, 11, 15, 16, 20, 21, 25, 29
Contracts (Bid on)	2, 20, 21, 25, 29
Cultivate	no ideal dates
Decorating	1, 18, 19, 26–28
Demolition	3–5, 12, 13, 31
Electronics (Buy)	9, 19, 28
Entertain Guests	no ideal dates
Floor Covering (Laying new)	3–9
Habits (Break)	14, 15
Hair (Cut to increase growth)	20, 21, 24–27, 30
Hair (Cut to decrease growth)	12–16
Harvest (Grain for storage)	3–5
Harvest (Root crops)	3, 4, 12–14, 31
Investments (New)	6, 27
Loan (Ask for)	24–26, 30, 31
Massage (Relaxing)	no ideal dates
Mow Lawn (Decrease growth)	2–15
Mow Lawn (Increase growth)	17–30
Mushrooms (Pick)	1, 2, 30, 31
Negotiate (Business for the elderly)	9, 19, 24
Prune for Better Fruit	9–12
Prune to Promote Healing	15, 16
Wean Children	12–19
Wood Floors (Installing)	14–16
Write Letters or Contracts	4, 14, 15, 19

Activity	February
Animals (Neuter or spay)	10–12
Animals (Sell or buy)	17, 21, 26
Automobile (Buy)	1, 11, 24
Brewing	6, 7
Build (Start foundation)	21
Business (Conducting for self and others)	4, 10, 20, 25
Business (Start new)	21, 22
Can Fruits and Vegetables	6, 7
Can Preserves	6, 7
Concrete (Pour)	14
Construction (Begin new)	3, 4, 10, 12, 20, 25, 26
Consultants (Begin work with)	3, 4, 7, 9, 12, 15, 17, 21, 25, 26
Contracts (Bid on)	17, 21, 25, 26
Cultivate	14, 15
Decorating	15, 23, 24
Demolition	9
Electronics (Buy)	4, 15, 24
Entertain Guests	5, 21, 26
Floor Covering (Laying new)	1–5, 14, 15
Habits (Break)	11–14
Hair (Cut to increase growth)	16–17, 20–23, 26
Hair (Cut to decrease growth)	9–12
Harvest (Grain for storage)	1
Harvest (Root crops)	1, 9, 10, 14
Investments (New)	4, 25
Loan (Ask for)	20–22, 26–28
Massage (Relaxing)	5, 21, 26
Mow Lawn (Decrease growth)	1–14
Mow Lawn (Increase growth)	16–28
Mushrooms (Pick)	1, 28
Negotiate (Business for the elderly)	1, 6, 16
Prune for Better Fruit	6–10
Prune to Promote Healing	11–13
Wean Children	9–15
Wood Floors (Installing)	10–13
Write Letters or Contracts	1, 10, 15, 24, 28

Activity	March
Animals (Neuter or spay)	8, 10, 11, 12, 15, 16
Animals (Sell or buy)	25, 28, 30
Automobile (Buy)	1, 10, 23, 29
Brewing	6, 7, 16
Build (Start foundation)	20
Business (Conducting for self and others)	6, 12, 22, 26
Business (Start new)	1, 20, 21, 29, 30
Can Fruits and Vegetables	6, 7, 16
Can Preserves	6, 7
Concrete (Pour)	13, 14
Construction (Begin new)	2, 12, 22, 25, 26, 30
Consultants (Begin work with)	2, 7, 12, 13, 17, 18, 23, 25, 27, 30
Contracts (Bid on)	18, 23, 25, 27, 30
Cultivate	8, 9, 13–15
Decorating	22–24, 30, 31
Demolition	7–9
Electronics (Buy)	13, 14, 23
Entertain Guests	23, 28
Floor Covering (Laying new)	2–5, 13, 14
Habits (Break)	10–13, 15
Hair (Cut to increase growth)	19–23, 26
Hair (Cut to decrease growth)	7–11, 16
Harvest (Grain for storage)	7, 8
Harvest (Root crops)	7–9, 13, 14
Investments (New)	6, 26
Loan (Ask for)	19–21, 26–28
Massage (Relaxing)	13, 28
Mow Lawn (Decrease growth)	2–16
Mow Lawn (Increase growth)	18–30
Mushrooms (Pick)	1, 2, 30, 31
Negotiate (Business for the elderly)	1, 5, 15, 20
Prune for Better Fruit	5–9
Prune to Promote Healing	10–12
Wean Children	8–15
Wood Floors (Installing)	10–12
Write Letters or Contracts	9, 14, 18, 23, 28

Activity	April
Animals (Neuter or spay)	4–8, 12, 13
Animals (Sell or buy)	26, 27
Automobile (Buy)	7, 18, 20, 25
Brewing	2, 12, 13, 30
Build (Start foundation)	16
Business (Conducting for self and others)	5, 10, 20, 25
Business (Start new)	16, 17, 25, 26
Can Fruits and Vegetables	2, 12, 13, 30
Can Preserves	2, 30
Concrete (Pour)	9, 10
Construction (Begin new)	5, 8, 10, 20, 21, 25, 26
Consultants (Begin work with)	3, 4, 8, 9, 13, 14, 18, 21, 23, 26, 30
Contracts (Bid on)	18, 21, 23, 26
Cultivate	4–6, 9–11, 14, 15
Decorating	18–20, 26–29
Demolition	4, 5, 14, 15
Electronics (Buy)	9, 11, 18, 20
Entertain Guests	22
Floor Covering (Laying new)	1, 9–11
Habits (Break)	9–11, 14
Hair (Cut to increase growth)	16–19, 22
Hair (Cut to decrease growth)	4–9, 12
Harvest (Grain for storage)	4–6
Harvest (Root crops)	4–6, 9–11, 14
Investments (New)	5, 25
Loan (Ask for)	16, 17, 22–24
Massage (Relaxing)	17, 22, 27
Mow Lawn (Decrease growth)	1–14, 30
Mow Lawn (Increase growth)	16–28
Mushrooms (Pick)	1, 28–30
Negotiate (Business for the elderly)	2, 12, 16, 25, 29
Prune for Better Fruit	1–5
Prune to Promote Healing	7–9
Wean Children	4–11
Wood Floors (Installing)	7–9
Write Letters or Contracts	6, 11, 14, 24

Activity	May
Animals (Neuter or spay)	1–4, 9, 10, 29–31
Animals (Sell or buy)	18, 22, 23, 27
Automobile (Buy)	4, 21–23, 31
Brewing	9, 10
Build (Start foundation)	no ideal dates
Business (Conducting for self and others)	5, 10, 19, 24
Business (Start new)	22, 23
Can Fruits and Vegetables	9, 10
Can Preserves	14, 15
Concrete (Pour)	7, 8, 14
Construction (Begin new)	5, 18, 19, 23, 24
Consultants (Begin work with)	2, 5, 8, 10, 13, 18, 23, 27
Contracts (Bid on)	18, 23, 27
Cultivate	2, 3, 7, 8, 12, 13, 29, 30
Decorating	15–17, 24, 25
Demolition	1, 2, 11, 12, 29, 30
Electronics (Buy)	8
Entertain Guests	17
Floor Covering (Laying new)	6–8, 13–15
Habits (Break)	11, 12
Hair (Cut to increase growth)	16, 19, 28
Hair (Cut to decrease growth)	1–5, 9, 10, 13–15, 30, 31
Harvest (Grain for storage)	1–3, 6, 7, 30
Harvest (Root crops)	1–3, 6–8, 11–13, 29, 30
Investments (New)	5, 24
Loan (Ask for)	19–21
Massage (Relaxing)	7
Mow Lawn (Decrease growth)	1–14, 30, 31
Mow Lawn (Increase growth)	16–28
Mushrooms (Pick)	28–30
Negotiate (Business for the elderly)	9, 22
Prune for Better Fruit	1–3, 29
Prune to Promote Healing	4–6, 31
Wean Children	2–8, 29–31
Wood Floors (Installing)	3–6, 31
Write Letters or Contracts	3, 8, 13, 17, 21, 31

Activity	June
Animals (Neuter or spay)	1, 2, 5–7, 29
Animals (Sell or buy)	14, 15, 19, 26
Automobile (Buy)	18, 19, 27
Brewing	6, 7
Build (Start foundation)	no ideal dates
Business (Conducting for self and others)	3, 9, 17, 22
Business (Start new)	18, 19
Can Fruits and Vegetables	6, 7
Can Preserves	10
Concrete (Pour)	3, 4, 10, 30
Construction (Begin new)	1, 3, 9, 15, 17, 19, 28
Consultants (Begin work with)	1, 3, 6, 9, 14, 15, 19, 23, 24, 28
Contracts (Bid on)	14, 15, 19, 23, 24, 28
Cultivate	8, 9, 12, 13
Decorating	13, 14, 20–22
Demolition	7–9
Electronics (Buy)	3
Entertain Guests	11
Floor Covering (Laying new)	2–4, 10–13, 30
Habits (Break)	7–9, 12
Hair (Cut to increase growth)	16, 25, 26
Hair (Cut to decrease growth)	1, 5, 6, 10–13, 29
Harvest (Grain for storage)	2–4, 30
Harvest (Root crops)	2–4, 7–9, 12, 30
Investments (New)	3, 22
Loan (Ask for)	16, 17
Massage (Relaxing)	11, 16, 20
Mow Lawn (Decrease growth)	1–12, 29, 30
Mow Lawn (Increase growth)	14–26
Mushrooms (Pick)	27–29
Negotiate (Business for the elderly)	5, 10, 18
Prune for Better Fruit	no ideal dates
Prune to Promote Healing	1, 2, 28, 29
Wean Children	1–4, 25–30
Wood Floors (Installing)	1, 2, 28, 29
Write Letters or Contracts	5, 14, 18, 27

Activity	July
Animals (Neuter or spay)	3, 4, 30, 31
Animals (Sell or buy)	16, 25, 26
Automobile (Buy)	10, 15, 24, 25
Brewing	3, 30, 31
Build (Start foundation)	15
Business (Conducting for self and others)	8, 17, 22
Business (Start new)	15, 16, 25
Can Fruits and Vegetables	3, 12, 30, 31
Can Preserves	8, 12
Concrete (Pour)	1, 8, 28, 29
Construction (Begin new)	8, 12, 16, 17, 25
Consultants (Begin work with)	3, 5, 10, 12, 14, 16, 19, 20, 24, 25, 30
Contracts (Bid on)	14, 16, 19, 20, 24, 25
Cultivate	6, 7, 10, 11
Decorating	17–19, 27
Demolition	5, 6
Electronics (Buy)	10, 19
Entertain Guests	15
Floor Covering (Laying new)	7–10, 28, 29
Habits (Break)	9, 11
Hair (Cut to increase growth)	13, 22–26
Hair (Cut to decrease growth)	3, 4, 7–10, 30, 31
Harvest (Grain for storage)	1, 5, 6, 28–29
Harvest (Root crops)	1, 2, 5, 6, 9–11, 28, 29
Investments (New)	3, 22
Loan (Ask for)	13, 14
Massage (Relaxing)	11
Mow Lawn (Decrease growth)	1–11, 28–31
Mow Lawn (Increase growth)	13–26
Mushrooms (Pick)	26–28
Negotiate (Business for the elderly)	7, 15
Prune for Better Fruit	no ideal dates
Prune to Promote Healing	no ideal dates
Wean Children	1, 2, 22–29
Wood Floors (Installing)	no ideal dates
Write Letters or Contracts	2, 11, 14, 15, 24, 30

Activity	August
Animals (Neuter or spay)	27, 28
Animals (Sell or buy)	12, 13, 19, 22, 24
Automobile (Buy)	7, 12, 21
Brewing	8, 27, 28
Build (Start foundation)	no ideal dates
Business (Conducting for self and others)	2, 6, 15, 21, 31
Business (Start new)	12, 13, 22
Can Fruits and Vegetables	8, 27
Can Preserves	4, 5, 8, 31
Concrete (Pour)	4, 5, 10, 31
Construction (Begin new)	2, 6, 8, 13, 15, 20, 22, 31
Consultants (Begin work with)	2, 7, 8, 10, 13, 14, 17, 19, 22, 27, 30
Contracts (Bid on)	13, 14, 17, 19, 22
Cultivate	6, 7, 10, 11
Decorating	14–16, 23–25
Demolition	1, 2, 10, 28, 29
Electronics (Buy)	7, 14
Entertain Guests	5
Floor Covering (Laying new)	3–7, 10, 11, 31
Habits (Break)	6, 7, 10
Hair (Cut to increase growth)	18–22
Hair (Cut to decrease growth)	3–7, 27, 30, 31
Harvest (Grain for storage)	1–3, 28–30
Harvest (Root crops)	1–3, 6, 7, 10, 28–30
Investments (New)	2, 20, 31
Loan (Ask for)	no ideal dates
Massage (Relaxing)	5, 10, 14, 25
Mow Lawn (Decrease growth)	1–10, 27–31
Mow Lawn (Increase growth)	12–25
Mushrooms (Pick)	25–27
Negotiate (Business for the elderly)	3, 16
Prune for Better Fruit	no ideal dates
Prune to Promote Healing	no ideal dates
Wean Children	19–25
Wood Floors (Installing)	no ideal dates
Write Letters or Contracts	8, 12, 21, 26

Activity	September
Animals (Neuter or spay)	no ideal dates
Animals (Sell or buy)	17, 18, 22, 23
Automobile (Buy)	4, 8, 17, 19, 30
Brewing	5
Build (Start foundation)	no ideal dates
Business (Conducting for self and others)	5, 14, 19, 29
Business (Start new)	9, 18
Can Fruits and Vegetables	5
Can Preserves	1, 5, 27, 28
Concrete (Pour)	1, 7, 27, 28
Construction (Begin new)	5, 9, 18, 19, 29
Consultants (Begin work with)	4, 5, 8, 9, 13, 14, 18, 19, 24, 30
Contracts (Bid on)	13, 14, 16, 18, 19, 24
Cultivate	2–4, 7–9
Decorating	10–12, 19–22
Demolition	6, 7, 24–26
Electronics (Buy)	4, 30
Entertain Guests	3
Floor Covering (Laying new)	6–9, 27–30
Habits (Break)	3, 4, 8
Hair (Cut to increase growth)	14–18
Hair (Cut to decrease growth)	1–3, 6, 27–30
Harvest (Grain for storage)	2, 25, 26, 29, 30
Harvest (Root crops)	2, 3, 6, 7, 25, 26, 29, 30
Investments (New)	19, 29
Loan (Ask for)	no ideal dates
Massage (Relaxing)	8
Mow Lawn (Decrease growth)	1–8, 25–30
Mow Lawn (Increase growth)	10–23
Mushrooms (Pick)	23–25
Negotiate (Business for the elderly)	8, 12, 22, 27
Prune for Better Fruit	no ideal dates
Prune to Promote Healing	no ideal dates
Wean Children	15–22
Wood Floors (Installing)	no ideal dates
Write Letters or Contracts	4, 8, 17, 22

Activity	October
Animals (Neuter or spay)	no ideal dates
Animals (Sell or buy)	no ideal dates
Automobile (Buy)	5, 6, 14, 15
Brewing	2, 3, 29, 30
Build (Start foundation)	10, 15, 20, 21
Business (Conducting for self and others)	4, 13, 19, 29
Business (Start new)	16
Can Fruits and Vegetables	2, 3, 29, 30
Can Preserves	2, 3, 25, 26, 29, 30
Concrete (Pour)	4, 5, 25, 26, 31
Construction (Begin new)	3, 4, 7, 13, 16, 19, 29, 30
Consultants (Begin work with)	3, 5, 7, 10, 11, 15, 16, 21, 30
Contracts (Bid on)	11, 15, 16, 21
Cultivate	4–7
Decorating	8, 9, 17–19
Demolition	3, 4, 30, 31
Electronics (Buy)	no ideal dates
Entertain Guests	2, 28
Floor Covering (Laying new)	3–8, 25–27, 30, 31
Habits (Break)	3
Hair (Cut to increase growth)	12–16, 20–22, 24
Hair (Cut to decrease growth)	3, 25–27, 30
Harvest (Grain for storage)	26–28, 30, 31
Harvest (Root crops)	1, 3–5, 26–28, 30, 31
Investments (New)	19, 29
Loan (Ask for)	no ideal dates
Massage (Relaxing)	2, 28
Mow Lawn (Decrease growth)	1–7, 25–31
Mow Lawn (Increase growth)	9–23
Mushrooms (Pick)	23–25
Negotiate (Business for the elderly)	24
Prune for Better Fruit	no ideal dates
Prune to Promote Healing	no ideal dates
Wean Children	12–19
Wood Floors (Installing)	no ideal dates
Write Letters or Contracts	1, 5, 10, 14, 19, 28

Activity	November
Animals (Neuter or spay)	no ideal dates
Animals (Sell or buy)	10, 13, 18
Automobile (Buy)	2, 11, 25, 29
Brewing	25, 26
Build (Start foundation)	6
Business (Conducting for self and others)	2, 12, 18, 27
Business (Start new)	21
Can Fruits and Vegetables	7, 25, 26
Can Preserves	7, 25, 26
Concrete (Pour)	27, 28
Construction (Begin new)	2, 4, 12, 13, 18, 27
Consultants (Begin work with)	4, 8, 9, 13, 14, 18, 19, 27
Contracts (Bid on)	8, 9, 13, 14, 18, 19
Cultivate	1–3, 30
Decorating	13–15
Demolition	1, 2, 27, 28
Electronics (Buy)	4, 14, 15, 25
Entertain Guests	2, 6, 24
Floor Covering (Laying new)	1–3, 5, 6, 23, 24, 27–30
Habits (Break)	2
Hair (Cut to increase growth)	8–12, 16, 17, 20, 21
Hair (Cut to decrease growth)	24, 25, 27
Harvest (Grain for storage)	27–29
Harvest (Root crops)	1, 23, 24, 27, 28
Investments (New)	18, 27
Loan (Ask for)	20–22
Massage (Relaxing)	2, 6, 15, 29
Mow Lawn (Decrease growth)	1–3, 5, 6, 24–30
Mow Lawn (Increase growth)	8–21
Mushrooms (Pick)	22–24
Negotiate (Business for the elderly)	2, 6, 16, 29
Prune for Better Fruit	6, 7
Prune to Promote Healing	no ideal dates
Wean Children	9–15
Wood Floors (Installing)	no ideal dates
Write Letters or Contracts	9, 10, 15, 25

Activity	December
Animals (Neuter or spay)	6, 7
Animals (Sell or buy)	8, 11, 13, 16
Automobile (Buy)	1, 9, 10, 22, 27
Brewing	4, 5, 23, 31
Build (Start foundation)	13
Business (Conducting for self and others)	2, 12, 17, 26, 31
Business (Start new)	18
Can Fruits and Vegetables	4, 5, 23, 31
Can Preserves	4, 5, 23, 31
Concrete (Pour)	25
Construction (Begin new)	1, 2, 11, 12, 16, 17, 25, 26, 29
Consultants (Begin work with)	1, 5, 6, 10, 11, 16, 25, 29, 30
Contracts (Bid on)	10, 11, 16, 21
Cultivate	1
Decorating	11–13, 20–22
Demolition	6, 7, 24, 25
Electronics (Buy)	13, 22, 30
Entertain Guests	3
Floor Covering (Laying new)	1–3, 24–30
Habits (Break)	no ideal dates
Hair (Cut to increase growth)	8, 9, 14, 18–21
Hair (Cut to decrease growth)	6, 7, 24
Harvest (Grain for storage)	24–26
Harvest (Root crops)	24–26
Investments (New)	17, 26
Loan (Ask for)	18–20
Massage (Relaxing)	23
Mow Lawn (Decrease growth)	1–5, 23–31
Mow Lawn (Increase growth)	8–21
Mushrooms (Pick)	21–23
Negotiate (Business for the elderly)	18, 31
Prune for Better Fruit	3–6, 31
Prune to Promote Healing	no ideal dates
Wean Children	6–13
Wood Floors (Installing)	no ideal dates
Write Letters or Contracts	5, 8, 22, 26

2017 © Ridd81 Image from BigStockPhoto.com

Choose the Best Time for Your Activities

When rules for elections refer to "favorable" and "unfavorable" aspects to your Sun or other planets, please refer to the Favorable and Unfavorable Days Tables and Lunar Aspectarian for more information. You'll find instructions beginning on page 129 and the tables beginning on page 136.

The material in this section came from several sources including: *The New A to Z Horoscope Maker and Delineator* by Llewellyn George (Llewellyn, 1999), *Moon Sign Book* (Llewellyn, 1945), and *Electional Astrology* by Vivian Robson (Slingshot Publishing, 2000). Robson's book was originally published in 1937.

Advertise (Internet)

The Moon should be conjunct, sextile, or trine Mercury or Uranus and in the sign of Gemini, Capricorn, or Aquarius.

Advertise (Print)

Write ads on a day favorable to your Sun. The Moon should be conjunct, sextile, or trine Mercury or Venus. Avoid hard aspects to Mars and Saturn. Ad campaigns produce the best results when the Moon is well aspected in Gemini (to enhance communication) or Capricorn (to build business).

Animals

Take home new pets when the day is favorable to your Sun, or when the Moon is trine, sextile, or conjunct Mercury, Jupiter or Venus, or in the sign of Virgo or Pisces. However, avoid days when the Moon is either square or opposing the Sun, Mars, Saturn, Uranus, Neptune, or Pluto. When selecting a pet, have the Moon well aspected by the planet that rules the animal. Cats are ruled by the Sun, dogs by Mercury, birds by Venus, horses by Jupiter, and fish by Neptune. Buy large animals when the Moon is in Sagittarius or Pisces and making favorable aspects to Jupiter or Mercury. Buy animals smaller than sheep when the Moon is in Virgo with favorable aspects to Mercury or Venus.

Animals (Breed)

Animals are easiest to handle when the Moon is in Taurus, Cancer, Libra, or Pisces, but try to avoid the Full Moon. To encourage healthy births, animals should be mated so births occur when the Moon is increasing in Taurus, Cancer, Pisces, or Libra. Those born during a semi-fruitful sign (Taurus and Capricorn) will produce leaner meat. Libra yields beautiful animals for showing and racing.

Animals (Declaw)

Declaw cats for medical purposes in the dark of the Moon. Avoid the week before and after the Full Moon and the sign of Pisces.

Animals (Neuter or Spay)

Have livestock and pets neutered or spayed when the Moon is in Sagittarius, Capricorn, or Pisces, after it has passed through Scorpio, the sign that rules reproductive organs. Avoid the week before and after the Full Moon.

Animals (Sell or Buy)

In either buying or selling, it is important to keep the Moon and Mercury free from any aspect to Mars. Aspects to Mars will create discord and increase the likelihood of wrangling over price and quality. The Moon should be passing from the first quarter to full and sextile or trine Venus or Jupiter. When buying racehorses, let the Moon be in an air sign. The Moon should be in air signs when you buy birds. If the birds are to be pets, let the Moon be in good aspect to Venus.

Animals (Train)

Train pets when the Moon is in Virgo or trine to Mercury.

Animals (Train Dogs to Hunt)

Let the Moon be in Aries in conjunction with Mars, which makes them courageous and quick to learn. But let Jupiter also be in aspect to preserve them from danger in hunting.

Automobiles

When buying an automobile, select a time when the Moon is conjunct, sextile, or trine to Mercury, Saturn, or Uranus and in the sign of Gemini or Capricorn. Avoid times when Mercury is in retrograde motion.

Baking Cakes

Your cakes will have a lighter texture if you see that the Moon is in Gemini, Libra, or Aquarius and in good aspect to Venus or Mercury. If you are decorating a cake or confections are being made, have the Moon placed in Libra.

Beauty Treatments (Massage, etc.)

See that the Moon is in Taurus, Cancer, Leo, Libra, or Aquarius and in favorable aspect to Venus. In the case of plastic surgery, aspects to Mars should be avoided, and the Moon should not be in the sign ruling the part to be operated on.

Borrow (Money or Goods)

See that the Moon is not placed between 15 degrees Libra and 15 degrees Scorpio. Let the Moon be waning and in Leo, Scorpio (16 to 30 degrees), Sagittarius, or Pisces. Venus should be in good aspect to the Moon, and the Moon should not be square, opposing, or conjunct either Saturn or Mars.

Brewing

Start brewing during the third or fourth quarter, when the Moon is in Cancer, Scorpio, or Pisces.

Build (Start Foundation)

Turning the first sod for the foundation marks the beginning of the building. For best results, excavate the site when the Moon is in the first quarter of a fixed sign and making favorable aspects to Saturn.

Business (Start New)

When starting a business, have the Moon be in Taurus, Virgo, or Capricorn and increasing. The Moon should be sextile or trine Jupiter or Saturn, but avoid oppositions or squares. The planet ruling the business should be well aspected, too.

Buy Goods

Buy during the third quarter, when the Moon is in Taurus for quality or in a mutable sign (Gemini, Sagittarius, Virgo, or Pisces) for savings. Good aspects to Venus or the Sun are desirable. If you are buying for yourself, it is good if the day is favorable for your Sun sign. You may also apply rules for buying specific items.

Canning

Can fruits and vegetables when the Moon is in either the third or fourth quarter and in the water sign Cancer or Pisces. Preserves and jellies use the same quarters and the signs Cancer, Pisces, or Taurus.

Clothing

Buy clothing on a day that is favorable for your Sun sign and when Venus or Mercury is well aspected. Avoid aspects to Mars and Saturn. Buy your clothing when the Moon is in Taurus if you want to remain satisfied. Do not buy clothing or jewelry when the Moon is in Scorpio or Aries. See that the Moon is sextile or trine the Sun during the first or second quarters.

Collections

Try to make collections on days when your natal Sun is well aspected. Avoid days when the Moon is opposing or square Mars or Saturn. If possible, the Moon should be in a cardinal sign (Aries, Cancer, Libra, or Capricorn). It is more difficult to collect when the Moon is in Taurus or Scorpio.

Concrete

Pour concrete when the Moon is in the third quarter of the fixed sign Taurus, Leo, or Aquarius.

Construction (Begin New)

The Moon should be sextile or trine Jupiter. According to Hermes, no building should be begun when the Moon is in Scorpio or Pisces. The best time to begin building is when the Moon is in Aquarius.

Consultants (Work with)

The Moon should be conjunct, sextile, or trine Mercury or Jupiter.

2017 © Stockcentral Image from BigStockPhoto.com

Contracts (Bid On)

The Moon should be in Gemini or Capricorn and either the Moon or Mercury should be conjunct, sextile, or trine Jupiter.

Copyrights/Patents

The Moon should be conjunct, trine, or sextile either Mercury or Jupiter.

Coronations and Installations

Let the Moon be in Leo and in favorable aspect to Venus, Jupiter, or Mercury. The Moon should be applying to these planets.

Cultivate

Cultivate when the Moon is in a barren sign and waning, ideally the fourth quarter in Aries, Gemini, Leo, Virgo, or Aquarius. The third quarter in the sign of Sagittarius will also work.

Cut Timber

Timber cut during the waning Moon does not become worm-eaten; it will season well and not warp, decay, or snap during burning. Cut when the Moon is in Taurus, Gemini, Virgo, or

Capricorn—especially in August. Avoid the water signs. Look for favorable aspects to Mars.

Decorating or Home Repairs
Have the Moon waxing and in the sign of Libra, Gemini, or Aquarius. Avoid squares or oppositions to either Mars or Saturn. Venus in good aspect to Mars or Saturn is beneficial.

Demolition
Let the waning Moon be in Leo, Sagittarius, or Aries.

Dental and Dentists
Visit the dentist when the Moon is in Virgo, or pick a day marked favorable for your Sun sign. Mars should be marked sextile, conjunct, or trine; avoid squares or oppositions to Saturn, Uranus, or Jupiter.

Teeth are best removed when the Moon is in Gemini, Virgo, Sagittarius, or Pisces and during the first or second quarter. Avoid the Full Moon! The day should be favorable for your lunar cycle, and Mars and Saturn should be marked conjunct, trine, or sextile. Fillings should be done in the third or fourth quarters in the sign of Taurus, Leo, Scorpio, or Pisces. The same applies for dentures.

Dressmaking
William Lilly wrote in 1676: "Make no new clothes, or first put them on when the Moon is in Scorpio or afflicted by Mars, for they will be apt to be torn and quickly worn out." Design, repair, and sew clothes in the first and second quarters of Taurus, Leo, or Libra on a day marked favorable for your Sun sign. Venus, Jupiter, and Mercury should be favorably aspected, but avoid hard aspects to Mars or Saturn.

Egg-Setting (see p. 161)

Eggs should be set so chicks will hatch during fruitful signs. To set eggs, subtract the number of days given for incubation or gestation from the fruitful dates. Chickens incubate in twenty-one days, turkeys and geese in twenty-eight days.

A freshly laid egg loses quality rapidly if it is not handled properly. Use plenty of clean litter in the nests to reduce the number of dirty or cracked eggs. Gather eggs daily in mild weather and at least two times daily in hot or cold weather. The eggs should be placed in a cooler immediately after gathering and stored at 50 to 55°F. Do not store eggs with foods or products that give off pungent odors since eggs may absorb the odors.

Eggs saved for hatching purposes should not be washed. Only clean and slightly soiled eggs should be saved for hatching. Dirty eggs should not be incubated. Eggs should be stored in a cool place with the large ends up. It is not advisable to store the eggs longer than one week before setting them in an incubator.

Electricity and Gas (Install)

The Moon should be in a fire sign, and there should be no squares, oppositions, or conjunctions with Uranus (ruler of electricity), Neptune (ruler of gas), Saturn, or Mars. Hard aspects to Mars can cause fires.

Electronics (Buying)

Choose a day when the Moon is in an air sign (Gemini, Libra, Aquarius) and well aspected by Mercury and/or Uranus when buying electronics.

Electronics (Repair)

The Moon should be sextile or trine Mars or Uranus and in a fixed sign (Taurus, Leo, Scorpio, Aquarius).

Entertain Friends

Let the Moon be in Leo or Libra and making good aspects to Venus. Avoid squares or oppositions to either Mars or Saturn by the Moon or Venus.

Eyes and Eyeglasses

Have your eyes tested and glasses fitted on a day marked favorable for your Sun sign, and on a day that falls during your favorable lunar cycle. Mars should not be in aspect with the Moon. The same applies for any treatment of the eyes, which should also be started during the Moon's first or second quarter.

Fence Posts

Set posts when the Moon is in the third or fourth quarter of the fixed sign Taurus or Leo.

Fertilize and Compost

Fertilize when the Moon is in a fruitful sign (Cancer, Scorpio, Pisces). Organic fertilizers are best when the Moon is waning. Use chemical fertilizers when the Moon is waxing. Start compost when the Moon is in the fourth quarter in a water sign.

Find Hidden Treasure

Let the Moon be in good aspect to Jupiter or Venus. If you erect a horoscope for this election, place the Moon in the Fourth House.

Find Lost Articles

Search for lost articles during the first quarter and when your Sun sign is marked favorable. Also check to see that the planet ruling the lost item is trine, sextile, or conjunct the Moon. The Moon rules household utensils; Mercury rules letters and books; and Venus rules clothing, jewelry, and money.

2017 © dobrinya Image from BigStockPhoto.com

Fishing

During the summer months, the best time of the day to fish is from sunrise to three hours after and from two hours before sunset until one hour after. Fish do not bite in cooler months until the air is warm, from noon to three pm. Warm, cloudy days are good. The most favorable winds are from the south and southwest. Easterly winds are unfavorable. The best days of the month for fishing are when the Moon changes quarters, especially if the change occurs on a day when the Moon is in a water sign (Cancer, Scorpio, Pisces). The best period in any month is the day after the Full Moon.

Friendship

The need for friendship is greater when the Moon is in Aquarius or when Uranus aspects the Moon. Friendship prospers when Venus or Uranus is trine, sextile, or conjunct the Moon. The

Moon in Gemini facilitates the chance meeting of acquaintances and friends.

Grafting or Budding

Grafting is the process of introducing new varieties of fruit on less desirable trees. For this process you should use the increasing phase of the Moon in fruitful signs such as Cancer, Scorpio, or Pisces. Capricorn may be used, too. Cut your grafts while trees are dormant, from December to March. Keep them in a cool, dark place, not too dry or too damp. Do the grafting before the sap starts to flow and while the Moon is waxing, preferably while it is in Cancer, Scorpio, or Pisces. The type of plant should determine both cutting and planting times.

Habit (Breaking)

To end an undesirable habit, and this applies to ending everything from a bad relationship to smoking, start on a day when the Moon is in the fourth quarter and in the barren sign of Gemini, Leo, or Aquarius. Aries, Virgo, and Capricorn may be suitable as well, depending on the habit you want to be rid of. Make sure that your lunar cycle is favorable. Avoid lunar aspects to Mars or Jupiter. However, favorable aspects to Pluto are helpful.

Haircuts

Cut hair when the Moon is in Gemini, Sagittarius, Pisces, Taurus, or Capricorn, but not in Virgo. Look for favorable aspects to Venus. For faster growth, cut hair when the Moon is increasing in Cancer or Pisces. To make hair grow thicker, cut when the Moon is full in the signs of Taurus, Cancer, or Leo. If you want your hair to grow more slowly, have the Moon be decreasing in Aries, Gemini, or Virgo, and have the Moon square or opposing Saturn.

Permanents, straightening, and hair coloring will take well if the Moon is in Taurus or Leo and trine or sextile Venus. Avoid hair treatments if Mars is marked as square or in opposition, especially if heat is to be used. For permanents, a trine to Jupiter is helpful. The Moon also should be in the first quarter. Check the lunar cycle for a favorable day in relation to your Sun sign.

Harvest Crops

Harvest root crops when the Moon is in a dry sign (Aries, Leo, Sagittarius, Gemini, Aquarius) and waning. Harvest grain for storage just after the Full Moon, avoiding Cancer, Scorpio, or Pisces. Harvest in the third and fourth quarters in dry signs. Dry crops in the third quarter in fire signs.

Health

A diagnosis is more likely to be successful when the Moon is in Aries, Cancer, Libra, or Capricorn and less so when in Gemini, Sagittarius, Pisces, or Virgo. Begin a recuperation program or enter a hospital when the Moon is in a cardinal or fixed sign and the day is favorable to your Sun sign. For surgery, see "Surgical Procedures." Buy medicines when the Moon is in Virgo or Scorpio.

Home (Buy New)

If you desire a permanent home, buy when the New Moon is in a fixed sign—Taurus or Leo, for example. Each sign will affect your decision in a different way. A house bought when the Moon is in Taurus is likely to be more practical and have a country look—right down to the split-rail fence. A house purchased when the Moon is in Leo will more likely be a real showplace.

If you're buying for speculation and a quick turnover, be certain that the Moon is in a cardinal sign (Aries, Cancer, Libra, Capricorn). Avoid buying when the Moon is in a fixed sign (Leo, Scorpio, Aquarius, Taurus).

Home (Make Repairs)

In all repairs, avoid squares, oppositions, or conjunctions to the planet ruling the place or thing to be repaired. For example, bathrooms are ruled by Scorpio and Cancer. You would not want to start a project in those rooms when the Moon or Pluto is receiving hard aspects. The front entrance, hall, dining room, and porch are ruled by the Sun. So you would want to avoid times when Saturn or Mars are square, opposing, or conjunct the Sun. Also, let the Moon be waxing.

Home (Sell)

Make a strong effort to list your property for sale when the Sun is marked favorable in your sign and in good aspect to Jupiter. Avoid adverse aspects to as many planets as possible.

Home Furnishings (Buy New)

Saturn days (Saturday) are good for buying, and Jupiter days (Thursday) are good for selling. Items bought on days when Saturn is well aspected tend to wear longer and purchases tend to be more conservative.

Job (Start New)

Jupiter and Venus should be sextile, trine, or conjunct the Moon. A day when your Sun is receiving favorable aspects is preferred.

Legal Matters

Good Moon-Jupiter aspects improve the outcome in legal decisions. To gain damages through a lawsuit, begin the process during the increasing Moon. To avoid paying damages, a court date during the decreasing Moon is desirable. Good Moon-Sun aspects strengthen your chance of success. A well-aspected Moon in Cancer or Leo, making good aspects to the Sun, brings the best results in custody cases. In divorce cases, a favorable Moon-Venus aspect is best.

Loan (Ask For)

A first and second quarter phase favors the lender, the third and fourth quarters favor the borrower. Good aspects of Jupiter and

Venus to the Moon are favorable to both, as is having the Moon in Leo or Taurus.

Machinery, Appliances, or Tools (Buy)

Tools, machinery, and other implements should be bought on days when your lunar cycle is favorable and when Mars and Uranus are trine, sextile, or conjunct the Moon. Any quarter of the Moon is suitable. When buying gas or electrical appliances, the Moon should be in Aquarius.

Make a Will

Let the Moon be in a fixed sign (Taurus, Leo, Scorpio, or Aquarius) to ensure permanence. If the Moon is in a cardinal sign (Aries, Cancer, Libra, or Capricorn), the will could be altered. Let the Moon be waxing—increasing in light—and in good aspect to Saturn, Venus, or Mercury. In case the will is made in an emergency during illness and the Moon is slow in motion, void-of-course, combust, or under the Sun's beams, the testator will die and the will remain unaltered. There is some danger that it will be lost or stolen, however.

Marriage

The best time for marriage to take place is when the Moon is increasing, but not yet full. Good signs for the Moon to be in are Taurus, Cancer, Leo, or Libra.

The Moon in Taurus produces the most steadfast marriages, but if the partners later want to separate, they may have a difficult time. Make sure that the Moon is well aspected, especially to Venus or Jupiter. Avoid aspects to Mars, Uranus, or Pluto and the signs Aries, Gemini, Virgo, Scorpio, or Aquarius.

The values of the signs are as follows:

- Aries is not favored for marriage
- Taurus from 0 to 19 degrees is good, the remaining degrees are less favorable

- Cancer is unfavorable unless you are marrying a widow
- Leo is favored, but it may cause one party to deceive the other as to his or her money or possessions
- Virgo is not favored except when marrying a widow
- Libra is good for engagements but not for marriage
- Scorpio from 0 to 15 degrees is good, but the last 15 degrees are entirely unfortunate. The woman may be fickle, envious, and quarrelsome
- Sagittarius is neutral
- Capricorn, from 0 to 10 degrees, is difficult for marriage; however, the remaining degrees are favorable, especially when marrying a widow
- Aquarius is not favored
- Pisces is favored, although marriage under this sign can incline a woman to chatter a lot

These effects are strongest when the Moon is in the sign. If the Moon and Venus are in a cardinal sign, happiness between the couple may not continue long.

On no account should the Moon apply to Saturn or Mars, even by good aspect.

Medical Treatment for the Eyes

Let the Moon be increasing in light and motion and making favorable aspects to Venus or Jupiter and be unaspected by Mars. Keep the Moon out of Taurus, Capricorn, or Virgo. If an aspect between the Moon and Mars is unavoidable, let it be separating.

Medical Treatment for the Head

If possible, have Mars and Saturn free of hard aspects. Let the Moon be in Aries or Taurus, decreasing in light, in conjunction or aspect with Venus or Jupiter and free of hard aspects. The Sun should not be in any aspect to the Moon.

Medical Treatment for the Nose

Let the Moon be in Cancer, Leo, or Virgo and not aspecting Mars or Saturn and also not in conjunction with a retrograde or weak planet.

Mining

Saturn rules mining. Begin work when Saturn is marked conjunct, trine, or sextile. Mine for gold when the Sun is marked conjunct, trine, or sextile. Mercury rules quicksilver, Venus rules copper, Jupiter rules tin, Saturn rules lead and coal, Uranus rules radioactive elements, Neptune rules oil, the Moon rules water. Mine for these items when the ruling planet is marked conjunct, trine, or sextile.

Move to New Home

If you have a choice, and sometimes you don't, make sure that Mars is not aspecting the Moon. Move on a day favorable to your Sun sign or when the Moon is conjunct, sextile, or trine the Sun.

Mow Lawn

Mow in the first and second quarters (waxing phase) to increase growth and lushness, and in the third and fourth quarters (waning phase) to decrease growth.

Negotiate

When you are choosing a time to negotiate, consider what the meeting is about and what you want to have happen. If it is agreement or compromise between two parties that you desire, have the Moon be in the sign of Libra. When you are making contracts, it is best to have the Moon in the same element. For example, if your concern is communication, then elect a time when the Moon is in an air sign. If, on the other hand, your concern is about possessions, an earth sign would be more appropriate.

Fixed signs are unfavorable, with the exception of Leo; so are cardinal signs, except for Capricorn. If you are negotiating the end of something, use the rules that apply to ending habits.

Occupational Training

When you begin training, see that your lunar cycle is favorable that day and that the planet ruling your occupation is marked conjunct or trine.

Paint

Paint buildings during the waning Libra or Aquarius Moon. If the weather is hot, paint when the Moon is in Taurus. If the weather is cold, paint when the Moon is in Leo. Schedule the painting to start in the fourth quarter as the wood is drier and paint will penetrate wood better. Avoid painting around the New Moon, though, as the wood is likely to be damp, making the paint subject to scalding when hot weather hits it. If the temperature is below 70°F, it is not advisable to paint while the Moon is in Cancer, Scorpio, or Pisces as the paint is apt to creep, check, or run.

Party (Host or Attend)

A party timed so the Moon is in Gemini, Leo, Libra, or Sagittarius, with good aspects to Venus and Jupiter, will be fun and well attended. There should be no aspects between the Moon and Mars or Saturn.

Pawn

Do not pawn any article when Jupiter is receiving a square or opposition from Saturn or Mars or when Jupiter is within 17 degrees of the Sun, for you will have little chance to redeem the items.

Pick Mushrooms

Mushrooms, one of the most promising traditional medicines in the world, should be gathered at the Full Moon.

Plant

Root crops, like carrots and potatoes, are best if planted in the sign Taurus or Capricorn. Beans, peas, tomatoes, peppers, and other fruit-bearing plants are best if planted in a sign that supports seed growth. Leaf plants, like lettuce, broccoli, or cauliflower, are best planted when the Moon is in a water sign.

It is recommended that you transplant during a decreasing Moon, when forces are streaming into the lower part of the plant. This helps root growth.

Promotion (Ask For)

Choose a day favorable to your Sun sign. Mercury should be marked conjunct, trine, or sextile. Avoid days when Mars or Saturn is aspected.

Prune

Prune during the third and fourth quarter of a Scorpio Moon to retard growth and to promote better fruit. Prune when the Moon is in cardinal Capricorn to promote healing.

Reconcile with People

If the reconciliation is with a woman, let Venus be strong and well aspected. If elders or superiors are involved, see that Saturn is receiving good aspects; if the reconciliation is between young people or between an older and younger person, see that Mercury is well aspected.

Romance

There is less control of when a romance starts, but romances begun under an increasing Moon are more likely to be permanent or satisfying, while those begun during the decreasing Moon tend to transform the participants. The tone of the relationship can be guessed from the sign the Moon is in. Romances begun with the Moon in Aries may be impulsive. Those begun in Capricorn will

2017 © kabVisio Image from BigStockPhoto.com

take greater effort to bring to a desirable conclusion, but they may be very rewarding. Good aspects between the Moon and Venus will have a positive influence on the relationship. Avoid unfavorable aspects to Mars, Uranus, and Pluto. A decreasing Moon, particularly the fourth quarter, facilitates ending a relationship and causes the least pain.

Roof a Building

Begin roofing a building during the third or fourth quarter, when the Moon is in Aries or Aquarius. Shingles laid during the New Moon have a tendency to curl at the edges.

Sauerkraut

The best-tasting sauerkraut is made just after the Full Moon in the fruitful signs of Cancer, Scorpio, or Pisces.

Select a Child's Sex

Count from the last day of menstruation to the first day of the next cycle and divide the interval between the two dates in half.

Pregnancy in the first half produces females, but copulation should take place with the Moon in a feminine sign. Pregnancy in the latter half, up to three days before the beginning of menstruation, produces males, but copulation should take place with the Moon in a masculine sign. The three-day period before the next period again produces females.

Sell or Canvass

Begin these activities during a day favorable to your Sun sign. Otherwise, sell on days when Jupiter, Mercury, or Mars is trine, sextile, or conjunct the Moon. Avoid days when Saturn is square or opposing the Moon, for that always hinders business and causes discord. If the Moon is passing from the first quarter to full, it is best to have the Moon swift in motion and in good aspect with Venus and/or Jupiter.

Sign Papers

Sign contracts or agreements when the Moon is increasing in a fruitful sign and on a day when the Moon is making favorable aspects to Mercury. Avoid days when Mars, Saturn, or Neptune are square or opposite the Moon.

Spray and Weed

Spray pests and weeds during the fourth quarter when the Moon is in the barren sign Leo or Aquarius and making favorable aspects to Pluto. Weed during a waning Moon in a barren sign.

Staff (Fire)

Have the Moon in the third or fourth quarter, but not full. The Moon should not be square any planets.

Staff (Hire)

The Moon should be in the first or second quarter, and preferably in the sign of Gemini or Virgo. The Moon should be conjunct, trine, or sextile Mercury or Jupiter.

Stocks (Buy)

The Moon should be in Taurus or Capricorn, and there should be a sextile or trine to Jupiter or Saturn.

Surgical Procedures

Blood flow, like ocean tides, appears to be related to Moon phases. To reduce hemorrhage after a surgery, schedule it within one week before or after a New Moon. Schedule surgery to occur during the increase of the Moon if possible, as wounds heal better and vitality is greater than during the decrease of the Moon. Avoid surgery within one week before or after the Full Moon. Select a date when the Moon is past the sign governing the part of the body involved in the operation. For example, abdominal operations should be done when the Moon is in Sagittarius, Capricorn, or Aquarius. The further removed the Moon sign is from the sign ruling the afflicted part of the body, the better.

For successful operations, avoid times when the Moon is applying to any aspect of Mars. (This tends to promote inflammation and complications.) See the Lunar Aspectarian on odd pages 137–159 to find days with negative Mars aspects and positive Venus and Jupiter aspects. Never operate with the Moon in the same sign as a person's Sun sign or Ascendant. Let the Moon be in a fixed sign and avoid square or opposing aspects. The Moon should not be void-of-course. Cosmetic surgery should be done in the increase of the Moon, when the Moon is not square or in opposition to Mars. Avoid days when the Moon is square or opposing Saturn or the Sun.

Travel (Air)

Start long trips when the Moon is making favorable aspects to the Sun. For enjoyment, aspects to Jupiter are preferable; for visiting, look for favorable aspects to Mercury. To prevent accidents, avoid squares or oppositions to Mars, Saturn, Uranus, or

Pluto. Choose a day when the Moon is in Sagittarius or Gemini and well aspected to Mercury, Jupiter, or Uranus. Avoid adverse aspects of Mars, Saturn, or Uranus.

Visit

On setting out to visit a person, let the Moon be in aspect with any retrograde planet, for this ensures that the person you're visiting will be at home. If you desire to stay a long time in a place, let the Moon be in good aspect to Saturn. If you desire to leave the place quickly, let the Moon be in a cardinal sign.

Wean Children

To wean a child successfully, do so when the Moon is in Sagittarius, Capricorn, Aquarius, or Pisces—signs that do not rule vital human organs. By observing this astrological rule, much trouble for parents and child may be avoided.

Weight (Reduce)

If you want to lose weight, the best time to get started is when the Moon is in the third or fourth quarter and in the barren sign of Virgo. Review the section on How to Use the Moon Tables and Lunar Aspectarian beginning on page 136 to help you select a date that is favorable to begin your weight-loss program.

Wine and Drink Other Than Beer

Start brewing when the Moon is in Pisces or Taurus. Sextiles or trines to Venus are favorable, but avoid aspects to Mars or Saturn.

Write

Write for pleasure or publication when the Moon is in Gemini. Mercury should be making favorable aspects to Uranus and Neptune.

2017 © GeorgeRudy Image from BigStockPhoto.com

How to Use the Moon Tables and Lunar Aspectarian

Timing activities is one of the most important things you can do to ensure success. In many Eastern countries, timing by the planets is so important that practically no event takes place without first setting up a chart for it. Weddings have occurred in the middle of the night because the influences were at the best then. You may not want to take it that far, but you can still make use of the influences of the Moon whenever possible. It's easy and it works!

Llewellyn's Moon Sign Book has information to help you plan just about any activity: weddings, fishing, making purchases, cutting your hair, traveling, and more. We provide the guidelines you need to pick the best day out of the several from which you have to choose. The Moon Tables are the *Moon Sign Book's* primary method for choosing dates. Following are instructions, examples, and directions on how to read the Moon Tables. More advanced information on using the tables containing the Lunar Aspectarian and favorable and unfavorable days (found on odd-numbered pages opposite the Moon Tables), Moon void-of-course and retrograde information to choose the dates best for you is also included.

The Five Basic Steps

Step 1: Directions for Choosing Dates

Look up the directions for choosing dates for the activity that you wish to begin, then go to step 2.

Step 2: Check the Moon Tables

You'll find two tables for each month of the year beginning on page 136. The Moon Tables (on the left-hand pages) include the day, date, and sign the Moon is in; the element and nature of the sign; the Moon's phase; and when it changes sign or phase. If there is a time listed after a date, that time is the time when the Moon moves into that zodiac sign. Until then, the Moon is considered to be in the sign for the previous day.

The abbreviation Full signifies Full Moon and New signifies New Moon. The times listed with dates indicate when the Moon changes sign. The times listed after the phase indicate when the Moon changes phase.

Turn to the month you would like to begin your activity. You will be using the Moon's sign and phase information most often when you begin choosing your own dates. Use the Time Zone Map on page 164 and the Time Zone Conversions table on page 165 to convert time to your own time zone.

When you find dates that meet the criteria for the correct Moon phase and sign for your activity, you may have completed the process. For certain simple activities, such as getting a haircut, the phase and sign information is all that is needed. If the directions for your activity include information on certain lunar aspects, however, you should consult the Lunar Aspectarian. An example of this would be if the directions told you not to perform a certain activity when the Moon is square (Q) Jupiter.

Step 3: Check the Lunar Aspectarian

On the pages opposite the Moon Tables you will find tables containing the Lunar Aspectarian and Favorable and Unfavorable Days. The Lunar Aspectarian gives the aspects (or angles) of the Moon to other planets. Some aspects are favorable, while others are not. To use the Lunar Aspectarian, find the planet that the directions list as favorable for your activity, and run down the column to the date desired. For example, you should avoid aspects to Mars if you are planning surgery. So you would look for Mars across the top and then run down that column looking for days where there are no aspects to Mars (as signified by empty boxes). If you want to find a *favorable* aspect (sextile (X) or trine (T)) to Mercury, run your finger down the column under Mercury until you find an X or T. *Adverse* aspects to planets are squares (Q) or oppositions (O). A conjunction (C) is sometimes beneficial, sometimes not, depending on the activity or planets involved.

Step 4: Favorable and Unfavorable Days

The tables listing favorable and unfavorable days are helpful when you want to choose your personal best dates because your Sun sign is taken into consideration. The twelve Sun signs are listed on the right side of the tables. Once you have determined which days meet your criteria for phase, sign, and aspects, you can determine whether or not those days are positive for you by checking the favorable and unfavorable days for your Sun sign.

To find out if a day is positive for you, find your Sun sign and then look down the column. If it is marked F, it is very favorable. The Moon is in the same sign as your Sun on a favorable day. If it is marked f, it is slightly favorable; U is very unfavorable; and u means slightly unfavorable. A day marked very unfavorable (U) indicates that the Moon is in the sign opposing your Sun.

Once you have selected good dates for the activity you are about to begin, you can go straight to "Using What You've Learned," beginning on the next page. To learn how to fine-tune your selections even further, read on.

Step 5: Void-of-Course Moon and Retrogrades

This last step is perhaps the most advanced portion of the procedure. It is generally considered poor timing to make decisions, sign important papers, or start special activities during a Moon void-of-course period or during a Mercury retrograde. Once you have chosen the best date for your activity based on steps one through four, you can check the Void-of-Course tables, beginning on page 76, to find out if any of the dates you have chosen have void periods.

The Moon is said to be void-of-course after it has made its last aspect to a planet within a particular sign, but before it has moved into the next sign. Put simply, the Moon is "resting" during the void-of-course period, so activities initiated at this time generally don't come to fruition. You will notice that there are many void periods during the year, and it is nearly impossible to avoid all of them. Some people choose to ignore these altogether and do not take them into consideration when planning activities.

Next, you can check the Retrograde Planets tables on page 160 to see what planets are retrograde during your chosen date(s).

A planet is said to be retrograde when it appears to move backward in the sky as viewed from Earth. Generally, the farther a planet is away from the Sun, the longer it can stay retrograde. Some planets will retrograde for several months at a time. Avoiding retrogrades is not as important in lunar planning as avoiding the Moon void-of-course, with the exception of the planet Mercury.

Mercury rules thought and communication, so it is advisable not to sign important papers, initiate important business or legal work, or make crucial decisions during these times. As with the Moon void-of-course, it is difficult to avoid all planetary retrogrades when beginning events, and you may choose to ignore this step of the process. Following are some examples using some or all of the steps outlined above.

Using What You've Learned

Let's say it's a new year and you want to have your hair cut. It's thin and you would like it to look fuller, so you find the directions for hair care and you see that for thicker hair you should cut hair while the Moon is Full and in the sign of Taurus, Cancer, or Leo. You should avoid the Moon in Aries, Gemini, or Virgo. Look at the January Moon Table on page 136. You see that the Full Moon is on January 1 at 9:24 pm. The Moon is in Cancer that day after 3:10 am and remains in Cancer until January 3 at 2:23 am, so January 1–3 meets both the phase and sign criteria.

Let's move on to a more difficult example using the sign and phase of the Moon. You want to buy a permanent home. After checking the instructions for purchasing a house: "Home (Buy New)" on page 118, you see that you should buy a home when the Moon is in Taurus, Cancer, or Leo. You need to get a loan, so you should also look under "Loan (Ask For)" on page 119. Here it says that the third and fourth quarters favor the borrower (you). You are going to buy the house in October, so go to page 154. The Moon is in the third quarter October 1 and 25–30 and fourth quarter Oct. 2–8. The Moon is in Taurus from 10:33 am on Oct. 24 until Oct. 26 at 3:41 pm; in Cancer from 2:00 pm Oct. 1 until Oct. 3 at 5:12 pm and from 7:27 pm on Oct. 28 until Oct. 30 at 10:42 pm; and in Leo from Oct. 3 at 5:12 pm until Oct. 5 at 7:19 pm. The best days for obtaining a loan would be October 1–5, 25, 26, 28, 29, or 30.

Just match up the best sign and phase (quarter) to come up with the best date. With all activities, be sure to check the favorable and unfavorable days for your Sun sign in the table adjoining the Lunar Aspectarian. If there is a choice between several dates, pick the one most favorable for you. Because buying a home is an important business decision, you may also wish to see if the Moon is void or if Mercury is retrograde during these dates.

Now let's look at an example that uses signs, phases, and aspects. Our example is starting new home construction. We will use the month of February. Look under "Build (Start Foundation)" on page 110 and you'll see that the Moon should be in the first quarter of a fixed sign—Leo, Taurus, Aquarius, or Scorpio. You should select a time when the Moon is not making unfavorable aspects to Saturn. (Conjunctions are usually considered unfavorable if they are to Mars, Saturn, or Neptune.) Look in the February Moon Table on page 138. You will see that the Moon is in the first quarter Feb. 20–22 and in Taurus from 2:12 pm on Feb. 20 until 7:07 pm on Feb. 22. Now, look to the February Lunar Aspectarian. We see that there is a favorable trine to Saturn on Feb. 21, with no unfavorable aspects on Feb. 20 and 22; therefore Feb. 21 would be the best date to start a foundation.

A Note About Time and Time Zones

All tables in the Moon Sign Book use Eastern Time. You must calculate the difference between your time zone and the Eastern Time Zone. Please refer to the Time Zone Conversions chart on page 165 for help with time conversions. The sign the Moon is in at midnight is the sign shown in the Aspectarian and Favorable and Unfavorable Days tables.

How Does the Time Matter?

Due to the three-hour time difference between the East and West Coasts of the United States, those of you living on the East Coast may be, for example, under the influence of a Virgo Moon, while those of you living on the West Coast will still have a Leo Moon influence.

We follow a commonly held belief among astrologers: whatever sign the Moon is in at the start of a day—12:00 am Eastern Time—is considered the dominant influence of the day. That sign is indicated in the Moon Tables. If the date you select for an activity shows the Moon changing signs, you can decide how important the sign change may be for your specific election and adjust your election date and time accordingly.

Use Common Sense

Some activities depend on outside factors. Obviously, you can't go out and plant when there is a foot of snow on the ground. You should adjust to the conditions at hand. If the weather was bad during the first quarter, when it was best to plant crops, do it during the second quarter while the Moon is in a fruitful sign. If the Moon is not in a fruitful sign during the first or second quarter, choose a day when it is in a semi-fruitful sign. The best advice is to choose either the sign or phase that is most favorable, when the two don't coincide.

To Summarize

First, look up the activity under the proper heading, then look for the information given in the tables. Choose the best date considering the number of positive factors in effect. If most of the dates are favorable, there is no problem choosing the one that will fit your schedule. However, if there aren't any really good dates, pick the ones with the least number of negative influences. Please keep in mind that the information found here applies in the broadest sense to the events you want to plan or are considering. To be the most effective, when you use electional astrology, you should also consider your own birth chart in relation to a chart drawn for the time or times you have under consideration. The best advice we can offer you is: read the entire introduction to each section.

January Moon Table

Date	Sign	Element	Nature	Phase
1 Mon 3:10 am	Cancer	Water	Fruitful	Full 9:24 pm
2 Tue	Cancer	Water	Fruitful	3rd
3 Wed 2:23 am	Leo	Fire	Barren	3rd
4 Thu	Leo	Fire	Barren	3rd
5 Fri 3:12 am	Virgo	Earth	Barren	3rd
6 Sat	Virgo	Earth	Barren	3rd
7 Sun 7:15 am	Libra	Air	Semi-fruitful	3rd
8 Mon	Libra	Air	Semi-fruitful	4th 5:25 pm
9 Tue 3:05 pm	Scorpio	Water	Fruitful	4th
10 Wed	Scorpio	Water	Fruitful	4th
11 Thu	Scorpio	Water	Fruitful	4th
12 Fri 2:04 am	Sagittarius	Fire	Barren	4th
13 Sat	Sagittarius	Fire	Barren	4th
14 Sun 2:42 pm	Capricorn	Earth	Semi-fruitful	4th
15 Mon	Capricorn	Earth	Semi-fruitful	4th
16 Tue	Capricorn	Earth	Semi-fruitful	New 9:17 pm
17 Wed 3:32 am	Aquarius	Air	Barren	1st
18 Thu	Aquarius	Air	Barren	1st
19 Fri 3:26 pm	Pisces	Water	Fruitful	1st
20 Sat	Pisces	Water	Fruitful	1st
21 Sun	Pisces	Water	Fruitful	1st
22 Mon 1:27 am	Aries	Fire	Barren	1st
23 Tue	Aries	Fire	Barren	1st
24 Wed 8:39 am	Taurus	Earth	Semi-fruitful	2nd 5:20 pm
25 Thu	Taurus	Earth	Semi-fruitful	2nd
26 Fri 12:40 pm	Gemini	Air	Barren	2nd
27 Sat	Gemini	Air	Barren	2nd
28 Sun 1:57 pm	Cancer	Water	Fruitful	2nd
29 Mon	Cancer	Water	Fruitful	2nd
30 Tue 1:53 pm	Leo	Fire	Barren	2nd
31 Wed	Leo	Fire	Barren	Full 8:27 am

January Aspectarian/Favorable & Unfavorable Days

Date	Sun	Mercury	Venus	Mars	Jupiter	Saturn	Uranus	Neptune	Pluto
1	O		O			O		T	
2				T	T		Q		O
3									
4		T		Q	Q		T		
5						T		O	
6	T	Q	T	X	X				T
7						Q			
8	Q		Q						Q
9		X					X	O	
10								T	
11	X		X	C	C				X
12									
13								Q	
14					C	T			
15		C						X	
16	C			X	X		Q		C
17			C						
18					Q				
19				Q			X	X	
20		X						C	
21				T	T				X
22	X		X			Q			
23		Q					C		Q
24	Q					T			
25		T	Q		O			X	T
26				O					
27	T		T					Q	
28						O	X		
29					T			T	O
30		O		T			Q		
31	O		O						

Date	Aries	Taurus	Gemini	Cancer	Leo	Virgo	Libra	Scorpio	Sagittarius	Capricorn	Aquarius	Pisces
1	f		F		f	u	f		U		f	u
2	u	f		F		f	u	f		U		f
3	f	u	f		F		f	u	f		U	
4	f	u	f		F		f	u	f		U	
5	f	u	f		F		f	u	f		U	
6		f	u	f		F		f	u	f		U
7		f	u	f		F		f	u	f		U
8	U		f	u	f		F		f	u	f	
9	U		f	u	f		F		f	u	f	
10		U		f	u	f		F		f	u	f
11		U		f	u	f		F		f	u	f
12	f		U		f	u	f		F		f	u
13	f		U		f	u	f		F		f	u
14	f		U		f	u	f		F		f	u
15	u	f		U		f	u	f		F		f
16	u	f		U		f	u	f		F		f
17	u	f		U		f	u	f		F		f
18	f	u	f		U		f	u	f		F	
19	f	u	f		U		f	u	f		F	
20		f	u	f		U		f	u	f		F
21		f	u	f		U		f	u	f		F
22	F		f	u	f		U		f	u	f	
23	F		f	u	f		U		f	u	f	
24	F		f	u	f		U		f	u	f	
25		F		f	u	f		U		f	u	f
26		F		f	u	f		U		f	u	f
27	f		F		f	u	f		U		f	u
28	f		F		f	u	f		U		f	u
29	u	f		F		f	u	f		U		f
30	u	f		F		f	u	f		U		f
31	f	u	f		F		f	u	f		U	

February Moon Table

Date	Sign	Element	Nature	Phase
1 Thu 2:13 pm	Virgo	Earth	Barren	3rd
2 Fri	Virgo	Earth	Barren	3rd
3 Sat 4:47 pm	Libra	Air	Semi-fruitful	3rd
4 Sun	Libra	Air	Semi-fruitful	3rd
5 Mon 10:56 pm	Scorpio	Water	Fruitful	3rd
6 Tue	Scorpio	Water	Fruitful	3rd
7 Wed	Scorpio	Water	Fruitful	4th 10:54 am
8 Thu 8:53 am	Sagittarius	Fire	Barren	4th
9 Fri	Sagittarius	Fire	Barren	4th
10 Sat 9:21 pm	Capricorn	Earth	Semi-fruitful	4th
11 Sun	Capricorn	Earth	Semi-fruitful	4th
12 Mon	Capricorn	Earth	Semi-fruitful	4th
13 Tue 10:11 am	Aquarius	Air	Barren	4th
14 Wed	Aquarius	Air	Barren	4th
15 Thu 9:42 pm	Pisces	Water	Fruitful	New 4:05 pm
16 Fri	Pisces	Water	Fruitful	1st
17 Sat	Pisces	Water	Fruitful	1st
18 Sun 7:05 am	Aries	Fire	Barren	1st
19 Mon	Aries	Fire	Barren	1st
20 Tue 2:12 pm	Taurus	Earth	Semi-fruitful	1st
21 Wed	Taurus	Earth	Semi-fruitful	1st
22 Thu 7:07 pm	Gemini	Air	Barren	1st
23 Fri	Gemini	Air	Barren	2nd 3:09 am
24 Sat 10:06 pm	Cancer	Water	Fruitful	2nd
25 Sun	Cancer	Water	Fruitful	2nd
26 Mon 11:42 pm	Leo	Fire	Barren	2nd
27 Tue	Leo	Fire	Barren	2nd
28 Wed	Leo	Fire	Barren	2nd

February Aspectarian/Favorable & Unfavorable Days

Date	Sun	Mercury	Venus	Mars	Jupiter	Saturn	Uranus	Neptune	Pluto
1				Q	Q	T	T		
2								O	T
3					X				
4	T	T		X		Q			
5			T					O	Q
6		Q				X		T	
7	Q				C				X
8			Q						
9		X		C				Q	
10	X		X				T		
11						C			
12					X			X	C
13							Q		
14				X					
15	C	C			Q		X		
16			C	Q		X		C	
17					T				X
18						Q			
19				T					Q
20	X						C		
21		X	X			T		X	
22				O					T
23	Q	Q	Q					Q	
24				O			X		
25	T	T				O		T	
26			T		T			Q	O
27									
28				T	Q		T		

Date	Aries	Taurus	Gemini	Cancer	Leo	Virgo	Libra	Scorpio	Sagittarius	Capricorn	Aquarius	Pisces
1	f	u	f		F		f	u	f		U	
2		f	u	f		F		f	u	f		U
3		f	u	f		F		f	u	f		U
4	U		f	u	f		F		f	u	f	
5	U		f	u	f		F		f	u	f	
6		U		f	u	f		F		f	u	f
7		U		f	u	f		F		f	u	f
8		U		f	u	f		F		f	u	f
9	f		U		f	u	f		F		f	u
10	f		U		f	u	f		F		f	u
11	u	f		U		f	u	f		F		f
12	u	f		U		f	u	f		F		f
13	u	f		U		f	u	f		F		f
14	f	u	f		U		f	u	f		F	
15	f	u	f		U		f	u	f		F	
16		f	u	f		U		f	u	f		F
17		f	u	f		U		f	u	f		F
18		f	u	f		U		f	u	f		F
19	F		f	u	f		U		f	u	f	
20	F		f	u	f		U		f	u	f	
21		F		f	u	f		U		f	u	f
22		F		f	u	f		U		f	u	f
23	f		F		f	u	f		U		f	u
24	f		F		f	u	f		U		f	u
25	u	f		F		f	u	f		U		f
26	u	f		F		f	u	f		U		f
27	f	u	f		F		f	u	f		U	
28	f	u	f		F		f	u	f		U	

March Moon Table

Date	Sign	Element	Nature	Phase
1 Thu 12:57 am	Virgo	Earth	Barren	Full 7:51 pm
2 Fri	Virgo	Earth	Barren	3rd
3 Sat 3:20 am	Libra	Air	Semi-fruitful	3rd
4 Sun	Libra	Air	Semi-fruitful	3rd
5 Mon 8:23 am	Scorpio	Water	Fruitful	3rd
6 Tue	Scorpio	Water	Fruitful	3rd
7 Wed 5:03 pm	Sagittarius	Fire	Barren	3rd
8 Thu	Sagittarius	Fire	Barren	3rd
9 Fri	Sagittarius	Fire	Barren	4th 6:20 am
10 Sat 4:52 am	Capricorn	Earth	Semi-fruitful	4th
11 Sun	Capricorn	Earth	Semi-fruitful	4th
12 Mon 6:44 pm	Aquarius	Air	Barren	4th
13 Tue	Aquarius	Air	Barren	4th
14 Wed	Aquarius	Air	Barren	4th
15 Thu 6:12 am	Pisces	Water	Fruitful	4th
16 Fri	Pisces	Water	Fruitful	4th
17 Sat 2:57 pm	Aries	Fire	Barren	New 9:12 am
18 Sun	Aries	Fire	Barren	1st
19 Mon 9:07 pm	Taurus	Earth	Semi-fruitful	1st
20 Tue	Taurus	Earth	Semi-fruitful	1st
21 Wed	Taurus	Earth	Semi-fruitful	1st
22 Thu 1:30 am	Gemini	Air	Barren	1st
23 Fri	Gemini	Air	Barren	1st
24 Sat 4:53 am	Cancer	Water	Fruitful	2nd 11:35 am
25 Sun	Cancer	Water	Fruitful	2nd
26 Mon 7:45 am	Leo	Fire	Barren	2nd
27 Tue	Leo	Fire	Barren	2nd
28 Wed 10:30 am	Virgo	Earth	Barren	2nd
29 Thu	Virgo	Earth	Barren	2nd
30 Fri 1:52 pm	Libra	Air	Semi-fruitful	2nd
31 Sat	Libra	Air	Semi-fruitful	Full 8:37 am

March Aspectarian/Favorable & Unfavorable Days

Date	Sun	Mercury	Venus	Mars	Jupiter	Saturn	Uranus	Neptune	Pluto
1	O					T		O	
2		O	O	Q	X				T
3						Q			
4				X					Q
5					X	O			
6	T							T	X
7		T	T		C				
8								Q	
9	Q				C		T		
10		Q	Q			C			
11								X	
12	X				X		Q		C
13		X	X						
14					Q		X		
15				X	X				
16								C	X
17	C			Q	T				
18		C	C			Q			
19				T			C		Q
20						T		X	
21				O					T
22	X								
23		X	X				X	Q	
24	Q				O	O			
25		Q	Q		T			T	O
26	T					Q			
27		T			Q				
28			T	T			T		
29						T		O	T
30				X					
31	O	O		Q		Q			

Date	Aries	Taurus	Gemini	Cancer	Leo	Virgo	Libra	Scorpio	Sagittarius	Capricorn	Aquarius	Pisces
1		f	u	f		F		f	u	f		U
2		f	u	f		F		f	u	f		U
3		f	u	f		F		f	u	f		U
4	U		f	u	f		F		f	u	f	
5	U		f	u	f		F		f	u	f	
6		U		f	u	f		F		f	u	f
7		U		f	u	f		F		f	u	f
8	f		U		f	u	f		F		f	u
9	f		U		f	u	f		F		f	u
10	f		U		f	u	f		F		f	u
11	u	f		U		f	u	f		F		f
12	u	f		U		f	u	f		F		f
13	f	u	f		U		f	u	f		F	
14	f	u	f		U		f	u	f		F	
15	f	u	f		U		f	u	f		F	
16		f	u	f		U		f	u	f		F
17		f	u	f		U		f	u	f		F
18	F		f	u	f		U		f	u	f	
19	F		f	u	f		U		f	u	f	
20		F		f	u	f		U		f	u	f
21		F		f	u	f		U		f	u	f
22	f		F		f	u	f		U		f	u
23	f		F		f	u	f		U		f	u
24	f		F		f	u	f		U		f	u
25	u	f		F		f	u	f		U		f
26	u	f		F		f	u	f		U		f
27	f	u	f		F		f	u	f		U	
28	f	u	f		F		f	u	f		U	
29		f	u	f		F		f	u	f		U
30		f	u	f		F		f	u	f		U
31	U		f	u	f		F		f	u	f	

April Moon Table

Date	Sign	Element	Nature	Phase
1 Sun 6:57 pm	Scorpio	Water	Fruitful	3rd
2 Mon	Scorpio	Water	Fruitful	3rd
3 Tue	Scorpio	Water	Fruitful	3rd
4 Wed 2:55 am	Sagittarius	Fire	Barren	3rd
5 Thu	Sagittarius	Fire	Barren	3rd
6 Fri 2:01 pm	Capricorn	Earth	Semi-fruitful	3rd
7 Sat	Capricorn	Earth	Semi-fruitful	3rd
8 Sun	Capricorn	Earth	Semi-fruitful	4th 3:18 am
9 Mon 2:50 am	Aquarius	Air	Barren	4th
10 Tue	Aquarius	Air	Barren	4th
11 Wed 2:40 pm	Pisces	Water	Fruitful	4th
12 Thu	Pisces	Water	Fruitful	4th
13 Fri 11:25 pm	Aries	Fire	Barren	4th
14 Sat	Aries	Fire	Barren	4th
15 Sun	Aries	Fire	Barren	New 9:57 pm
16 Mon 4:51 am	Taurus	Earth	Semi-fruitful	1st
17 Tue	Taurus	Earth	Semi-fruitful	1st
18 Wed 8:02 am	Gemini	Air	Barren	1st
19 Thu	Gemini	Air	Barren	1st
20 Fri 10:26 am	Cancer	Water	Fruitful	1st
21 Sat	Cancer	Water	Fruitful	1st
22 Sun 1:09 pm	Leo	Fire	Barren	2nd 5:46 pm
23 Mon	Leo	Fire	Barren	2nd
24 Tue 4:40 pm	Virgo	Earth	Barren	2nd
25 Wed	Virgo	Earth	Barren	2nd
26 Thu 9:13 pm	Libra	Air	Semi-fruitful	2nd
27 Fri	Libra	Air	Semi-fruitful	2nd
28 Sat	Libra	Air	Semi-fruitful	2nd
29 Sun 3:11 am	Scorpio	Water	Fruitful	Full 8:58 pm
30 Mon	Scorpio	Water	Fruitful	3rd

April Aspectarian/Favorable & Unfavorable Days

Date	Sun	Mercury	Venus	Mars	Jupiter	Saturn	Uranus	Neptune	Pluto
1			O					O	Q
2				X		X		T	
3					C				X
4		T							
5	T							Q	
6							T		
7		Q	T	C		C		X	
8	Q				X		Q		C
9		X							
10	X		Q		Q				
11							X		
12			X	X		X		C	
13					T				X
14		C				Q			
15	C			Q					Q
16						T	C		
17			C	T	O			X	T
18		X							
19								Q	
20	X	Q					X		
21				O	T	O		T	O
22	Q		X				Q		
23		T			Q				
24			Q				T		
25	T					T		O	
26				T	X				T
27		O	T			Q			
28			Q						Q
29	O						X	O	
30				X	C			T	X

Date	Aries	Taurus	Gemini	Cancer	Leo	Virgo	Libra	Scorpio	Sagittarius	Capricorn	Aquarius	Pisces
1	U		f	u	f		F		f	u	f	
2		U		f	u	f		F		f	u	f
3		U		f	u	f		F		f	u	f
4	f		U		f	u	f		F		f	u
5	f		U		f	u	f		F		f	u
6	f		U		f	u	f		F		f	u
7	u	f		U		f	u	f		F		f
8	u	f		U		f	u	f		F		f
9	f	u	f		U		f	u	f		F	
10	f	u	f		U		f	u	f		F	
11	f	u	f		U		f	u	f		F	
12		f	u	f		U		f	u	f		F
13		f	u	f		U		f	u	f		F
14	F		f	u	f		U		f	u	f	
15	F		f	u	f		U		f	u	f	
16	F		f	u	f		U		f	u	f	
17		F		f	u	f		U		f	u	f
18		F		f	u	f		U		f	u	f
19	f		F		f	u	f		U		f	u
20	f		F		f	u	f		U		f	u
21	u	f		F		f	u	f		U		f
22	u	f		F		f	u	f		U		f
23	f	u	f		F		f	u	f		U	
24	f	u	f		F		f	u	f		U	
25		f	u	f		F		f	u	f		U
26		f	u	f		F		f	u	f		U
27	U		f	u	f		F		f	u	f	
28	U		f	u	f		F		f	u	f	
29	U		f	u	f		F		f	u	f	
30		U		f	u	f		F		f	u	f

May Moon Table

Date	Sign	Element	Nature	Phase
1 Tue 11:20 am	Sagittarius	Fire	Barren	3rd
2 Wed	Sagittarius	Fire	Barren	3rd
3 Thu 10:06 pm	Capricorn	Earth	Semi-fruitful	3rd
4 Fri	Capricorn	Earth	Semi-fruitful	3rd
5 Sat	Capricorn	Earth	Semi-fruitful	3rd
6 Sun 10:48 am	Aquarius	Air	Barren	3rd
7 Mon	Aquarius	Air	Barren	4th 10:09 pm
8 Tue 11:11 pm	Pisces	Water	Fruitful	4th
9 Wed	Pisces	Water	Fruitful	4th
10 Thu	Pisces	Water	Fruitful	4th
11 Fri 8:40 am	Aries	Fire	Barren	4th
12 Sat	Aries	Fire	Barren	4th
13 Sun 2:15 pm	Taurus	Earth	Semi-fruitful	4th
14 Mon	Taurus	Earth	Semi-fruitful	4th
15 Tue 4:43 pm	Gemini	Air	Barren	New 7:48 am
16 Wed	Gemini	Air	Barren	1st
17 Thu 5:47 pm	Cancer	Water	Fruitful	1st
18 Fri	Cancer	Water	Fruitful	1st
19 Sat 7:11 pm	Leo	Fire	Barren	1st
20 Sun	Leo	Fire	Barren	1st
21 Mon 10:03 pm	Virgo	Earth	Barren	2nd 11:49 pm
22 Tue	Virgo	Earth	Barren	2nd
23 Wed	Virgo	Earth	Barren	2nd
24 Thu 2:52 am	Libra	Air	Semi-fruitful	2nd
25 Fri	Libra	Air	Semi-fruitful	2nd
26 Sat 9:39 am	Scorpio	Water	Fruitful	2nd
27 Sun	Scorpio	Water	Fruitful	2nd
28 Mon 6:29 pm	Sagittarius	Fire	Barren	2nd
29 Tue	Sagittarius	Fire	Barren	Full 10:20 am
30 Wed	Sagittarius	Fire	Barren	3rd
31 Thu 5:27 am	Capricorn	Earth	Semi-fruitful	3rd

May Aspectarian/Favorable & Unfavorable Days

Date	Sun	Mercury	Venus	Mars	Jupiter	Saturn	Uranus	Neptune	Pluto
1									
2		T	O					Q	
3							T		
4					C				
5	T	Q			X			X	C
6				C		Q			
7	Q		T						
8		X		Q			X		
9					X				
10	X		Q		T			C	X
11				X					
12						Q			Q
13		C	X	Q			C		
14				O	T			X	
15	C			T					T
16								Q	
17			C				X		
18		X			T	O		T	
19	X		O			Q			O
20		Q		Q					
21	Q						T		
22			X		T				
23		T		X				O	T
24	T		Q	T	Q				
25									Q
26			Q				O		
27		T			C	X		T	
28		O							X
29	O			X					
30								Q	
31						C	T		

Date	Aries	Taurus	Gemini	Cancer	Leo	Virgo	Libra	Scorpio	Sagittarius	Capricorn	Aquarius	Pisces
1		U		f	u	f		F		f	u	f
2	f		U		f	u	f		F		f	u
3	f		U		f	u	f		F		f	u
4	u	f		U		f	u	f		F		f
5	u	f		U		f	u	f		F		f
6	u	f		U		f	u	f		F		f
7	f	u	f		U		f	u	f		F	
8	f	u	f		U		f	u	f		F	
9		f	u	f		U		f	u	f		F
10		f	u	f		U		f	u	f		F
11		f	u	f		U		f	u	f		F
12	F		f	u	f		U		f	u	f	
13	F		f	u	f		U		f	u	f	
14		F		f	u	f		U		f	u	f
15		F		f	u	f		U		f	u	f
16	f		F		f	u	f		U		f	u
17	f		F		f	u	f		U		f	u
18	u	f		F		f	u	f		U		f
19	u	f		F		f	u	f		U		f
20	f	u	f		F		f	u	f		U	
21	f	u	f		F		f	u	f		U	
22		f	u	f		F		f	u	f		U
23		f	u	f		F		f	u	f		U
24	U		f	u	f		F		f	u	f	
25	U		f	u	f		F		f	u	f	
26	U		f	u	f		F		f	u	f	
27		U		f	u	f		F		f	u	f
28		U		f	u	f		F		f	u	f
29	f		U		f	u	f		F		f	u
30	f		U		f	u	f		F		f	u
31	f		U		f	u	f		F		f	u

June Moon Table

Date	Sign	Element	Nature	Phase
1 Fri	Capricorn	Earth	Semi-fruitful	3rd
2 Sat 6:06 pm	Aquarius	Air	Barren	3rd
3 Sun	Aquarius	Air	Barren	3rd
4 Mon	Aquarius	Air	Barren	3rd
5 Tue 6:53 am	Pisces	Water	Fruitful	3rd
6 Wed	Pisces	Water	Fruitful	4th 2:32 pm
7 Thu 5:26 pm	Aries	Fire	Barren	4th
8 Fri	Aries	Fire	Barren	4th
9 Sat	Aries	Fire	Barren	4th
10 Sun 12:04 am	Taurus	Earth	Semi-fruitful	4th
11 Mon	Taurus	Earth	Semi-fruitful	4th
12 Tue 2:53 am	Gemini	Air	Barren	4th
13 Wed	Gemini	Air	Barren	New 3:43 pm
14 Thu 3:20 am	Cancer	Water	Fruitful	1st
15 Fri	Cancer	Water	Fruitful	1st
16 Sat 3:21 am	Leo	Fire	Barren	1st
17 Sun	Leo	Fire	Barren	1st
18 Mon 4:41 am	Virgo	Earth	Barren	1st
19 Tue	Virgo	Earth	Barren	1st
20 Wed 8:29 am	Libra	Air	Semi-fruitful	2nd 6:51 am
21 Thu	Libra	Air	Semi-fruitful	2nd
22 Fri 3:11 pm	Scorpio	Water	Fruitful	2nd
23 Sat	Scorpio	Water	Fruitful	2nd
24 Sun	Scorpio	Water	Fruitful	2nd
25 Mon 12:29 am	Sagittarius	Fire	Barren	2nd
26 Tue	Sagittarius	Fire	Barren	2nd
27 Wed 11:52 am	Capricorn	Earth	Semi-fruitful	2nd
28 Thu	Capricorn	Earth	Semi-fruitful	Full 12:53 am
29 Fri	Capricorn	Earth	Semi-fruitful	3rd
30 Sat 12:37 am	Aquarius	Air	Barren	3rd

June Aspectarian/Favorable & Unfavorable Days

Date	Sun	Mercury	Venus	Mars	Jupiter	Saturn	Uranus	Neptune	Pluto
1			O	X				X	C
2							Q		
3	T	T		C					
4					Q				
5						X	X		
6	Q	Q			T			C	X
7			T						
8				X		Q			
9	X	X	Q						Q
10			·	Q		T	C		
11			X		O			X	T
12				T					
13	C							Q	
14		C				O	X		
15					T			T	O
16			C	O		Q			
17	X				Q				
18						T	T		
19		X		X				O	T
20	Q		X		Q				
21		Q		T					Q
22	T						O		
23			Q	Q	C	X		T	
24		T							X
25				X					
26			T					Q	
27						C	T		
28	O				X			X	
29									C
30		O		C			Q		

Date	Aries	Taurus	Gemini	Cancer	Leo	Virgo	Libra	Scorpio	Sagittarius	Capricorn	Aquarius	Pisces
1	u	f		U		f	u	f		F		f
2	u	f		U		f	u	f		F		f
3	f	u	f		U		f	u	f		F	
4	f	u	f		U		f	u	f		F	
5	f	u	f		U		f	u	f		F	
6		f	u	f		U		f	u	f		F
7		f	u	f		U		f	u	f		F
8	F		f	u	f		U		f	u	f	
9	F		f	u	f		U		f	u	f	
10		F		f	u	f		U		f	u	f
11		F		f	u	f		U		f	u	f
12	f		F		f	u	f		U		f	u
13	f		F		f	u	f		U		f	u
14	f		F		f	u	f		U		f	u
15	u	f	F		f	u	f		U		f	
16	u	f	F		f	u	f		U		f	
17	f	u	f		F		f	u	f		U	
18	f	u	f		F		f	u	f		U	
19		f	u	f	F		f	u	f			U
20		f	u	f	F		f	u	f			U
21	U		f	u	f	F		f	u	f		
22	U		f	u	f	F		f	u	f		
23		U		f	u	f	F		f	u	f	
24		U		f	u	f	F		f	u	f	
25	f		U		f	u	f	F		f		u
26	f		U		f	u	f	F		f		u
27	f		U		f	u	f	F		f		u
28	u	f		U		f	u	f		F		f
29	u	f		U		f	u	f		F		f
30	f	u	f	U		f	u	f		F		

July Moon Table

Date	Sign	Element	Nature	Phase
1 Sun	Aquarius	Air	Barren	3rd
2 Mon 1:31 pm	Pisces	Water	Fruitful	3rd
3 Tue	Pisces	Water	Fruitful	3rd
4 Wed	Pisces	Water	Fruitful	3rd
5 Thu 12:50 am	Aries	Fire	Barren	3rd
6 Fri	Aries	Fire	Barren	4th 3:51 am
7 Sat 8:51 am	Taurus	Earth	Semi-fruitful	4th
8 Sun	Taurus	Earth	Semi-fruitful	4th
9 Mon 12:58 pm	Gemini	Air	Barren	4th
10 Tue	Gemini	Air	Barren	4th
11 Wed 1:59 pm	Cancer	Water	Fruitful	4th
12 Thu	Cancer	Water	Fruitful	New 10:48 pm
13 Fri 1:31 pm	Leo	Fire	Barren	1st
14 Sat	Leo	Fire	Barren	1st
15 Sun 1:31 pm	Virgo	Earth	Barren	1st
16 Mon	Virgo	Earth	Barren	1st
17 Tue 3:42 pm	Libra	Air	Semi-fruitful	1st
18 Wed	Libra	Air	Semi-fruitful	1st
19 Thu 9:13 pm	Scorpio	Water	Fruitful	2nd 3:52 pm
20 Fri	Scorpio	Water	Fruitful	2nd
21 Sat	Scorpio	Water	Fruitful	2nd
22 Sun 6:12 am	Sagittarius	Fire	Barren	2nd
23 Mon	Sagittarius	Fire	Barren	2nd
24 Tue 5:49 pm	Capricorn	Earth	Semi-fruitful	2nd
25 Wed	Capricorn	Earth	Semi-fruitful	2nd
26 Thu	Capricorn	Earth	Semi-fruitful	2nd
27 Fri 6:41 am	Aquarius	Air	Barren	Full 4:20 pm
28 Sat	Aquarius	Air	Barren	3rd
29 Sun 7:28 pm	Pisces	Water	Fruitful	3rd
30 Mon	Pisces	Water	Fruitful	3rd
31 Tue	Pisces	Water	Fruitful	3rd

July Aspectarian/Favorable & Unfavorable Days

Date	Sun	Mercury	Venus	Mars	Jupiter	Saturn	Uranus	Neptune	Pluto
1			O		Q				
2							X		
3	T				T	X		C	
4									X
5		T		X		Q			
6	Q								Q
7			T	Q		T	C		
8	X	Q			O			X	T
9			Q						
10		X		T				Q	
11		X				O	X		
12	C				T			T	O
13							Q		
14		C		O	Q				
15						T	T		
16			C		X			O	T
17	X					Q			
18				T					
19	Q	X							Q
20			X	Q	C	X	O		
21		Q						T	X
22	T			X					
23			Q					Q	
24		T					T		
25					X	C			
26			T					X	C
27	O			C			Q		
28					Q				
29		O							
30						T	X	X	
31			O					C	X

Date	Aries	Taurus	Gemini	Cancer	Leo	Virgo	Libra	Scorpio	Sagittarius	Capricorn	Aquarius	Pisces
1	f	u	f		U		f	u	f		F	
2	f	u	f		U		f	u	f		F	
3		f	u	f		U		f	u	f		F
4		f	u	f		U		f	u	f		F
5	F		f	u	f		U		f	u	f	
6	F		f	u	f		U		f	u	f	
7	F		f	u	f		U		f	u	f	
8		F		f	u	f		U		f	u	f
9		F		f	u	f		U		f	u	f
10	f		F		f	u	f		U		f	u
11	f		F		f	u	f		U		f	u
12	u	f		F		f	u	f		U		f
13	u	f		F		f	u	f		U		f
14	f	u	f		F		f	u	f		U	
15	f	u	f		F		f	u	f		U	
16		f	u	f		F		f	u	f		U
17		f	u	f		F		f	u	f		U
18	U		f	u	f		F		f	u	f	
19	U		f	u	f		F		f	u	f	
20		U		f	u	f		F		f	u	f
21		U		f	u	f		F		f	u	f
22		U		f	u	f		F		f	u	f
23	f		U		f	u	f		F		f	u
24	f		U		f	u	f		F		f	u
25	u	f		U		f	u	f		F		f
26	u	f		U		f	u	f		F		f
27	u	f		U		f	u	f		F		f
28	f	u	f		U		f	u	f		F	
29	f	u	f		U		f	u	f		F	
30		f	u	f		U		f	u	f		F
31		f	u	f		U		f	u	f		F

August Moon Table

Date	Sign	Element	Nature	Phase
1 Wed 6:54 am	Aries	Fire	Barren	3rd
2 Thu	Aries	Fire	Barren	3rd
3 Fri 3:51 pm	Taurus	Earth	Semi-fruitful	3rd
4 Sat	Taurus	Earth	Semi-fruitful	4th 2:18 pm
5 Sun 9:32 pm	Gemini	Air	Barren	4th
6 Mon	Gemini	Air	Barren	4th
7 Tue	Gemini	Air	Barren	4th
8 Wed 12:01 am	Cancer	Water	Fruitful	4th
9 Thu	Cancer	Water	Fruitful	4th
10 Fri 12:18 am	Leo	Fire	Barren	4th
11 Sat 11:59 pm	Virgo	Earth	Barren	New 5:58 am
12 Sun	Virgo	Earth	Barren	1st
13 Mon	Virgo	Earth	Barren	1st
14 Tue 12:57 am	Libra	Air	Semi-fruitful	1st
15 Wed	Libra	Air	Semi-fruitful	1st
16 Thu 4:54 am	Scorpio	Water	Fruitful	1st
17 Fri	Scorpio	Water	Fruitful	1st
18 Sat 12:45 pm	Sagittarius	Fire	Barren	2nd 3:49 am
19 Sun	Sagittarius	Fire	Barren	2nd
20 Mon	Sagittarius	Fire	Barren	2nd
21 Tue 12:00 am	Capricorn	Earth	Semi-fruitful	2nd
22 Wed	Capricorn	Earth	Semi-fruitful	2nd
23 Thu 12:56 pm	Aquarius	Air	Barren	2nd
24 Fri	Aquarius	Air	Barren	2nd
25 Sat	Aquarius	Air	Barren	2nd
26 Sun 1:32 am	Pisces	Water	Fruitful	Full 7:56 am
27 Mon	Pisces	Water	Fruitful	3rd
28 Tue 12:35 pm	Aries	Fire	Barren	3rd
29 Wed	Aries	Fire	Barren	3rd
30 Thu 9:30 pm	Taurus	Earth	Semi-fruitful	3rd
31 Fri	Taurus	Earth	Semi-fruitful	3rd

August Aspectarian/Favorable & Unfavorable Days

Date	Sun	Mercury	Venus	Mars	Jupiter	Saturn	Uranus	Neptune	Pluto
1				X		Q			
2	T	T							Q
3				Q		T	C		
4	Q				O			X	
5		Q	T						T
6	X			T					
7		X						Q	
8			Q			T	O	X	
9								T	O
10		C	X	O	Q		Q		
11	C								
12							T	T	
13						X		O	T
14		X	C	T		Q			
15	X								Q
16				Q			X	O	
17		Q			C			T	X
18	Q			X					
19		T	X					Q	
20	T								
21						C	T		
22			Q	X				X	C
23				C			Q		
24		O			Q				
25			T						
26	O					X	X		
27					T			C	X
28				X		Q			
29									
30		T	O	Q					Q
31	T					T	C		

Date	Aries	Taurus	Gemini	Cancer	Leo	Virgo	Libra	Scorpio	Sagittarius	Capricorn	Aquarius	Pisces
1		f	u	f		U		f	u	f		F
2	F		f	u	f		U		f	u	f	
3	F		f	u	f		U		f	u	f	
4		F		f	u	f		U		f	u	f
5		F		f	u	f		U		f	u	f
6	f		F		f	u	f		U		f	u
7	f		F		f	u	f		U		f	u
8	u	f		F		f	u	f		U		f
9	u	f		F		f	u	f		U		f
10	f	u	f		F		f	u	f		U	
11	f	u	f		F		f	u	f		U	
12		f	u	f		F		f	u	f		U
13		f	u	f		F		f	u	f		U
14	U		f	u	f		F		f	u	f	
15	U		f	u	f		F		f	u	f	
16	U		f	u	f		F		f	u	f	
17		U		f	u	f		F		f	u	f
18		U		f	u	f		F		f	u	f
19	f		U		f	u	f		F		f	u
20	f		U		f	u	f		F		f	u
21	u	f		U		f	u	f		F		f
22	u	f		U		f	u	f		F		f
23	u	f		U		f	u	f		F		f
24	f	u	f		U		f	u	f		F	
25	f	u	f		U		f	u	f		F	
26		f	u	f		U		f	u	f		F
27		f	u	f		U		f	u	f		F
28		f	u	f		U		f	u	f		F
29	F		f	u	f		U		f	u	f	
30	F		f	u	f		U		f	u	f	
31		F		f	u	f		U		f	u	f

September Moon Table

Date	Sign	Element	Nature	Phase
1 Sat	Taurus	Earth	Semi-fruitful	3rd
2 Sun 4:02 am	Gemini	Air	Barren	4th 10:37 pm
3 Mon	Gemini	Air	Barren	4th
4 Tue 8:03 am	Cancer	Water	Fruitful	4th
5 Wed	Cancer	Water	Fruitful	4th
6 Thu 9:54 am	Leo	Fire	Barren	4th
7 Fri	Leo	Fire	Barren	4th
8 Sat 10:29 am	Virgo	Earth	Barren	4th
9 Sun	Virgo	Earth	Barren	New 2:01 pm
10 Mon 11:20 am	Libra	Air	Semi-fruitful	1st
11 Tue	Libra	Air	Semi-fruitful	1st
12 Wed 2:15 pm	Scorpio	Water	Fruitful	1st
13 Thu	Scorpio	Water	Fruitful	1st
14 Fri 8:45 pm	Sagittarius	Fire	Barren	1st
15 Sat	Sagittarius	Fire	Barren	1st
16 Sun	Sagittarius	Fire	Barren	2nd 7:15 pm
17 Mon 7:07 am	Capricorn	Earth	Semi-fruitful	2nd
18 Tue	Capricorn	Earth	Semi-fruitful	2nd
19 Wed 7:52 pm	Aquarius	Air	Barren	2nd
20 Thu	Aquarius	Air	Barren	2nd
21 Fri	Aquarius	Air	Barren	2nd
22 Sat 8:27 am	Pisces	Water	Fruitful	2nd
23 Sun	Pisces	Water	Fruitful	2nd
24 Mon 7:04 pm	Aries	Fire	Barren	Full 10:52 pm
25 Tue	Aries	Fire	Barren	3rd
26 Wed	Aries	Fire	Barren	3rd
27 Thu 3:16 am	Taurus	Earth	Semi-fruitful	3rd
28 Fri	Taurus	Earth	Semi-fruitful	3rd
29 Sat 9:26 am	Gemini	Air	Barren	3rd
30 Sun	Gemini	Air	Barren	3rd

September Aspectarian/Favorable & Unfavorable Days

Date	Sun	Mercury	Venus	Mars	Jupiter	Saturn	Uranus	Neptune	Pluto
1		Q			O			X	T
2	Q			T					
3								Q	
4		X	T			O	X		
5	X				T			T	O
6			Q	O			Q		
7					Q				
8		C	X			T	T		
9	C				X			O	T
10				T	Q				
11									Q
12			C	Q		X	O		
13		X						T	X
14	X			X	C				
15									
16	Q	Q						Q	
17			X			C	T		
18					X			X	C
19	T	T						Q	
20			Q	C					
21					Q				
22						X	X		
23			T					C	X
24	O				T				
25		O		X		Q			
26									Q
27			O	Q		T	C		
28					O			X	T
29	T			T					
30		T						Q	

Date	Aries	Taurus	Gemini	Cancer	Leo	Virgo	Libra	Scorpio	Sagittarius	Capricorn	Aquarius	Pisces
1		F		f	u	f		U		f	u	f
2		F		f	u	f		U		f	u	f
3	f		F		f	u	f		U		f	u
4	f		F		f	u	f		U		f	u
5	u	f		F		f	u	f		U		f
6	u	f		F		f	u	f		U		f
7	f	u	f		F		f	u	f		U	
8	f	u	f		F		f	u	f		U	
9		f	u	f		F		f	u	f		U
10		f	u	f		F		f	u	f		U
11	U		f	u	f		F		f	u	f	
12	U		f	u	f		F		f	u	f	
13		U		f	u	f		F		f	u	f
14		U		f	u	f		F		f	u	f
15	f		U		f	u	f		F		f	u
16	f		U		f	u	f		F		f	u
17	f		U		f	u	f		F		f	u
18	u	f		U		f	u	f		F		f
19	u	f		U		f	u	f		F		f
20	f	u	f		U		f	u	f		F	
21	f	u	f		U		f	u	f		F	
22	f	u	f		U		f	u	f		F	
23		f	u	f		U		f	u	f		F
24		f	u	f		U		f	u	f		F
25	F		f	u	f		U		f	u	f	
26	F		f	u	f		U		f	u	f	
27	F		f	u	f		U		f	u	f	
28		F		f	u	f		U		f	u	f
29		F		f	u	f		U		f	u	f
30	f		F		f	u	f		U		f	u

October Moon Table

Date	Sign	Element	Nature	Phase
1 Mon 2:00 pm	Cancer	Water	Fruitful	3rd
2 Tue	Cancer	Water	Fruitful	4th 5:45 am
3 Wed 5:12 pm	Leo	Fire	Barren	4th
4 Thu	Leo	Fire	Barren	4th
5 Fri 7:19 pm	Virgo	Earth	Barren	4th
6 Sat	Virgo	Earth	Barren	4th
7 Sun 9:10 pm	Libra	Air	Semi-fruitful	4th
8 Mon	Libra	Air	Semi-fruitful	New 11:47 pm
9 Tue	Libra	Air	Semi-fruitful	1st
10 Wed 12:09 am	Scorpio	Water	Fruitful	1st
11 Thu	Scorpio	Water	Fruitful	1st
12 Fri 5:53 am	Sagittarius	Fire	Barren	1st
13 Sat	Sagittarius	Fire	Barren	1st
14 Sun 3:17 pm	Capricorn	Earth	Semi-fruitful	1st
15 Mon	Capricorn	Earth	Semi-fruitful	1st
16 Tue	Capricorn	Earth	Semi-fruitful	2nd 2:02 pm
17 Wed 3:36 am	Aquarius	Air	Barren	2nd
18 Thu	Aquarius	Air	Barren	2nd
19 Fri 4:20 pm	Pisces	Water	Fruitful	2nd
20 Sat	Pisces	Water	Fruitful	2nd
21 Sun	Pisces	Water	Fruitful	2nd
22 Mon 2:58 am	Aries	Fire	Barren	2nd
23 Tue	Aries	Fire	Barren	2nd
24 Wed 10:33 am	Taurus	Earth	Semi-fruitful	Full 12:45 pm
25 Thu	Taurus	Earth	Semi-fruitful	3rd
26 Fri 3:41 pm	Gemini	Air	Barren	3rd
27 Sat	Gemini	Air	Barren	3rd
28 Sun 7:27 pm	Cancer	Water	Fruitful	3rd
29 Mon	Cancer	Water	Fruitful	3rd
30 Tue 10:42 pm	Leo	Fire	Barren	3rd
31 Wed	Leo	Fire	Barren	4th 12:40 pm

October Aspectarian/Favorable & Unfavorable Days

Date	Sun	Mercury	Venus	Mars	Jupiter	Saturn	Uranus	Neptune	Pluto
1						O	X		
2	Q	Q	T					T	O
3					T		Q		
4	X		Q	O					
5		X			Q		T		
6			X			T		O	
7					X				T
8	C			T		Q			
9									Q
10		C	C	Q		X	O		
11					C			T	X
12									
13	X			X				Q	
14						C	T		
15		X	X					X	
16	Q				X				C
17			Q				Q		
18		Q		C					
19	T				Q		X		
20			T			X		C	
21		T			T				X
22						Q			
23				X					Q
24	O		O			T	C		
25				Q				X	T
26		O		O					
27							Q		
28			T	T			X		
29	T					O		T	
30		T	Q		T		Q		O
31	Q								

Date	Aries	Taurus	Gemini	Cancer	Leo	Virgo	Libra	Scorpio	Sagittarius	Capricorn	Aquarius	Pisces
1	f		F		f	u	f		U		f	u
2	u	f		F		f	u	f		U		f
3	u	f		F		f	u	f		U		f
4	f	u	f		F		f	u	f		U	
5	f	u	f		F		f	u	f		U	
6		f	u	f		F		f	u	f		U
7		f	u	f		F		f	u	f		U
8	U		f	u	f		F		f	u	f	
9	U		f	u	f		F		f	u	f	
10		U		f	u	f		F		f	u	f
11		U		f	u	f		F		f	u	f
12		U		f	u	f		F		f	u	f
13	f		U		f	u	f		F		f	u
14	f		U		f	u	f		F		f	u
15	u	f		U		f	u	f		F		f
16	u	f		U		f	u	f		F		f
17	u	f		U		f	u	f		F		f
18	f	u	f		U		f	u	f		F	
19	f	u	f		U		f	u	f		F	
20		f	u	f		U		f	u	f		F
21		f	u	f		U		f	u	f		F
22	F		f	u	f		U		f	u	f	
23	F		f	u	f		U		f	u	f	
24	F		f	u	f		U		f	u	f	
25		F		f	u	f		U		f	u	f
26		F		f	u	f		U		f	u	f
27	f		F		f	u	f		U		f	u
28	f		F		f	u	f		U		f	u
29	u	f		F		f	u	f		U		f
30	u	f		F		f	u	f		U		f
31	f	u	f		F		f	u	f		U	

November Moon Table

Date	Sign	Element	Nature	Phase
1 Thu	Leo	Fire	Barren	4th
2 Fri 1:48 am	Virgo	Earth	Barren	4th
3 Sat	Virgo	Earth	Barren	4th
4 Sun 4:01 am	Libra	Air	Semi-fruitful	4th
5 Mon	Libra	Air	Semi-fruitful	4th
6 Tue 8:02 am	Scorpio	Water	Fruitful	4th
7 Wed	Scorpio	Water	Fruitful	New 11:02 am
8 Thu 1:59 pm	Sagittarius	Fire	Barren	1st
9 Fri	Sagittarius	Fire	Barren	1st
10 Sat 10:55 pm	Capricorn	Earth	Semi-fruitful	1st
11 Sun	Capricorn	Earth	Semi-fruitful	1st
12 Mon	Capricorn	Earth	Semi-fruitful	1st
13 Tue 10:45 am	Aquarius	Air	Barren	1st
14 Wed	Aquarius	Air	Barren	1st
15 Thu 11:41 pm	Pisces	Water	Fruitful	2nd 9:54 am
16 Fri	Pisces	Water	Fruitful	2nd
17 Sat	Pisces	Water	Fruitful	2nd
18 Sun 10:56 am	Aries	Fire	Barren	2nd
19 Mon	Aries	Fire	Barren	2nd
20 Tue 6:43 pm	Taurus	Earth	Semi-fruitful	2nd
21 Wed	Taurus	Earth	Semi-fruitful	2nd
22 Thu 11:10 pm	Gemini	Air	Barren	2nd
23 Fri	Gemini	Air	Barren	Full 12:39 am
24 Sat	Gemini	Air	Barren	3rd
25 Sun 1:38 am	Cancer	Water	Fruitful	3rd
26 Mon	Cancer	Water	Fruitful	3rd
27 Tue 3:35 am	Leo	Fire	Barren	3rd
28 Wed	Leo	Fire	Barren	3rd
29 Thu 6:08 am	Virgo	Earth	Barren	4th 7:19 pm
30 Fri	Virgo	Earth	Barren	4th

November Aspectarian/Favorable & Unfavorable Days

Date	Sun	Mercury	Venus	Mars	Jupiter	Saturn	Uranus	Neptune	Pluto
1				O	Q				
2	X	Q	X			T	T		
3								O	T
4		X			X	Q			
5				T					Q
6		C				X	O		
7	C							T	X
8				Q	C				
9		C						Q	
10			X	X			T		
11					C				
12	X							X	C
13			Q		X		Q		
14		X							
15	Q		T				X		
16				C	Q	X			
17		Q						C	X
18	T				T	Q			
19		T							Q
20			O			C			
21			X		T		X		
22									T
23	O	O		Q	O			Q	
24			T						
25				T		O	X		
26		Q						T	O
27	T	T			T		Q		
28									
29	Q	Q	X	O	Q	T	T		
30								O	T

Date	Aries	Taurus	Gemini	Cancer	Leo	Virgo	Libra	Scorpio	Sagittarius	Capricorn	Aquarius	Pisces
1	f		u	f	F		f	u	f		U	
2		f		u	f	F		f	u	f		U
3		f		u	f	F		f	u	f		U
4		f		u	f	F		f	u	f		U
5	U		f		u	f	F		f	u	f	
6	U		f		u	f	F		f	u	f	
7		U		f		u	f	F		f	u	f
8		U		f		u	f	F		f	u	f
9	f		U		f		u	f	F		f	u
10	f		U		f		u	f	F		f	u
11	u	f		U		f		u	f	F		f
12	u	f		U		f		u	f	F		f
13	u	f		U		f		u	f	F		f
14	f	u	f		U		f		u	f	F	
15	f	u	f		U		f		u	f	F	
16		f	u	f		U		f		u	f	F
17		f	u	f		U		f		u	f	F
18		f	u	f		U		f		u	f	F
19	F		f	u	f		U		f		u	f
20	F		f	u	f		U		f		u	f
21	f	F		f	u	f		U		f		u
22	f	F		f	u	f		U		f		u
23	u	f	F		f	u	f		U		f	
24	u	f	F		f	u	f		U		f	
25		u	f	F		f	u	f		U		f
26		u	f	F		f	u	f		U		f
27		u	f	F		f	u	f		U		f
28	f		u	f	F		f	u	f		U	
29	f		u	f	F		f	u	f		U	
30		f		u	f	F		f	u	f		U

December Moon Table

Date	Sign	Element	Nature	Phase
1 Sat 9:49 am	Libra	Air	Semi-fruitful	4th
2 Sun	Libra	Air	Semi-fruitful	4th
3 Mon 2:55 pm	Scorpio	Water	Fruitful	4th
4 Tue	Scorpio	Water	Fruitful	4th
5 Wed 9:49 pm	Sagittarius	Fire	Barren	4th
6 Thu	Sagittarius	Fire	Barren	4th
7 Fri	Sagittarius	Fire	Barren	New 2:20 am
8 Sat 7:01 am	Capricorn	Earth	Semi-fruitful	1st
9 Sun	Capricorn	Earth	Semi-fruitful	1st
10 Mon 6:39 pm	Aquarius	Air	Barren	1st
11 Tue	Aquarius	Air	Barren	1st
12 Wed	Aquarius	Air	Barren	1st
13 Thu 7:40 am	Pisces	Water	Fruitful	1st
14 Fri	Pisces	Water	Fruitful	1st
15 Sat 7:44 pm	Aries	Fire	Barren	2nd 6:49 am
16 Sun	Aries	Fire	Barren	2nd
17 Mon	Aries	Fire	Barren	2nd
18 Tue 4:37 am	Taurus	Earth	Semi-fruitful	2nd
19 Wed	Taurus	Earth	Semi-fruitful	2nd
20 Thu 9:34 am	Gemini	Air	Barren	2nd
21 Fri	Gemini	Air	Barren	2nd
22 Sat 11:28 am	Cancer	Water	Fruitful	Full 12:49 pm
23 Sun	Cancer	Water	Fruitful	3rd
24 Mon 11:59 am	Leo	Fire	Barren	3rd
25 Tue	Leo	Fire	Barren	3rd
26 Wed 12:50 pm	Virgo	Earth	Barren	3rd
27 Thu	Virgo	Earth	Barren	3rd
28 Fri 3:23 pm	Libra	Air	Semi-fruitful	3rd
29 Sat	Libra	Air	Semi-fruitful	4th 4:34 am
30 Sun 8:23 pm	Scorpio	Water	Fruitful	4th
31 Mon	Scorpio	Water	Fruitful	4th

December Aspectarian/Favorable & Unfavorable Days

Date	Sun	Mercury	Venus	Mars	Jupiter	Saturn	Uranus	Neptune	Pluto
1	O		O			O		T	
2				T	T			Q	O
3									
4		T		Q	Q		T		
5						T		O	
6	T	Q	T	X	X				T
7							Q		
8	Q		Q						Q
9		X					X	O	
10								T	
11	X		X	C	C				X
12									
13								Q	
14						C	T		
15		C						X	
16	C			X	X			Q	C
17			C						
18					Q				
19				Q		X	X		
20		X						C	
21				T	T				X
22	X		X			Q			
23		Q					C		Q
24	Q					T			
25		T	Q		O			X	T
26				O					
27	T		T					Q	
28						O	X		
29					T			T	O
30		O		T				Q	
31	O		O						

Date	Aries	Taurus	Gemini	Cancer	Leo	Virgo	Libra	Scorpio	Sagittarius	Capricorn	Aquarius	Pisces
1		f	u	f		F		f	u	f		U
2	U		f	u	f		F		f	u	f	
3	U		f	u	f		F		f	u	f	
4		U		f	u	f		F		f	u	f
5		U		f	u	f		F		f	u	f
6	f		U		f	u	f		F		f	u
7	f		U		f	u	f		F		f	u
8	f		U		f	u	f		F		f	u
9	u	f		U		f	u	f		F		f
10	u	f		U		f	u	f		F		f
11	f	u	f		U		f	u	f		F	
12	f	u	f		U		f	u	f		F	
13	f	u	f		U		f	u	f		F	
14		f	u	f		U		f	u	f		F
15		f	u	f		U		f	u	f		F
16	F		f	u	f		U		f	u	f	
17	F		f	u	f		U		f	u	f	
18	F		f	u	f		U		f	u	f	
19		F		f	u	f		U		f	u	f
20		F		f	u	f		U		f	u	f
21	f		F		f	u	f		U		f	u
22	f		F		f	u	f		U		f	u
23	u	f		F		f	u	f		U		f
24	u	f		F		f	u	f		U		f
25	f	u	f		F		f	u	f		U	
26	f	u	f		F		f	u	f		U	
27		f	u	f		F		f	u	f		U
28		f	u	f		F		f	u	f		U
29	U		f	u	f		F		f	u	f	
30	U		f	u	f		F		f	u	f	
31		U		f	u	f		F		f	u	f

2018 Retrograde Planets

Planet	Begin	Eastern	Pacific	End	Eastern	Pacific
Uranus	8/2/17		**10:31 am**	1/2/18	9:13 am	**6:13 am**
Uranus	8/3/17	1:31 am		1/2/18	9:13 am	**6:13 am**
Jupiter	3/8/18	11:45 pm	**8:45 pm**	7/10/18	1:02 pm	**10:02 am**
Mercury	3/22/18	8:19 pm	**5:19 pm**	4/15/18	5:21 am	**2:21 am**
Saturn	4/17/18	9:47 pm	**6:47 pm**	9/6/18	7:09 am	**4:09 am**
Pluto	4/22/18	11:26 am	**8:26 am**	9/30/18	10:03 pm	**7:03 pm**
Neptune	6/18/18	7:26 pm	**4:26 pm**	11/24/18	8:08 pm	**5:08 pm**
Mars	6/26/18	5:04 pm	**2:04 pm**	8/27/18	10:05 am	**7:05 am**
Mercury	7/25/18		**10:02 pm**	8/18/18		**9:25 pm**
Mercury	7/26/18	1:02 am		8/19/18	12:25 am	
Uranus	8/7/17	12:48 pm	**9:48 pm**	1/6/19	3:27 pm	**12:27 pm**
Venus	10/5/18	3:04 pm	**12:04 pm**	11/16/18	5:51 am	**2:51 am**
Mercury	11/16/18	8:33 pm	**5:33 pm**	12/6/18	4:22 pm	**1:22 pm**

Eastern Time in plain type, **Pacific Time in bold type**

	Dec 17	Jan 18	Feb	Mar	Apr	May	Jun	Jul	Aug	Sep	Oct	Nov	Dec	Jan 19
☿				▓	▓			▓				▓		
♃				▓	▓	▓	▓	▓						
♀											▓			
♄					▓	▓	▓	▓	▓					
♇					▓	▓	▓	▓	▓	▓				
♆							▓	▓	▓	▓	▓	▓		
♅	▓	▓							▓	▓	▓	▓	▓	▓
♂							▓	▓	▓					

Egg-Setting Dates

To Have Eggs by this Date	Sign	Qtr.	Date to Set Eggs
Jan 19, 3:26 pm–Jan 22, 1:27 am	Pisces	1st	Dec 29, 2017
Jan 24, 8:39 am–Jan 26, 12:40 pm	Taurus	1st	Jan 03, 2018
Jan 28, 1:57 pm–Jan 30, 1:53 pm	Cancer	2nd	Jan 07
Feb 15, 9:42 pm–Feb 18, 7:05 am	Pisces	1st	Jan 25
Feb 20, 2:12 pm–Feb 22, 7:07 pm	Taurus	1st	Jan 30
Feb 24, 10:06 pm–Feb 26, 11:42 pm	Cancer	2nd	Feb 03
Mar 17, 9:12 am–Mar 17, 2:57 pm	Pisces	1st	Feb 24
Mar 19, 9:07 am–Mar 22, 1:30 am	Taurus	1st	Feb 26
Mar 24, 4:53 am–Mar 26, 7:45 am	Cancer	1st	Mar 03
Mar 30, 1:52 pm–Mar 31, 8:37 am	Libra	2nd	Mar 09
Apr 16, 4:51 am–Apr 18, 8:02 am	Taurus	1st	Mar 26
Apr 20, 10:26 am–Apr 22, 1:09 pm	Cancer	1st	Mar 30
Apr 26, 9:13 pm–Apr 29, 3:11 am	Libra	2nd	Apr 05
May 15, 7:48 am–May 15, 4:43 pm	Taurus	1st	Apr 24
May 17, 5:47 pm–May 19, 7:11 pm	Cancer	1st	Apr 26
May 24, 2:52 am–May 26, 9:39 am	Libra	2nd	May 03
Jun 14, 3:20 am–Jun 16, 3:21 am	Cancer	1st	May 24
Jun 20, 8:29 am–Jun 22, 3:11 pm	Libra	2nd	May 30
Jul 12, 10:48 pm–Jul 13, 1:31 pm	Cancer	1st	Jun 21
Jul 17, 3:42 pm–Jul 19, 9:13 pm	Libra	1st	Jun 26
Aug 14, 12:57 am–Aug 16, 4:54 am	Libra	1st	Jul 24
Aug 26, 1:32 am–Aug 26, 7:56 am	Pisces	2nd	Aug 05
Sep 10, 11:20 am–Sep 12, 2:15 pm	Libra	1st	Aug 20
Sep 22, 8:27 am–Sep 24, 7:04 pm	Pisces	2nd	Sep 01
Oct 8, 11:47 pm–Oct 10, 12:09 am	Libra	1st	Sep 17
Oct 19, 4:20 pm–Oct 22, 2:58 am	Pisces	2nd	Sep 28
Oct 24, 10:33 am–Oct 24, 12:45 pm	Taurus	2nd	Oct 03
Nov 15, 11:41 pm–Nov 18, 10:56 am	Pisces	2nd	Oct 25
Nov 20, 6:43 pm–Nov 22, 11:10 pm	Taurus	2nd	Oct 30
Dec 13, 7:40 am–Dec 15, 7:44 pm	Pisces	1st	Nov 22
Dec 18, 4:37 am–Dec 20, 9:34 am	Taurus	2nd	Nov 27
Dec 22, 11:28 am–Dec 22, 12:49 pm	Cancer	2nd	Dec 01

Dates to Hunt and Fish

Date	Quarter	Sign
Jan 1, 3:10 am–Jan 3, 2:23 am	2nd	Cancer
Jan 9, 3:05 pm–Jan 12, 2:04 am	4th	Scorpio
Jan 19, 3:26 am–Jan 22, 1:27 am	1st	Pisces
Jan 28, 1:57 pm–Jan 30, 1:53 pm	2nd	Cancer
Feb 5, 10:56 pm–Feb 8, 8:53 am	3rd	Scorpio
Feb 15, 9:42 pm–Feb 18, 7:05 am	1st	Pisces
Feb 24, 10:06 pm–Feb 26, 11:42 pm	2nd	Cancer
Mar 5, 8:23 am–Mar 7, 5:03 pm	3rd	Scorpio
Mar 7, 5:03 pm–Mar 10, 4:52 am	3rd	Sagittarius
Mar 15, 6:12 am–Mar 17, 2:57 pm	4th	Pisces
Mar 24, 4:53 am–Mar 26, 7:45 am	1st	Cancer
Apr 1, 6:57 pm–Apr 4, 2:55 am	3rd	Scorpio
Apr 4, 2:55 am–Apr 6, 2:01 pm	3rd	Sagittarius
Apr 11, 2:40 pm–Apr 13, 11:25 pm	4th	Pisces
Apr 20, 10:26 am–Apr 22, 1:09 pm	1st	Cancer
Apr 29, 3:11 am–May 1, 11:20 am	2nd	Scorpio
May 1, 11:20 am–May 3, 10:06 pm	3rd	Sagittarius
May 8, 11:11 pm–May 11, 8:40 am	4th	Pisces
May 17, 5:47 pm–May 19, 7:11 pm	1st	Cancer
May 26, 9:39 am–May 28, 6:29 pm	2nd	Scorpio
May 28, 6:29 pm–May 31, 5:27 am	2nd	Sagittarius
Jun 5, 6:53 am–Jun 7, 5:26 pm	3rd	Pisces
Jun 14, 3:20 am–Jun 16, 3:21 am	1st	Cancer
Jun 22, 3:11 pm–Jun 25, 12:29 am	2nd	Scorpio
Jun 25, 12:29 am–Jun 27, 11:52 am	2nd	Sagittarius
Jul 2, 1:31 pm–Jul 5, 12:50 am	3rd	Pisces
Jul 5, 12:50 am–Jul 7, 8:51 am	3rd	Aries
Jul 11, 1:59 pm–Jul 13, 1:31 pm	4th	Cancer
Jul 19, 9:13 pm–Jul 22, 6:12 am	2nd	Scorpio
Jul 22, 6:12 am–Jul 24, 5:49 pm	2nd	Sagittarius
Jul 29, 7:28 pm–Aug 1, 6:54 am	3rd	Pisces
Aug 1, 6:54 am–Aug 3, 3:51 pm	3rd	Aries
Aug 8, 12:01 am–Aug 10, 12:18 am	4th	Cancer
Aug 16, 4:54 am–Aug 18, 12:45 pm	1st	Scorpio
Aug 18, 12:45 pm–Aug 21, 12:00 am	2nd	Sagittarius
Aug 26, 1:32 am–Aug 28, 12:35 pm	2nd	Pisces
Aug 28, 12:35 pm–Aug 30, 9:30 pm	3rd	Aries
Sep 4, 8:03 am–Sep 6, 9:54 am	4th	Cancer
Sep 12, 2:15 pm–Sep 14, 8:45 pm	1st	Scorpio
Sep 22, 8:27 am–Sep 24, 7:04 pm	2nd	Pisces
Sep 24, 7:04 pm–Sep 27, 3:16 am	2nd	Aries
Oct 1, 2:00 pm–Oct 3, 5:12 pm	3rd	Cancer
Oct 10, 12:09 am–Oct 12, 5:53 pm	1st	Scorpio
Oct 19, 4:20 pm–Oct 22, 2:58 am	2nd	Pisces
Oct 22, 2:58 am–Oct 24, 10:33 am	2nd	Aries
Oct 28, 7:27 pm–Oct 30, 10:42 pm	3rd	Cancer
Nov 6, 8:02 am–Nov 8, 1:59 pm	4th	Scorpio
Nov 15, 11:41 pm–Nov 18, 10:56 am	2nd	Pisces
Nov 18, 10:56 am–Nov 20, 6:43 pm	2nd	Aries
Nov 25, 1:38 am–Nov 27, 3:35 am	3rd	Cancer
Dec 3, 2:55 pm–Dec 5, 9:49 pm	4th	Scorpio
Dec 13, 7:40 am–Dec 15, 7:44 pm	1st	Pisces
Dec 15, 7:44 pm–Dec 18, 4:37 am	2nd	Aries
Dec 22, 11:28 am–Dec 24, 11:59 am	2nd	Cancer

Dates to Destroy Weeds and Pests

Date	Sign	Qtr.
Jan 3 2:23 am–Jan 5 3:12 am	Leo	3rd
Jan 5 3:12 am–Jan 7 7:15 am	Virgo	3rd
Jan 12 2:04 am–Jan 14 2:42 pm	Sagittarius	4th
Jan 31 8:27 am–Feb 1 2:13 pm	Leo	3rd
Feb 1 2:13 pm–Feb 3 4:47 pm	Virgo	3rd
Feb 8 8:53 am–Feb 10 9:21 pm	Sagittarius	4th
Feb 13 10:11 am–Feb 15 4:05 pm	Aquarius	4th
Mar 1 7:51 pm–Mar 3 3:20 am	Virgo	3rd
Mar 7 5:03 pm–Mar 9 6:20 am	Sagittarius	3rd
Mar 9 6:20 am–Mar 10 4:52 am	Sagittarius	4th
Mar 12 6:44 pm–Mar 15 6:12 am	Aquarius	4th
Apr 4 2:55 am–Apr 6 2:01 pm	Sagittarius	3rd
Apr 9 2:50 am–Apr 11 2:40 pm	Aquarius	4th
Apr 13 11:25 pm–Apr 15 9:57 pm	Aries	4th
May 1 11:20 am–May 3 10:06 pm	Sagittarius	3rd
May 6 10:48 am–May 7 10:09 pm	Aquarius	3rd
May 7 10:09 pm–May 8 11:11 pm	Aquarius	4th
May 11 8:40 am–May 13 2:15 pm	Aries	4th
May 29 10:20 am–May 31 5:27 am	Sagittarius	3rd
Jun 2 6:06 pm–Jun 5 6:53 am	Aquarius	3rd
Jun 7 5:26 pm–Jun 10 12:04 am	Aries	4th
Jun 12 2:53 am–Jun 13 3:43 pm	Gemini	4th
Jun 30 12:37 am–Jul 2 1:31 pm	Aquarius	3rd
Jul 5 12:50 am–Jul 6 3:51 am	Aries	3rd
Jul 6 3:51 am–Jul 7 8:51 am	Aries	4th
Jul 9 12:58 pm–Jul 11 1:59 pm	Gemini	4th
Jul 27 4:20 pm–Jul 29 7:28 pm	Aquarius	3rd
Aug 1 6:54 am–Aug 3 3:51 pm	Aries	3rd
Aug 5 9:32 pm–Aug 8 12:01 am	Gemini	4th
Aug 10 12:18 am–Aug 11 5:58 am	Leo	4th
Aug 28 12:35 pm–Aug 30 9:30 pm	Aries	3rd
Sep 2 4:02 am–Sep 2 10:37 pm	Gemini	3rd
Sep 2 10:37 pm–Sep 4 8:03 am	Gemini	4th
Sep 6 9:54 am–Sep 8 10:29 am	Leo	4th
Sep 8 10:29 am–Sep 9 2:01 pm	Virgo	4th
Sep 24 10:52 pm–Sep 27 3:16 am	Aries	3rd
Sep 29 9:26 am–Oct 1 2:00 pm	Gemini	3rd
Oct 3 5:12 pm–Oct 5 7:19 pm	Leo	4th
Oct 5 7:19 pm–Oct 7 9:10 pm	Virgo	4th
Oct 26 3:41 pm–Oct 28 7:27 pm	Gemini	3rd
Oct 30 10:42 pm–Oct 31 12:40 pm	Leo	3rd
Oct 31 12:40 pm–Nov 2 1:48 am	Leo	4th
Nov 2 1:48 am–Nov 4 4:01 am	Virgo	4th
Nov 23 12:39 am–Nov 25 1:38 am	Gemini	3rd
Nov 27 3:35 am–Nov 29 6:08 am	Leo	3rd
Nov 29 6:08 am–Nov 29 7:19 pm	Virgo	3rd
Nov 29 7:19 pm–Dec 1 9:49 am	Virgo	4th
Dec 5 9:49 pm–Dec 7 2:20 am	Sagittarius	4th
Dec 24 11:59 am–Dec 26 12:50 pm	Leo	3rd
Dec 26 12:50 pm–Dec 28 3:23 pm	Virgo	3rd

Time Zone Map

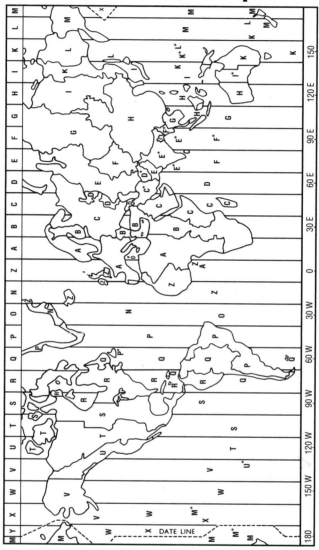

Time Zone Conversions

(R) EST—Used in book
(S) CST—Subtract 1 hour
(T) MST—Subtract 2 hours
(U) PST—Subtract 3 hours
(V) Subtract 4 hours
(V*) Subtract 4½ hours
(U*) Subtract 3½ hours
(W) Subtract 5 hours
(X) Subtract 6 hours
(Y) Subtract 7 hours
(Q) Add 1 hour
(P) Add 2 hours
(P*) Add 2½ hours
(O) Add 3 hours
(N) Add 4 hours
(Z) Add 5 hours
(A) Add 6 hours
(B) Add 7 hours
(C) Add 8 hours
(C*) Add 8½ hours

(D) Add 9 hours
(D*) Add 9½ hours
(E) Add 10 hours
(E*) Add 10½ hours
(F) Add 11 hours
(F*) Add 11½ hours
(G) Add 12 hours
(H) Add 13 hours
(I) Add 14 hours
(I*) Add 14½ hours
(K) Add 15 hours
(K*) Add 15½ hours
(L) Add 16 hours
(L*) Add 16½ hours
(M) Add 17 hours
(M*) Add 18 hours
(P*) Add 2½ hours

Important!

All times given in the *Moon Sign Book* are set in Eastern Time. The conversions shown here are for standard times only. Use the time zone conversions map and table to calculate the difference in your time zone. You must make the adjustment for your time zone and adjust for Daylight Saving Time where applicable.

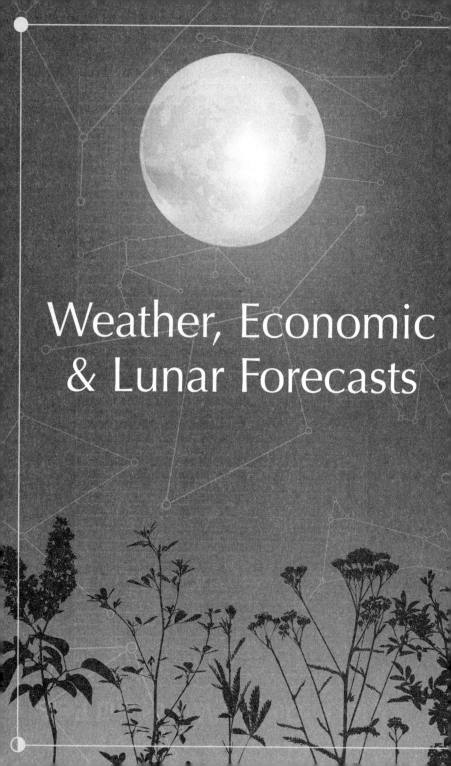

Weather, Economic & Lunar Forecasts

2017 © kropic Image from BigStockPhoto.com

Forecasting the Weather

by Kris Brandt Riske

Astrometeorology—astrological weather forecasting—reveals seasonal and weekly weather trends based on the cardinal ingresses (Summer and Winter Solstices, and Spring and Autumn Equinoxes) and the four monthly lunar phases. The planetary alignments and the longitudes and latitudes they influence have the strongest effect, but the zodiacal signs are also involved in creating weather conditions.

The components of a thunderstorm, for example, are heat, wind, and electricity. A Mars-Jupiter configuration generates the necessary heat and Mercury adds wind and electricity. A severe thunderstorm, and those that produce tornados, usually involve Mercury, Mars, Uranus, or Neptune. The zodiacal signs add their energy to the planetary mix to increase or decrease the chance for weather phenomena and their severity.

In general, the fire signs (Aries, Leo, Sagittarius) indicate heat and dryness, both of which peak when Mars, the planet with a similar nature, is in these signs. Water signs (Cancer, Scorpio, Pisces) are conducive to precipitation, and air signs (Gemini, Libra, Aquarius) are conducive to cool temperatures and wind. Earth signs (Taurus, Virgo, Capricorn) vary from wet to dry, heat to cold. The signs and their prevailing weather conditions are listed here:

Aries: Heat, dry, wind
Taurus: Moderate temperatures, precipitation
Gemini: Cool temperatures, wind, dry
Cancer: Cold, steady precipitation
Leo: Heat, dry, lightning
Virgo: Cold, dry, windy
Libra: Cool, windy, fair
Scorpio: Extreme temperatures, abundant precipitation
Sagittarius: Warm, fair, moderate wind
Capricorn: Cold, wet, damp
Aquarius: Cold, dry, high pressure, lightning
Pisces: Wet, cool, low pressure

Take note of the Moon's sign at each lunar phase. It reveals the prevailing weather conditions for the next six to seven days. The same is true of Mercury and Venus. These two influential weather planets transit the entire zodiac each year, unless retrograde patterns add their influence.

Planetary Influences

People relied on astrology to forecast weather for thousands of years. They were able to predict drought, floods, and temperature variations through interpreting planetary alignments. In recent years there has been a renewed interest in astrometeorology.

A weather forecast can be composed for any date—tomorrow, next week, or a thousand years in the future. According to astrometeorology, each planet governs certain weather phenomena. When certain planets are aligned with other planets, weather—precipitation, cloudy or clear skies, tornados, hurricanes, and other conditions—are generated.

Sun and Moon

The Sun governs the constitution of the weather and, like the Moon, it serves as a trigger for other planetary configurations that result in weather events. When the Sun is prominent in a cardinal ingress or lunar phase chart, the area is often warm and sunny. The Moon can bring or withhold moisture, depending upon its sign placement.

Mercury

Mercury is also a triggering planet, but its main influence is wind direction and velocity. In its stationary periods, Mercury reflects high winds, and its influence is always prominent in major weather events, such as hurricanes and tornadoes, when it tends to lower the temperature.

Venus

Venus governs moisture, clouds, and humidity. It brings warming trends that produce sunny, pleasant weather if in positive aspect to other planets. In some signs—Libra, Virgo, Gemini, Sagittarius—Venus is drier. It is at its wettest when placed in Cancer, Scorpio, Pisces, or Taurus.

Mars

Mars is associated with heat, drought, and wind, and can raise the temperature to record-setting levels when in a fire sign (Aries, Leo, Sagittarius). Mars is also the planet that provides the spark that generates thunderstorms and is prominent in tornado and hurricane configurations.

Jupiter

Jupiter, a fair-weather planet, tends toward higher temperatures when in Aries, Leo, or Sagittarius. It is associated with high-pressure systems and is a contributing factor at times to dryness. Storms are often amplified by Jupiter.

Saturn

Saturn is associated with low-pressure systems, cloudy to overcast skies, and excessive precipitation. Temperatures drop when Saturn is involved. Major winter storms always have a strong Saturn influence, as do storms that produce a slow, steady downpour for hours or days.

Uranus

Like Jupiter, Uranus indicates high-pressure systems. It reflects descending cold air and, when prominent, is responsible for a jet stream that extends far south. Uranus can bring drought in winter, and it is involved in thunderstorms, tornados, and hurricanes.

Neptune

Neptune is the wettest planet. It signals low-pressure systems and is dominant when hurricanes are in the forecast. When Neptune is strongly placed, flood danger is high. It's often associated with winter thaws. Temperatures, humidity, and cloudiness increase where Neptune influences weather.

Pluto

Pluto is associated with weather extremes, as well as unseasonably warm temperatures and drought. It reflects the high winds involved in major hurricanes, storms, and tornados.

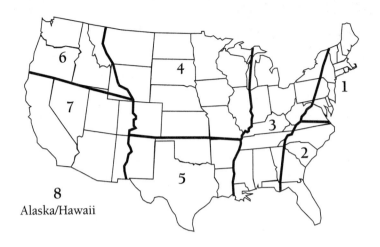

6

4

1

7

3

2

5

8
Alaska/Hawaii

Weather Forecast for 2018

by Kris Brandt Riske

Winter

Zones 1 and 2 will see generally warmer temperatures and periodic significant precipitation that could result in flooding. Strong thunderstorms with tornado potential are possible in central and southern areas of zone 2, and northern areas of zone 1 will see abundant downfall from storms. Western areas of zone 3 are also prone to significant precipitation that could result in flooding, along with strong thunderstorms in southern areas. Conditions will be overall windy in zone 3 with periods of very cold temperatures. Temperatures and conditions in zones 4 and 5 will be generally seasonal with precipitation that ranges from average to below. The exception is eastern areas of these zones, which will see some notable storms and precipitation. Zones 6 and 7 will experience temperatures that range from seasonal to above along with lower levels of moisture. Northern California and the western Rockies have a better chance for average precipitation.

In zone 8, central Alaska see an above-average number of cloudy days with precipitation, which at times will be abundant. Precipitation in other parts of the state will be average to above, and temperatures across Alaska will range from seasonal to below. Hawaii can expect temperatures that range from seasonal to below and average precipitation, with higher levels in western parts of the state.

Full Moon, January 1–7

Zone 1: The zone is windy and partly cloudy to cloudy with temperatures seasonal to below and precipitation, some locally heavy.

Zone 2: Much of the zone sees scattered precipitation under partly cloudy to cloudy skies, windy conditions, and temperatures seasonal to below.

Zone 3: Temperatures are seasonal, skies are variably cloudy, and central and eastern areas see precipitation.

Zone 4: The zone is windy, partly cloudy to cloudy, and windy with precipitation, and eastern areas could see stormy conditions with abundant precipitation.

Zone 5: Skies are windy and partly cloudy to cloudy, temperatures are seasonal, and eastern areas could see abundant precipitation and strong thunderstorms.

Zone 6: Western and central areas see precipitation, and the zone is variably cloudy and windy with temperatures seasonal to below.

Zone 7: The zone is windy and seasonal under skies that are fair to partly cloudy.

Zone 8: Alaska is variably cloudy, western areas and central areas see precipitation, some abundant, central and eastern areas are windy, and temperatures are seasonal. Hawaii is windy, seasonal, and partly cloudy with locally heavy precipitation possible in central areas.

4th Quarter Moon, January 8–15

Zone 1: Partly cloudy to cloudy skies accompany temperatures seasonal to below, southern areas have a chance for precipitation, and some northern areas see abundant downfall.

Zone 2: Northern areas are fair to partly cloudy, central and southern areas are cloudy with potential for abundant precipitation and stormy conditions, and temperatures are seasonal to below.

Zone 3: Much of the zone is windy, western skies are fair to partly cloudy, temperatures are seasonal to below, and central and eastern areas are partly cloudy to cloudy with locally heavy precipitation east, possibly from stormy conditions.

Zone 4: The zone is windy, western and central areas see precipitation, skies are partly cloudy to cloudy, and temperatures are seasonal to below.

Zone 5: Seasonal temperatures accompany variably cloudy skies, western and central parts of the zone have a chance for precipitation, and strong thunderstorms are possible in eastern areas, which are windy.

Zone 6: Much of the zone is windy, temperatures range from seasonal to above, western and central areas have a chance for precipitation, eastern areas see precipitation, and skies are fair to partly cloudy.

Zone 7: Northern coastal areas are windy with precipitation that moves into central parts of the zone, eastern areas see scattered precipitation, temperatures are seasonal, and skies are variably cloudy.

Zone 8: Central and eastern Alaska see precipitation, western areas are windy, and temperatures are seasonal. Temperatures in Hawaii range from seasonal to above, skies are variably cloudy, and much of the state sees precipitation.

New Moon, January 16–23

Zone 1: The zone is fair to partly cloudy and seasonal with scattered precipitation south.

Zone 2: Much of the zone sees precipitation under partly cloudy to cloudy skies, temperatures are seasonal to above, and locally heavy downfall is possible central and south.

Zone 3: Temperatures are seasonal to above, and skies are partly cloudy with more cloudiness east along with precipitation, some abundant.

Zone 4: Western skies are cloudy with precipitation, central and eastern areas are partly cloudy with a chance for precipitation, and temperatures are seasonal to above.

Zone 5: Skies are variably cloudy with a chance for precipitation, temperatures are seasonal to above, and central and eastern areas are windy.

Zone 6: Precipitation in western areas moves into central parts of the zone under cloudy skies, temperatures are seasonal to above, and eastern areas are fair to partly cloudy.

Zone 7: Western and central skies are partly cloudy to cloudy, eastern areas are fair to partly cloudy, and temperatures are seasonal.

Zone 8: Western areas see abundant precipitation, skies are variably cloudy and temperatures seasonal, and central and eastern areas are windy. Hawaii is fair to partly cloudy and seasonal with a chance for showers central and east.

2nd Quarter Moon, January 24–30

Zone 1: Temperatures range from seasonal to below, with cloudy skies and precipitation developing later in the week.

Zone 2: Northern areas see precipitation later in the week, temperatures are seasonal to below, central and southern areas see precipitation, and the zone is windy.

Zone 3: The zone is windy with temperatures seasonal to below, skies are partly cloudy to cloudy, and a front brings precipitation across much of the zone with heaviest downfall east.

Zone 4: Western areas are fair to partly cloudy, central and eastern areas see precipitation, and temperatures range from seasonal to below.

Zone 5: The zone is fair to partly cloudy and windy with more cloudiness and precipitation east; temperatures are seasonal to below.

Zone 6: Seasonal temperatures accompany partly cloudy to cloudy skies and precipitation across much of the zone, possibly abundant in eastern areas.

Zone 7: The zone is variably cloudy with precipitation in western and central areas, some abundant in the mountains, and temperatures are seasonal.

Zone 8: Temperatures in Alaska range from seasonal to below, central and eastern areas see precipitation, and western areas are windy. Hawaii is fair to partly cloudy and seasonal with scattered precipitation.

Full Moon, January 31–February 6

Zone 1: The zone is variably cloudy and seasonal with scattered precipitation.

Zone 2: Partly cloudy to cloudy skies, and seasonal temperatures become much cooler central and south later in the week, along with windy conditions and scattered precipitation.

Zone 3: Western and central areas are windy, temperatures range from seasonal to below, skies are fair to partly cloudy, and the zone sees scattered precipitation, which could be locally heavy in central and eastern areas.

Zone 4: Precipitation in western areas moves into central parts of the zone, which is windy and seasonal under variably cloudy skies; eastern areas see precipitation early in the week.

Zone 5: Much of the zone sees precipitation, skies are partly cloudy to cloudy, eastern areas are windy, and temperatures are seasonal.

Zone 6: Conditions are windy, temperatures seasonal, and skies fair to partly cloudy; western areas see more cloudiness with scattered precipitation.

Zone 7: The zone is fair to partly cloudy and seasonal with precipitation in northern coastal areas that moves into central parts of the zone.

Zone 8: Alaska is seasonal to below and windy under variably cloudy skies; central and eastern areas see precipitation, which is scattered in western parts of the state. Hawaii is seasonal and fair to partly cloudy.

4th Quarter Moon, February 7–14

Zone 1: Southern areas have a chance for precipitation, skies are mostly fair to partly cloudy, and temperatures are seasonal.

Zone 2: Temperatures are seasonal to blow and skies partly cloudy to cloudy, with strong thunderstorms with tornado potential possible in southern areas and sleet in central parts of the zone.

Zone 3: The zone is windy as a front brings precipitation and possibly stormy conditions to western and central areas, skies are variably cloudy and temperatures seasonal to below, and southern areas could see strong thunderstorms with tornado potential.

Zone 4: Partly cloudy to cloudy skies accompany seasonal temperatures and a chance for precipitation in central areas.

Zone 5: Central and eastern areas are windy with precipitation, temperatures are seasonal, and skies are partly cloudy to cloudy.

Zone 6: Skies are partly cloudy to cloudy, temperatures range from seasonal to below, and western and central areas see precipitation.

Zone 7: Temperatures are seasonal to above, skies are fair to partly cloudy, and the zone has a chance for precipitation.

Zone 8: Central and eastern Alaska are windy with precipitation, skies are variably cloudy, and temperatures range from seasonal to below. Hawaii is fair to partly cloudy and seasonal with scattered showers.

New Moon, February 15–22

Zone 1: The zone is windy and partly cloudy to cloudy with temperatures seasonal to below, precipitation south, and a chance for precipitation north.

Zone 2: Much of the zone sees precipitation, some locally heavy, skies are variably cloudy and temperatures seasonal, and central and southern areas could see strong thunderstorms with tornado potential.

Zone 3: Windy conditions accompany temperatures seasonal to below, western and central areas have a chance for precipitation, and eastern areas are stormy with potential for strong thunderstorms and tornados.

Zone 4: Western skies are fair to partly cloudy, central and eastern areas are partly cloudy to cloudy, eastern areas are windy with precipitation later in the week, and temperatures are seasonal to below.

Zone 5: Temperatures are seasonal to below under variably cloudy skies with precipitation east later in the week.

Zone 6: Western areas see precipitation that moves into central parts of the zone, bringing locally heavy downfall under partly cloudy to cloudy skies and seasonal temperatures; eastern parts of the zone are mostly fair and windy.

Zone 7: Temperatures are seasonal, eastern skies are fair to partly cloudy, and western and central parts of the zone are partly cloudy to cloudy with precipitation, some abundant.

Zone 8: Alaska is fair to partly cloudy and seasonal. Hawaii is seasonal and fair to partly cloudy with precipitation in western areas later in the week.

2nd Quarter Moon, February 23–28

Zone 1: Abundant precipitation and stormy conditions are possible across the zone, along with temperatures ranging from seasonal to below.

Zone 2: Northern areas see precipitation, central and southern areas have a chance for precipitation, skies are partly cloudy to cloudy, and the zone is seasonal but colder north.

Zone 3: Temperatures range from seasonal to below, conditions are windy in eastern areas, and central and eastern parts of the zone see precipitation.

Zone 4: The zone is windy with temperatures seasonal to below, and abundant precipitation is possible in northwest parts of the zone that moves into central and eastern areas.

Zone 5: Strong thunderstorms with tornado potential and abundant precipitation are possible across much of the zone, which is windy and seasonal under partly cloudy to cloudy skies.

Zone 6: Partly cloudy to cloudy skies accompany temperatures seasonal to above and windy conditions; central and eastern areas see precipitation, which could be abundant east and trigger flooding.

Zone 7: Much of the zone sees precipitation, which could be locally heavy precipitation in eastern areas, and the zone is windy and partly cloudy to cloudy with temperatures seasonal to above.

Zone 8: Alaska is variably cloudy with precipitation and temperatures seasonal to below. Temperatures in Hawaii are seasonal to above, skies are partly cloudy to cloudy, and abundant precipitation in central areas moves into eastern parts of the state.

Full Moon, March 1–8

Zone 1: Southern areas see more cloudiness than northern areas, which are partly cloudy, and the zone is seasonal with scattered precipitation.

Zone 2: Northern areas are cloudy with precipitation, central and southern areas are mostly fair with increasing cloudiness and precipitation later in the week, and temperatures are seasonal.

Zone 3: Strong thunderstorms with tornado potential and abundant precipitation are possible across the zone under variably cloudy skies and seasonal temperatures.

Zone 4: Western areas are fair to partly cloudy, central areas see abundant precipitation with flood potential, thunderstorms with tornado potential are possible in eastern areas, and temperatures are seasonal to above.

Zone 5: Strong thunderstorms with tornado potential are possible across the zone with abundant precipitation that could trigger flooding in western and central areas, and temperatures range from seasonal to above.

Zone 6: The zone is fair to partly cloudy and seasonal with a chance for scattered precipitation.

Zone 7: Much of the zone is windy and seasonal under partly cloudy to cloudy skies with a chance for precipitation.

Zone 8: Alaska is partly cloudy to cloudy and seasonal with a chance for precipitation. Hawaii is fair to partly cloudy with temperatures seasonal to above.

4th Quarter Moon, March 9–16

Zone 1: Much of the zone is windy with precipitation under partly cloudy to cloudy skies with temperatures seasonal to below.

Zone 2: Northern areas are partly cloudy to cloudy with more cloudiness central and south along with scattered precipitation; temperatures are seasonal to above.

Zone 3: Temperatures range from seasonal to below, skies are partly cloudy to cloudy, and western and central areas see precipitation later in the week.

Zone 4: Western areas are cloudy with precipitation, central and eastern areas are partly cloudy with a chance for precipitation east later in the week, and temperatures are seasonal to below.

Zone 5: Western areas see scattered precipitation later in the week, central and eastern areas have a chance for precipitation, temperatures are seasonal, and skies are variably cloudy.

Zone 6: The zone is windy and seasonal with partly cloudy to cloudy skies and precipitation in eastern areas later in the week.

Zone 7: Temperatures are seasonal to above, skies are windy and partly cloudy, and eastern areas see scattered precipitation.

Zone 8: Central and eastern Alaska see precipitation, some locally heavy, skies are partly cloudy to cloudy and windy, and temperatures are seasonal. Hawaii is variably cloudy and seasonal to above with showers and windy conditions east.

New Moon, March 17–23

Zone 1: Temperatures seasonal to above accompany windy conditions and partly cloudy skies.

Zone 2: The zone is fair to partly cloudy and windy, and temperatures range from seasonal to above.

Zone 3: Precipitation, including thunderstorms, in western areas moves into central and eastern parts of the zone under variably cloudy and windy skies and seasonal temperatures.

Zone 4: Seasonal temperatures and windy conditions accompany partly cloudy to cloudy skies and precipitation in eastern areas.

Zone 5: Western areas are windy, skies are partly cloudy to cloudy, and temperatures are seasonal.

Zone 6: The zone is seasonal and partly cloudy to cloudy.

Zone 7: Seasonal temperatures accompany partly cloudy to cloudy skies and a chance for precipitation in eastern areas.

Zone 8: Eastern Alaska sees precipitation, central areas are windy, skies are variably cloudy, and temperatures range from seasonal to above. Hawaii is seasonal and fair to partly cloudy.

Spring

Above-average temperatures will be the norm in zone 1, along with moisture ranging from average to below. Zone 2 will see the same conditions overall except for inland areas of the mid-Atlantic states, where periods of high precipitation could trigger flooding. Northeastern parts of zone 3 will see the same periodic abundant precipitation with increased flooding potential. Temperatures in zone 3 will range from seasonal to above and precipitation from seasonal to below west and central. Precipitation in zones 4 and 5 will range from average to below with temperatures average to above. Some storms with significant precipitation will enter zone 4 near Montana and the Dakotas and travel southeast across zones 4 and 5. Overall, there will be fewer periods with strong thunderstorms with tornado potential. Western areas of both zones will be generally windy. Zones 6 and 7 will also experience temperatures ranging from average to above, along with dryness. Moisture will be below average. In zone 8, moisture in western Alaska will be average, while other parts of the state will experience below average totals. Temperatures will be above average in western and central parts of the state and average in eastern locations. Eastern and central Hawaii will experience above average temperatures, which will be average in western parts of the state. Precipitation will be below average across the state.

2nd Quarter Moon, March 24–30

Zone 1: The zone is cloudy with temperatures seasonal to below and precipitation, some locally heavy, in northern areas later in the week.

Zone 2: Northern areas see precipitation, southern areas are humid with scattered precipitation, skies are variably cloudy and temperatures seasonal to above.

Zone 3: Much of the zone sees precipitation under skies that are windy and partly cloudy to cloudy and temperatures seasonal to below; stormy conditions are possible, along with locally heavy downfall and flooding in western areas.

Zone 4: The zone is fair to partly cloudy and seasonal with a chance for precipitation in eastern areas later in the week.

Zone 5: Central and eastern areas have a chance for precipitation, skies are partly cloudy, and temperatures are seasonal.

Zone 6: The zone is cloudy, windy, and stormy with precipitation and temperatures seasonal to below.

Zone 7: Skies are variably cloudy, western and central areas see precipitation, and temperatures are seasonal but colder west.

Zone 8: Alaska is fair to partly cloudy and seasonal with precipitation in western areas. Hawaii is humid and partly cloudy with temperatures seasonal to above.

Full Moon, March 31–April 7

Zone 1: Temperatures seasonal to below accompany partly cloudy to cloudy skies and precipitation across much of the zone and locally heavy south.

Zone 2: Central and southern areas are fair to partly cloudy, temperatures are seasonal to below, and northern areas are partly cloudy to cloudy with precipitation.

Zone 3: Skies are variably cloudy and temperatures seasonal to below; western areas see scattered precipitation and downfall is locally heavy in some eastern areas.

Zone 4: Western and central areas see stormy conditions with abundant downfall in some locations, eastern areas are partly cloudy with scattered precipitation, and temperatures are seasonal to below.

Zone 5: The zone is windy and partly cloudy to cloudy with precipitation, some abundant, central and east, and temperatures seasonal to below.

Zone 6: Precipitation across the zone could be abundant in western and central areas under cloudy skies and seasonal temperatures; eastern areas are partly cloudy to cloudy.

Zone 7: Northern coastal and central areas see precipitation under partly cloudy to cloudy skies, southern coastal areas are partly cloudy with a chance for precipitation, eastern areas are fair to partly cloudy, and temperatures are seasonal to above.

Zone 8: Western Alaska sees precipitation, western and central areas are partly cloudy to cloudy, eastern areas are mostly fair, and temperatures are seasonal. Hawaii is fair to partly cloudy and seasonal.

4th Quarter Moon, April 8–14

Zone 1: Windy conditions, seasonal temperatures, and partly cloudy skies accompany a chance for precipitation in southern areas.

2017 © pikappa Image from BigStockPhoto.com

Zone 2: Much of the zone sees precipitation later in the week, temperatures are seasonal, and skies are partly cloudy to cloudy.

Zone 3: Temperatures are seasonal to below, conditions are windy, skies are partly cloudy to cloudy, and much of the zone sees precipitation.

Zone 4: Variably cloudy skies and windy conditions accompany temperatures seasonal to below with precipitation in eastern areas.

Zone 5: The zone is windy and fair to partly cloudy with temperatures seasonal to below.

Zone 6: Western skies are partly cloudy and windy with precipitation, central and eastern areas see more cloudiness, and temperatures are seasonal.

Zone 7: Western and central parts of the zone are windy with partly cloudy to cloudy skies and precipitation, eastern areas are fair to partly cloudy with a chance for precipitation, and temperatures are seasonal but warmer east.

Zone 8: Temperatures in Alaska are seasonal, skies are partly cloudy to cloudy, and western areas see precipitation. Hawaii is fair to partly cloudy with temperatures seasonal to above.

New Moon, April 15–21

Zone 1: The zone is fair to partly cloudy with temperatures seasonal to below and a chance for precipitation later in the week.

Zone 2: Central and southern areas could see thunderstorms, northern areas see scattered precipitation, and the zone is windy and seasonal.

Zone 3: Precipitation in western areas moves into central parts of the zone under mostly cloudy skies and the zone is windy and seasonal; eastern areas are fair to partly cloudy with a chance for precipitation.

Zone 4: Western and central skies are fair, conditions are windy, temperatures are seasonal to below, and eastern areas see precipitation, some locally heavy.

Zone 5: Skies are partly cloudy west and central, eastern areas see more cloudiness with precipitation, and temperatures are seasonal.

Zone 6: The zone is windy, fair to partly cloudy, and seasonal to below, with a chance for precipitation west.

Zone 7: Temperatures are seasonal to above, skies are windy and fair to partly cloudy, and northern coastal areas have a chance for precipitation.

Zone 8: Central Alaska sees precipitation, temperatures are seasonal to above, and skies are fair to partly cloudy. Hawaii is variably cloudy skies accompany temperatures seasonal to above and showers across much of the state with locally heavy downfall west.

2nd Quarter Moon, April 22–28

Zone 1: The zone is windy and seasonal under partly cloudy to cloudy skies with precipitation.

Zone 2: Northern areas are cloudy with precipitation, some locally heavy; central and southern areas are partly cloudy to cloudy with precipitation; and temperatures are seasonal.

Zone 3: Eastern areas are cloudy with abundant precipitation, central areas are partly cloudy with a chance for precipitation, western skies are fair to partly cloudy, and temperatures are seasonal.

Zone 4: Western areas could see abundant precipitation and flooding, central and eastern areas are mostly fair to partly cloudy with a chance for precipitation, and temperatures are seasonal to above.

Zone 5: Temperatures are seasonal to above, eastern areas are mostly fair, and western and central parts of the zone could see significant precipitation and flooding.

Zone 6: Precipitation in western areas moves into central and eastern areas, conditions are windy, skies are partly cloudy to cloudy, and temperatures are seasonal.

Zone 7: Western and central areas see precipitation under variably cloudy, and windy skies and temperatures are seasonal to above.

Zone 8: Western and central Alaska see precipitation under partly cloudy to cloudy and windy skies, eastern areas are mostly fair, and temperatures are seasonal. Temperatures in Hawaii are seasonal to above and skies are mostly fair; western areas see scattered precipitation.

Full Moon, April 29–May 6

Zone 1: Skies are windy and partly cloudy to cloudy, temperatures are seasonal to below, and much of the zone sees precipitation.

Zone 2: Central and southern areas are fair to partly cloudy, northern areas are cloudy with precipitation, and temperatures are seasonal.

Zone 3: Skies are variably cloudy and windy with a chance for precipitation, and temperatures are seasonal.

Zone 4: Western areas see precipitation later in the week, central areas are fair to partly cloudy, eastern areas see more cloudiness and precipitation, and the zone is windy and seasonal.

Zone 5: The zone is partly cloudy and seasonal with a chance for precipitation west.

Zone 6: Temperatures seasonal to below accompany partly

cloudy to cloudy skies and precipitation, some locally heavy in central and eastern areas, which are windy.

Zone 7: Much of the zone sees precipitation as the week progresses, temperatures are seasonal to above, western areas are very windy, and skies are variably cloudy.

Zone 8: Temperatures in Alaska are seasonal, eastern areas are fair, and western and central parts of the state see precipitation, some abundant. Skies in Hawaii are partly cloudy to cloudy, temperatures are seasonal, and western and central areas see showers.

4th Quarter Moon, May 7–14

Zone 1: Much of the zone sees precipitation, some locally heavy under partly cloudy to cloudy skies; strong thunderstorms are possible.

Zone 2: Strong thunderstorms with tornado potential are possible along with scattered showers under partly cloudy to cloudy skies and temperatures ranging from seasonal to above.

Zone 3: Abundant precipitation could trigger flooding in western and central areas, along with strong thunderstorms with tornado potential, skies are variably cloudy, and temperatures are seasonal.

Zone 4: The zone is windy, seasonal, and partly cloudy to cloudy, and central and eastern areas could see strong thunderstorms with tornado potential and locally heavy precipitation and flooding.

Zone 5: Skies are windy and fair to partly cloudy, temperatures are seasonal, and central and eastern areas could see strong thunderstorms with tornado potential.

Zone 6: Western and central areas are partly cloudy, eastern areas are cloudy with precipitation, some locally heavy, and temperatures are seasonal.

Zone 7: Eastern parts of the zone are windy partly cloudy to cloudy with precipitation, western and central areas have a chance for precipitation under partly cloudy skies, and temperatures are seasonal to above.

Zone 8: Western and central Alaska are cloudy with precipitation, eastern areas are mostly fair, and temperatures are seasonal. Hawaii is variably cloudy and seasonal.

New Moon, May 15–20

Zone 1: Temperatures are seasonal to below, skies are variably cloudy, and much of the zone sees precipitation.

Zone 2: Northern areas see precipitation, strong thunderstorms with tornado potential are possible central and south along with locally heavy precipitation and flooding, and temperatures are seasonal under variably cloudy skies.

Zone 3: Central parts of the zone have a chance for thunderstorms with tornado potential, skies are fair to partly cloudy, and temperatures are seasonal.

Zone 4: Thunderstorms with tornado potential are possible in western areas, central parts of the zone see scattered precipitation, eastern areas are fair, and temperatures are seasonal.

Zone 5: The zone is windy and variably cloudy with temperatures ranging from seasonal to below and showers and thunderstorms with tornado potential.

Zone 6: Skies are fair to partly cloudy central and east with a chance for precipitation, eastern areas are windy, and temperatures are seasonal to below.

Zone 7: The zone is fair to partly cloudy with temperatures seasonal to above.

Zone 8: Alaska is variably cloudy and windy with precipitation east and central, and temperatures are seasonal. Much of Hawaii sees scattered precipitation under partly cloudy to cloudy and windy skies and temperatures ranging from seasonal to above.

2nd Quarter Moon, May 21–28

Zone 1: The zone sees scattered showers and thunderstorms under windy and variably cloudy skies with seasonal temperatures.

Zone 2: Much of the zone is windy and partly cloudy to cloudy, with precipitation, including strong thunderstorms with tornado potential, central and south, and seasonal temperatures.

Zone 3: The zone is windy and partly cloudy to cloudy with thunderstorms with tornado potential and locally heavy downfall possible west and central; temperatures are seasonal to below.

Zone 4: Temperatures are seasonal to above, skies are windy and fair to partly cloudy, and eastern areas sees showers and thunderstorms with locally heavy downfall.

Zone 5: The zone is partly cloudy and seasonal to above with a chance for showers and thunderstorms east.

Zone 6: Skies are fair to partly cloudy, and temperatures are seasonal; eastern areas see more cloudiness and locally heavy precipitation that could trigger flooding.

Zone 7: Western and central areas are partly cloudy and windy with a chance for precipitation, eastern areas are cloudy with showers and potential for locally heavy downfall, and temperatures are seasonal.

Zone 8: Central and eastern parts of Alaska see precipitation under partly cloudy to cloudy skies, western areas are mostly fair, and temperatures are seasonal to below. Hawaii is fair to partly cloudy with temperatures seasonal to above and scattered showers.

Full Moon, May 29–June 5

Zone 1: Skies are partly cloudy, temperatures are seasonal to above, and northern areas are windy with thunderstorms.

Zone 2: Humidity and fair to partly cloudy skies accompany temperatures seasonal to above and scattered showers and thunderstorms.

Zone 3: Temperatures and humidity are seasonal to above and precipitation moves across western and central areas, bringing locally heavy downfall in central areas with flood potential.

Zone 4: Central and eastern areas see precipitation under partly cloudy to cloudy skies and windy conditions, temperatures are seasonal to above, and western areas are fair.

Zone 5: Scattered showers and thunderstorms accompany fair to partly cloudy skies, with more cloudiness east, and temperatures seasonal to above.

Zone 6: Much of the zone sees scattered showers and thunderstorms under partly cloudy to cloudy skies with temperatures seasonal to above.

Zone 7: Central and eastern areas are humid with scattered showers, skies are fair to partly cloudy, and temperatures are seasonal to above.

Zone 8: Alaska is seasonal with scattered precipitation west and central and fair to partly cloudy skies. Hawaii is humid and windy with temperatures seasonal to above and scattered showers and thunderstorms.

4th Quarter Moon, June 6–12

Zone 1: The zone is seasonal and mostly fair north with more cloudiness south with scattered showers and thunderstorms.

Zone 2: Central and southern parts of the zone are fair to partly cloudy, northern areas see more cloudiness and scattered thunderstorms, and temperatures are seasonal to above.

Zone 3: Temperatures are seasonal to above, western and central areas see showers and scattered thunderstorms under skies that are fair to partly cloudy, and eastern areas see more cloudiness and precipitation.

Zone 4: Temperatures are seasonal to above, conditions are humid, eastern areas see scattered showers and thunderstorms, skies are variably cloudy, and central areas see some locally heavy downfall with flood potential.

Zone 5: Humidity and temperatures seasonal to above accompany precipitation, some abundant, from strong thunderstorms with tornado potential central and east with flood potential, and western areas are partly cloudy to cloudy.

Zone 6: Eastern areas have a chance for precipitation, skies are partly cloudy, and temperatures are seasonal.

Zone 7: Skies are fair to partly cloudy and temperatures seasonal to above.

2017 © otsphoto image from BigStockPhoto.com

Zone 8: Central and eastern areas of Alaska see precipitation under partly cloudy to cloudy skies, western skies are mostly fair, and temperatures are seasonal. Much of Hawaii sees showers and thunderstorms under variably cloudy skies with temperatures seasonal to above.

New Moon, June 13–19

Zone 1: The zone is humid and partly cloudy to cloudy with showers and thunderstorms; temperatures are seasonal to above and then much cooler.

Zone 2: Central and southern parts of the zone are mostly fair, northern areas are partly cloudy to cloudy with showers and thunderstorms, and temperatures are seasonal to above.

Zone 3: Temperatures range from seasonal to above, skies are fair west and central, and eastern areas see more cloudiness with precipitation.

Zone 4: Stormy conditions west and central result in abundant precipitation in some areas under cloudy skies, eastern areas are partly cloudy and humid, and temperatures are seasonal but warmer east.

Zone 5: Western and central areas see precipitation under partly cloudy to cloudy skies, eastern parts of the zone see thunderstorms, and temperatures are seasonal to above.

Zone 6: Skies are variably cloudy, temperatures are seasonal to above, and much of the zone sees scattered thunderstorms and showers, some with abundant downfall and flood potential.

Zone 7: Temperatures seasonal to above accompany partly cloudy to cloudy skies and scattered precipitation, heaviest west.

Zone 8: Alaska is fair to partly cloudy, temperatures are seasonal to above, and western areas see precipitation. Hawaii is fair to partly cloudy and humid with temperatures seasonal to above.

Summer

Temperatures and precipitation will be average this summer in zone 1, but with an increased number of windy days. Northern and central parts of zone 2 can expect more cool, cloudy days along with above average precipitation, while southern areas will see some dryness and above average temperatures. Northeastern areas of zone 3 will also experience above average precipitation and cool, cloudy days, but much of the rest of the zone will be generally fair with temperatures above average and precipitation below. Zones 4 and 5 can expect seasonal temperatures and precipitation. However, western parts of these zones and states from the Dakotas southeast to Louisiana will see significant precipitation at times. These zones will also experience an increased number of windy days. Average precipitation and seasonal temperatures will be the norm in zone 6, but with above average temperatures in eastern areas. Drought will continue to be a major theme in zone 7, but there will be some relief in central and eastern parts of the zone. High pressure systems will elevate temperatures in zone 7, increasing the chance for fire weather. In zone 8, temperatures in Alaska will range from seasonal to above and precipitation will be generally average except for western parts of the state, which will see increased precipitation. Temperatures in Hawaii will be above average and precipitation average to below.

2nd Quarter Moon, June 20–27

Zone 1: The zone is windy and fair with temperatures seasonal to above; increasing cloudiness later in the week brings showers and scattered thunderstorms.

Zone 2: Much of the zone sees scattered showers and thunderstorms along with wind and humidity, variably cloudy skies, and temperatures seasonal to above.

Zone 3: Windy and partly cloudy to cloudy skies accompany humidity and scattered showers and thunderstorms.

Zone 4: Variably cloudy skies across the zone yield scattered showers and thunderstorms, conditions are humid, and temperatures are seasonal to above.

Zone 5: The zone is partly cloudy and humid with temperatures ranging from seasonal to above and scattered thunderstorms central and east.

Zone 6: Much of the zone is windy and cloudy with precipitation and thunderstorms and temperatures seasonal to above.

Zone 7: Western and central areas see precipitation, eastern areas have a chance for precipitation, skies are variably cloudy, and temperatures are seasonal to above.

Zone 8: Alaska is mostly cloudy with precipitation and temperatures seasonal to below. Hawaii is variably cloudy and seasonal with showers west.

Full Moon, June 28–July 5

Zone 1: The zone is cloudy and seasonal with abundant precipitation.

Zone 2: Northern and central coastal areas see abundant downfall, southern and central inland areas see scattered thunderstorms, temperatures are seasonal, and skies are partly cloudy to cloudy.

Zone 3: Eastern areas see abundant precipitation under cloudy skies, western and central parts of the zone are humid and partly cloudy with scattered thunderstorms, eastern areas are cooler and western and central areas are seasonal to above.

Zone 4: Strong thunderstorms with tornado potential across much of the zone accompany variably cloudy skies, temperatures seasonal to above, and humidity, with some eastern areas seeing locally heavy precipitation and flooding; western skies are fair to partly cloudy with scattered thunderstorms.

Zone 5: Much of the zone sees showers and thunderstorms with the heaviest downfall, and potential flooding, in eastern areas, skies are variably cloudy, and temperatures are seasonal to above with humidity; western parts of the zone are partly cloudy with scattered thunderstorms.

Zone 6: Western and central parts of the zone are cloudy with precipitation, eastern areas are partly cloudy, and temperatures are seasonal to above.

Zone 7: Eastern areas see scattered thunderstorms, western and central parts of the zone see precipitation, skies are variably cloudy, and temperatures are seasonal to above.

Zone 8: Alaska is fair to partly cloudy and seasonal with scattered precipitation west. Hawaii is partly cloudy and seasonal with a chance for precipitation.

4th Quarter Moon, July 6–11

Zone 1: Skies are partly cloudy to cloudy and much of the zone sees precipitation with humidity and seasonal temperatures.

Zone 2: Northern areas see precipitation under mostly partly cloudy skies, central and southern areas have a chance for scattered thunderstorms, and temperatures are seasonal.

Zone 3: Eastern areas are humid with showers, western and central parts of the zone see thunderstorms, and temperatures are seasonal to above.

Zone 4: The zone is fair to partly cloudy and seasonal with humidity and thunderstorms in eastern areas.

Zone 5: Temperatures range from seasonal to above, conditions are humid, skies are fair to partly cloudy, and the zone has a chance for scattered thunderstorms.

Zone 6: Skies are variably cloudy and temperatures seasonal to above and much of the zone sees showers and scattered thunderstorms.

Zone 7: Western and central areas see scattered showers, eastern areas are humid, skies are fair to partly cloudy, and temperatures range from seasonal to above.

Zone 8: Alaska is partly cloudy and windy with seasonal temperatures. Hawaii is partly cloudy, temperatures are seasonal, and the state sees scattered showers.

New Moon, July 12–18

Zone 1: Seasonal temperatures accompany partly cloudy skies and scattered showers.

Zone 2: Northern areas are windy, the zone is humid, temperatures range from seasonal to above, and much of the zone sees scattered showers.

Zone 3: Western and central areas see scattered showers and thunderstorms, eastern areas are humid with more precipitation and possible locally heavy downfall, and temperatures are seasonal to above.

Zone 4: Western areas are windy, skies are variably cloudy, eastern areas see showers and thunderstorms, and temperatures are seasonal.

Zone 5: Skies are fair to partly cloudy, temperatures are seasonal, western areas see scattered precipitation, and eastern parts of the zone have a chance for showers.

Zone 6: Western areas see precipitation, some abundant, skies are partly cloudy to cloudy, western areas are cooler than central and eastern parts of the zone, where temperatures range from seasonal to above.

Zone 7: Western and central parts of the zone have a chance for thunderstorms, eastern areas are windy and humid, temperatures are seasonal to above, and skies are partly cloudy.

Zone 8: Western parts of Alaska could see abundant precipitation that triggers flooding, central and eastern areas are mostly fair, and temperatures are seasonal. Western areas of Hawaii are windy, skies are partly cloudy, temperatures are seasonal to above, and the state is humid with scattered showers.

2nd Quarter Moon, July 19–26

Zone 1: Temperatures are seasonal to below and the zone sees precipitation, some locally heavy north, under partly cloudy to cloudy skies, possibly from a tropical storm.

Zone 2: Skies are windy and partly cloudy to cloudy, and much of the zone sees precipitation.

Zone 3: The zone is windy, skies are partly cloudy to cloudy, temperatures are seasonal to below, and western and eastern areas see precipitation, some locally heavy.

Zone 4: Seasonal temperatures accompany fair to partly cloudy skies, conditions are windy and humid, central areas have a chance for showers, and western areas see scattered thunderstorms and showers, some locally heavy.

Zone 5: Much of the zone sees scattered showers and thunderstorms under variably cloudy skies, with seasonal temperatures and humidity.

Zone 6: Temperatures are seasonal to above, skies are fair to partly cloudy, and much of the zone sees scattered precipitation; central areas have more cloudiness and potential for abundant downfall.

Zone 7: Fair to partly cloudy skies accompany temperatures seasonal to above and scattered showers west and central; eastern areas are humid with precipitation, some locally heavy, possibly from a tropical storm.

Zone 8: Precipitation in western areas of Alaska moves into central parts of the state, skies are variably cloudy and windy, temperatures are seasonal, and eastern skies are fair. Hawaii is windy with showers and temperatures seasonal to above.

Full Moon, July 27–August 3

Zone 1: Southern areas see showers, skies are partly cloudy, and temperatures are seasonal.

Zone 2: Abundant precipitation is possible along with strong thunderstorms with tornado potential central and south, skies are windy and variably cloudy, and temperatures are seasonal to above.

Zone 3: Western skies are mostly fair, central and eastern areas are partly cloudy to cloudy with abundant precipitation possible from strong thunderstorms with tornado potential, and temperatures range from seasonal to above.

Zone 4: The zone is fair to partly cloudy and humid with temperatures seasonal to above and a chance for showers in central areas.

Zone 5: The zone has a chance for showers, skies are partly cloudy, and temperatures seasonal.

Zone 6: Much of the zone sees showers and thunderstorms, some with locally heavy precipitation, skies are partly cloudy to cloudy, and temperatures are seasonal.

Zone 7: Showers and thunderstorms bring precipitation to much of the zone under variably cloudy skies and temperatures seasonal to above.

Zone 8: Alaska is partly cloudy to cloudy with precipitation west and central, some locally heavy, and temperatures are seasonal. Hawaii is mostly cloudy and seasonal.

4th Quarter Moon, August 4–10

Zone 1: The zone is partly cloudy and seasonal with showers.

Zone 2: Skies are windy and partly cloudy with precipitation, and temperatures range from seasonal to below.

Zone 3: Much of the zone sees precipitation, possibly abundant west and central, skies are partly cloudy to cloudy, and temperatures are seasonal.

Zone 4: Strong thunderstorms with tornado potential are possible west and central, eastern areas see precipitation, skies are variably cloudy, and temperatures range from seasonal to above.

Zone 5: Skies are partly cloudy to cloudy, eastern areas see showers, and western and central parts of the zone see thunderstorms with tornado potential.

Zone 6: Skies are fair to partly cloudy, and temperatures are seasonal to above.

Zone 7: Temperatures ranging from seasonal to above accompany fair to partly cloudy skies.

Zone 8: Eastern Alaska sees precipitation, skies are variably cloudy and windy, and temperatures are seasonal. Much of Hawaii sees showers and thunderstorms under partly cloudy to cloudy skies, humidity, and temperatures ranging from seasonal to above.

New Moon, August 11–17

Zone 1: Fair to partly cloudy skies and temperatures ranging from seasonal to above accompany a chance for precipitation.

Zone 2: The zone is windy with scattered thunderstorms, some strong with tornado potential, skies are partly cloudy, and temperatures are seasonal to above.

Zone 3: Skies are partly cloudy west and central with a chance for precipitation, eastern areas see more cloudiness and precipitation, and temperatures are seasonal to above.

Zone 4: Precipitation in western areas moves into the western plains, temperatures range from seasonal to above, central and eastern areas are humid with scattered thunderstorms and potential for locally heavy downfall that could trigger flooding.

Zone 5: Western areas see precipitation and are partly cloudy to cloudy, central and eastern parts of the zone are mostly fair, and seasonal temperatures accompany humidity.

Zone 6: The zone is fair to partly cloudy with scattered showers and thunderstorms and temperatures seasonal to above.

Zone 7: Northern coastal areas see precipitation, the zone is variably cloudy, eastern areas are humid with a chance for thunderstorms, and temperatures are seasonal.

Zone 8: Alaska is seasonal, windy, and variably cloudy with precipitation. Hawaii is windy with scattered showers and temperatures seasonal to below.

2nd Quarter Moon, August 18–25

Zone 1: The zone is humid and seasonal with precipitation, some locally heavy north.

Zone 2: Northern areas see precipitation, central and southern parts of the zone see scattered showers, skies are partly cloudy to cloudy, and temperatures are seasonal to below.

Zone 3: Skies are variably cloudy, western and central areas see scattered showers, eastern areas are windy with precipitation, and humidity accompanies temperatures seasonal to above.

Zone 4: Fair to partly cloudy skies and a chance for precipitation accompany humid and temperatures seasonal to above.

Zone 5: Temperatures are seasonal to above, skies are fair to partly cloudy, and the zone is humid with a chance for precipitation.

Zone 6: Scattered showers and partly cloudy skies accompany temperatures seasonal to above.

Zone 7: Much of the zone sees scattered showers, skies are variably cloudy, and temperatures range from seasonal to above.

Zone 8: Western and central Alaska see precipitation, eastern areas are windy, skies are variably cloudy and temperatures are seasonal. Hawaii is fair to partly cloudy with temperatures seasonal to above.

Full Moon, August 26–September 1

Zone 1: The zone is fair to partly cloudy and seasonal with a chance for precipitation south.

Zone 2: The zone could see abundant precipitation, possibly from a tropical storm, temperatures are seasonal to below, and skies are partly cloudy to cloudy.

Zone 3: Much of the zone sees precipitation, some abundant, possibly from a tropical storm, skies are variably cloudy, and temperatures are seasonal.

Zone 4: Temperatures are seasonal to above, skies are fair to partly cloudy, eastern areas see more cloudiness and wind with precipitation.

Zone 5: Skies are variably cloudy, temperatures range from seasonal to above, and eastern areas are windy with showers.

Zone 6: Temperatures are seasonal to above, skies are fair to partly cloudy, and eastern areas have a chance for precipitation.

Zone 7: Eastern parts of the zone see showers and scattered thunderstorms, temperatures are seasonal to above, and skies are partly cloudy.

Zone 8: Alaska is fair to partly cloudy and seasonal, and western skies are windy. Temperatures in Hawaii range from seasonal to above accompany partly cloudy and windy skies.

4th Quarter Moon, September 2–8

Zone 1: The zone is partly cloudy and seasonal with showers and thunderstorms later in the week.

Zone 2: Northern areas see scattered precipitation, central and southern areas could see abundant downfall with strong thunderstorms with tornado potential, temperatures are seasonal to above with humidity, and skies are partly cloudy to cloudy and windy.

Zone 3: Western areas have a chance for precipitation, central and eastern areas see showers, skies are partly cloudy to cloudy, and temperatures are seasonal to above.

Zone 4: Western skies are cloudy, central areas are partly cloudy with precipitation, eastern parts of the zone see more cloudiness and precipitation, and temperatures are seasonal.

Zone 5: Seasonal temperatures accompany partly cloudy to cloudy skies, western areas could see abundant downfall, and central and eastern parts of the zone see showers and thunderstorms.

Zone 6: Much of the zone sees precipitation, some abundant, skies are partly cloudy to cloudy, and temperatures are seasonal to below.

Zone 7: Skies are fair to partly cloudy with a chance for precipitation west and central, more cloudiness east with scattered thunderstorms, and seasonal temperatures.

Zone 8: Central and eastern parts of Alaska see precipitation, some abundant, skies are variably cloudy, temperatures are seasonal, and western parts of the state are mostly fair. Hawaii is partly cloudy, seasonal, and humid with showers.

New Moon, September 9–15

Zone 1: The zone is cloudy and seasonal with abundant precipitation, possibly from a tropical storm or hurricane.

Zone 2: Some areas see abundant downfall, possibly from a tropical storm or hurricane, temperatures are seasonal, and skies are variably cloudy.

Zone 3: Much of the zone sees showers and thunderstorms with heavy downfall possible from a tropical storm or hurricane; skies are variably cloudy and windy, and temperatures are seasonal.

Zone 4: Thunderstorms and precipitation, some locally heavy, possibly from a tropical storm or hurricane, accompany seasonal temperatures and variably cloudy skies.

Zone 5: Western and eastern parts of the zone sees scattered showers and thunderstorms, eastern areas could see abundant downfall, possibly form a tropical storm or hurricane, and temperatures are seasonal.

Zone 6: Seasonal temperatures accompany fair to partly cloudy skies and scattered precipitation west and central.

Zone 7: The zone is partly cloudy and seasonal with a chance for precipitation.

Zone 8: Alaska is fair to partly cloudy and seasonal. Hawaii is humid, partly cloudy, and seasonal.

2nd Quarter Moon, September 16–23

Zone 1: Skies are partly cloudy to cloudy, and precipitation accompanies temperatures seasonal to below.

Zone 2: Northern areas have a chance for precipitation, central and southern areas see showers and thunderstorms, some with locally heavy downfall, conditions are humid, skies are variably cloudy, and temperatures are seasonal.

Zone 3: Humidity accompanies partly cloudy to cloudy skies and temperatures seasonal to above; strong thunderstorms with tornado potential are possible west and central.

Zone 4: The zone is partly cloudy and seasonal with thunderstorms, possibly with tornado potential, east.

Zone 5: Skies are partly cloudy to cloudy, temperatures are seasonal, and the zone sees scattered precipitation.

Zone 6: Skies are fair to partly cloudy, temperatures are seasonal, eastern areas see scattered thunderstorms, and western parts of the zone see increasing cloudiness with abundant precipitation later in the week.

Zone 7: Much of the zone sees precipitation under variably cloudy skies with seasonal temperatures, and northern coastal areas see precipitation later in the week.

Zone 8: Central and eastern areas of Alaska are fair to partly cloudy, western Alaska is windy with precipitation, and temperatures are seasonal. Hawaii is windy, partly cloudy, and seasonal to above.

Autumn

Conditions will alternate between warm and fair and wet and cloudy in zone 1, where abundant precipitation will be the norm

2017 © Minerva Studio Image from BigStockPhoto.com

rather than the exception, along with seasonal temperatures. Zone 2 will be windy with temperatures ranging from seasonal to above and precipitation below average. Inland areas of central parts of the zone will see more precipitation, however. There will be an increased number of strong thunderstorms with tornado potential in zone 3, along with overall precipitation levels, and temperatures will range from seasonal to above. Zones 4 and 5 will see average precipitation, although temperatures will range from seasonal to below. These zones can also expect some major storms, primarily in western and central areas. Although central areas of zone 6 will see above average numbers of cloudy, wet, windy days, the zone will overall tend toward dryness and above average temperatures. Western and central parts of zone 7 could finally see some significant relief from drought conditions as storms move through these areas. Eastern areas, however, will tend toward above average temperatures and dryness. In zone 8, eastern Alaska will see above average levels of precipitation, with average precipitation in other parts of the state, where seasonal temperatures will be the norm. Precipitation will range from average to above in western and central parts of Hawaii and below average in eastern parts of the states; temperatures will be seasonal.

Full Moon, September 24–October 1
Zone 1: Temperatures are seasonal to below, skies are partly cloudy to cloudy, and much of the zone sees precipitation, some abundant.
Zone 2: The zone is windy and fair to partly cloudy with seasonal temperatures.
Zone 3: Western areas see precipitation, eastern areas see scattered precipitation, temperatures are seasonal, and skies are variably cloudy.
Zone 4: Western areas could see strong thunderstorms with tornado potential, eastern areas see precipitation, skies are variably cloudy and windy, and temperatures are seasonal to above.
Zone 5: Partly cloudy to cloudy skies accompany temperatures seasonal to above and precipitation, with strong thunderstorms with tornado potential in central areas.
Zone 6: Temperatures are seasonal to above, eastern areas see precipitation, and skies are partly cloudy to cloudy.
Zone 7: Skies are fair to partly cloudy, eastern areas have a chance for precipitation, and temperatures are seasonal to above.
Zone 8: Much of Alaska sees precipitation, temperatures are seasonal to below, and skies are partly cloudy to cloudy. Hawaii is seasonal, humid, and partly cloudy.

4th Quarter Moon, October 2–7
Zone 1: Skies are partly cloudy to cloudy and windy, temperatures are seasonal, and the zone sees precipitation.
Zone 2: Partly cloudy to cloudy skies and humid conditions bring precipitation, some abundant, and thunderstorms are possible; temperatures are seasonal.

Zone 3: Temperatures range from seasonal to above, skies are variably cloudy, eastern areas are windy, western areas see scattered precipitation, and central parts of the zone could see abundant downfall.

Zone 4: The zone is windy and seasonal to above with partly cloudy skies; central parts of the zone see scattered showers and thunderstorms.

Zone 5: Skies are fair to partly cloudy, temperatures are seasonal to above, and central and eastern areas see scattered showers and thunderstorms.

Zone 6: Seasonal temperatures and variably cloudy skies accompany windy conditions west and precipitation central and east.

Zone 7: Western and central areas see precipitation, some locally heavy, skies are partly cloudy to cloudy, and temperatures are seasonal.

Zone 8: Western Alaska sees precipitation while central areas of the state have a chance for precipitation, skies are variably cloudy, and temperatures are seasonal. Hawaii is partly cloudy and seasonal with scattered showers.

New Moon, October 8–15

Zone 1: Temperatures range from seasonal to below under partly cloudy to cloudy skies with scattered precipitation.

Zone 2: Skies are partly cloudy, temperatures are seasonal to below, and the zone sees scattered precipitation.

Zone 3: Western areas see precipitation, some abundant, central areas see scattered thunderstorms, eastern areas see precipitation, skies are partly cloudy to cloudy, and temperatures are seasonal to below.

Zone 4: Eastern areas see precipitation, some abundant, western and central parts of the zone have a chance for precipitation, skies are variably cloudy, and temperatures are seasonal.

Zone 5: The zone is partly cloudy and seasonal with scattered showers and thunderstorms west and central.

Zone 6: Temperatures are seasonal, skies are partly cloudy to cloudy, and western and central parts of the zone see precipitation.

Zone 7: Western skies are cloudy and the area sees precipitation, central and eastern parts of the zone are partly cloudy, and temperatures are seasonal.

Zone 8: Alaska is variably cloudy and seasonal with precipitation in many areas and abundant in western parts of the state. Hawaii is partly cloudy and seasonal.

2nd Quarter Moon, October 16–23

Zone 1: Seasonal temperatures accompany fair to partly cloudy and windy skies and scattered precipitation.

Zone 2: Central and southern parts of the zone see precipitation, northern areas see scattered showers, temperatures are seasonal, and skies are partly cloudy to cloudy.

Zone 3: Much of the zone sees precipitation, some locally heavy, under variably cloudy and windy skies and seasonal temperatures.

Zone 4: Temperatures range from seasonal to above, skies are partly cloudy to cloudy, and eastern areas see precipitation, some locally heavy.

Zone 5: Partly cloudy skies have a chance for precipitation across the zone, and temperatures are seasonal to above.

Zone 6: Western and central areas are partly cloudy with a chance for precipitation, eastern areas see more cloudiness with scattered precipitation, and temperatures are seasonal.

Zone 7: Eastern areas see precipitation, some locally heavy, western and central parts of the zone are windy with scattered precipitation, skies are partly cloudy to cloudy, and temperatures are seasonal.

Zone 8: Western and central Alaska see precipitation, eastern areas are fair, skies are partly cloudy to cloudy, and temperatures are seasonal. Hawaii is windy with scattered showers and temperatures seasonal to above.

Full Moon, October 24–30

Zone 1: Temperatures range from seasonal to below, skies are partly cloudy, and southern areas see precipitation.

Zone 2: Skies are fair to partly cloudy central and south with seasonal temperatures and northern areas are partly cloudy to cloudy and colder with precipitation.

Zone 3: The zone is mostly fair to partly cloudy with temperatures seasonal to above and scattered precipitation west, and eastern areas are cooler with precipitation.

Zone 4: Western skies are partly cloudy to cloudy with showers and thunderstorms, temperatures are seasonal to above, and central and eastern areas are fair to partly cloudy.

Zone 5: Skies are variably cloudy, temperatures are seasonal to above, and western and central parts of the zone see scattered showers and thunderstorms.

Zone 6: The zone is fair to partly cloudy with temperatures seasonal to above and precipitation in central areas, some locally heavy.

Zone 7: Partly cloudy to cloudy skies west and central bring precipitation, some possibly abundant, temperatures are seasonal, and eastern areas are fair to partly cloudy.

Zone 8: Western and central areas of Alaska see precipitation, some abundant, temperatures are seasonal to below, and eastern areas are windy. Western Hawaii sees showers, temperatures are seasonal to below, and skies are variably cloudy.

4th Quarter Moon, October 31–November 6

Zone 1: Skies are partly cloudy and temperatures are seasonal.

Zone 2: Temperatures range from seasonal to below and partly cloudy to cloudy skies bring precipitation, some abundant, to central and southern areas.

Zone 3: Temperatures are seasonal but warmer west and windy, skies are variably cloudy, and central areas see precipitation, some abundant.

Zone 4: The zone is partly cloudy to cloudy and seasonal to above with precipitation west.

Zone 5: Central and eastern areas are partly cloudy with a chance for precipitation, western areas are cloudy with precipitation, and temperatures are seasonal.

Zone 6: Skies are variably cloudy, temperatures are seasonal, western areas see precipitation, some abundant, and central and eastern areas have a chance for precipitation.

Zone 7: Northern coastal areas see precipitation, some abundant, temperatures are seasonal, skies are variably cloudy, and eastern parts of the zone have a chance for precipitation.

Zone 8: Alaska is fair to partly cloudy and seasonal. Hawaii is partly cloudy and seasonal with scattered showers.

New Moon, November 7–14

Zone 1: The zone is partly cloudy and seasonal.

Zone 2: Temperatures range from seasonal to below, skies are partly cloudy to cloudy, and much of the zone sees precipitation, some abundant.

Zone 3: Temperatures are seasonal, western and central parts of the zone are mostly fair, and eastern areas are cloudy with precipitation, some abundant.

Zone 4: Scattered precipitation accompanies partly cloudy to cloudy skies and seasonal temperatures.

Zone 5: The zone is partly cloudy to cloudy and seasonal with scattered precipitation west and central.

Zone 6: Western areas see precipitation, some abundant, skies are variably cloudy, and temperatures are seasonal.

Zone 7: Skies are partly cloudy to cloudy, temperatures are seasonal, and the zone has a chance for precipitation.

Zone 8: Alaska is fair to partly cloudy and seasonal. Hawaii is seasonal and partly cloudy.

2nd Quarter Moon, November 15–22

Zone 1: The zone is cloudy with precipitation and temperatures seasonal to below.

Zone 2: Central and southern areas see scattered thunderstorms, northern areas see precipitation, temperatures are seasonal to above, and skies are partly cloudy to cloudy.

Zone 3: Western and central areas see scattered showers and thunderstorms, eastern are see precipitation, skies are partly cloudy to cloudy, and temperatures range from seasonal to above.

Zone 4: Partly cloudy to cloudy skies and precipitation in central parts of the zone accompany seasonal temperatures.

Zone 5: Temperatures are seasonal, skies are partly cloudy to cloudy, western areas see scattered precipitation, and central and eastern parts of the zone see precipitation and possible strong thunderstorms.

Zone 6: Seasonal to below temperatures accompany precipitation across the zone, some abundant, and cloudy skies.

Zone 7: Western and central areas are partly cloudy to cloudy with scattered precipitation, temperatures are seasonal, and eastern parts of the zone see more cloudiness with precipitation, some abundant.

Zone 8: Much of Alaska sees precipitation under variably cloudy skies and temperatures seasonal to below. In Hawaii, mostly cloudy skies accompany precipitation across the state, some abundant, possibly from a tropical storm or hurricane.

Full Moon, November 23–28

Zone 1: The zone is seasonal and partly cloudy to cloudy with precipitation, some abundant, south.

Zone 2: Temperatures are seasonal to below, central and southern areas are windy and stormy with possible strong thunderstorms, and northern areas see precipitation.

Zone 3: Much of the zone sees precipitation, cloudy skies, and temperatures seasonal to below; central and eastern areas are stormy.

Zone 4: Western parts of the zone are fair to partly cloudy, central and eastern areas see more cloudiness with precipitation, and temperatures are seasonal.

Zone 5: Partly cloudy skies accompany seasonal temperatures and a chance for precipitation.

Zone 6: Western and central areas see precipitation, skies are partly cloudy to cloudy, temperatures are seasonal to below, and eastern parts of the zone see scattered precipitation.

Zone 7: Precipitation in western areas moves into central parts of the zone with partly cloudy to cloudy skies and seasonal temperatures; eastern areas are fair to partly cloudy.

Zone 8: Western Alaska is cloudy with precipitation, central and eastern areas are fair to partly cloudy, and temperatures are seasonal. Hawaii is mostly fair and seasonal.

4th Quarter Moon, November 29–December 6

Zone 1: Skies are partly cloudy and windy with scattered precipitation and temperatures seasonal to below.

Zone 2: The zone is fair to partly cloudy and seasonal with scattered precipitation.

Zone 3: Eastern areas are fair to partly cloudy with a chance for precipitation, western and central parts of the zone are partly cloudy to cloudy with precipitation, some abundant, and temperatures are seasonal; western areas could see strong thunderstorms with tornado potential.

Zone 4: Western skies are fair, central and eastern parts of the zone are partly cloudy to cloudy with precipitation, some abundant, and temperatures are seasonal; eastern areas could be stormy.

Zone 5: Western parts of the zone are partly cloudy, central and eastern areas see more cloudiness with precipitation, eastern areas are windy, and temperatures are seasonal.

Zone 6: Skies are variably cloudy with scattered precipitation, possibly abundant in central parts of the zone, and temperatures are seasonal.

Zone 7: The zone is partly cloudy and seasonal.

Zone 8: Alaska is partly cloudy to cloudy with seasonal temperatures and precipitation east. Hawaii is partly cloudy to cloudy with showers and thunderstorms in central areas; temperatures are seasonal to above.

New Moon, December 7–14

Zone 1: The zone is partly cloudy and seasonal.

Zone 2: Temperatures range from seasonal to above, skies are partly cloudy, and the zone has a chance for precipitation.

Zone 3: Partly cloudy to cloudy skies accompany precipitation across much of the zone with seasonal temperatures.

Zone 4: Western areas are mostly fair, central and eastern parts of the zone are partly cloudy to cloudy, and temperatures are seasonal.

Zone 5: Seasonal temperatures accompany fair to partly cloudy skies.

Zone 6: Skies are variably cloudy with precipitation east and temperatures ranging from seasonal to above.

Zone 7: Temperatures are seasonal to above, skies are partly cloudy to cloudy, and eastern areas see precipitation with thunderstorms with possible abundant downfall.

Zone 8: Central Alaska is cloudy with precipitation, western and eastern areas of Alaska are fair to partly cloudy, and temperatures are seasonal. Much of Hawaii sees showers, skies are partly cloudy to cloudy, and temperatures are seasonal to above.

2nd Quarter Moon, December 15–21

Zone 1: Skies are partly cloudy to cloudy and windy, and temperatures are seasonal to below.

Zone 2: Seasonal temperatures accompany skies that are windy and partly cloudy.

Zone 3: Eastern areas are windy with scattered precipitation, temperatures are seasonal, and western and central areas are fair to partly cloudy.

Zone 4: Variably cloudy skies and seasonal temperatures accompany precipitation, some abundant, central and east.

Zone 5: Western areas are windy and partly cloudy, central and eastern areas see more cloudiness with a chance for precipitation, and temperatures are seasonal.

Zone 6: The zone is partly cloudy and seasonal with precipitation west.

Zone 7: Temperatures are seasonal, skies are partly cloudy to cloudy, and western and central parts of the zone see scattered precipitation.

Zone 8: Western and central parts of Alaska are cloudy with precipitation, eastern areas are mostly fair and windy, and temperatures are seasonal to below. Hawaii is partly cloudy to cloudy and seasonal but cooler west with scattered precipitation.

Full Moon, December 22–28
Zone 1: The zone is partly cloudy and seasonal.

Zone 2: Seasonal temperatures accompany partly cloudy to cloudy skies and a chance for precipitation central and south.

Zone 3: Partly cloudy to cloudy skies bring a chance for precipitation across much of the zone with temperatures seasonal to below.

Zone 4: Western and central skies are cloudy and windy with precipitation, some abundant, temperatures are seasonal, and eastern areas are partly cloudy.

Zone 5: Eastern areas are windy and partly cloudy, temperatures are seasonal, and western and central parts of the zone are cloudy with precipitation.

Zone 6: Skies are partly cloudy and windy, temperatures are seasonal, and eastern areas have a chance for precipitation.

Zone 7: Temperatures are seasonal, skies are partly cloudy, and western and central parts of the zone see scattered precipitation.

Zone 8: Alaska is seasonal to below and partly cloudy to cloudy with precipitation in central areas. Hawaii is partly cloudy and seasonal with precipitation east.

Full Moon, December 29–January 5, 2019

Zone 1: Partly cloudy to cloudy and windy skies accompany seasonal temperatures and precipitation south, possibly locally heavy.

Zone 2: Northern areas see precipitation, some abundant, central and southern areas see scattered precipitation, skies are partly cloudy to cloudy, and temperatures are seasonal.

Zone 3: Temperatures are seasonal to below, skies are variably cloudy, and much of the zone sees precipitation, some possibly abundant.

Zone 4: Much of the zone is windy with precipitation, skies are partly cloudy to cloudy, and temperatures are seasonal.

Zone 5: Central and eastern parts of the zone see precipitation, temperatures are seasonal, and the zone is variably cloudy.

Zone 6: Seasonal temperatures accompany fair to partly cloudy skies.

Zone 7: Central and eastern areas have a chance for precipitation, skies are partly cloudy to cloudy, and temperatures are seasonal.

Zone 8: Alaska is seasonal with partly cloudy to cloudy skies and abundant precipitation east. Hawaii is windy, skies are fair, and temperatures are seasonal to above.

About the Author

Kris Brandt Riske is the executive director and a professional member of the American Federation of Astrologers (AFA), the oldest US astrological organization, founded in 1938; and a member of the National Council for Geocosmic Research (NCGR). She has a master's degree in journalism and a certificate of achievement in weather forecasting from Penn State. Kris is the author of several books, including **Llewellyn's Complete Book of Astrology: The Easy Way to Learn Astrology, Mapping Your Money,** *and* **Mapping Your Future.** *She is also the coauthor of* **Mapping Your Travels and Relocation** *and* **Astrometeorology: Planetary Powers in Weather Forecasting.** *Her newest book is* **Llewellyn's Complete Book of Predictive Astrology.** *She writes for astrology publications and contributes to the annual weather forecast for* **Llewellyn's Moon Sign Book.** *In addition to* *astrometeorology, she specializes in predictive astrology. Kris is an avid NASCAR fan, although she'd rather be a driver than a spectator. In 2011, she fulfilled her dream when she drove a stock car for twelve fast laps. She posts a weather forecast for each of the thirty-six race weekends (qualifying and race day) for NASCAR drivers and fans. Visit her at www.pitstopforecasting.com. Kris also enjoys gardening, reading, jazz, and her three cats.*

2017 © www.BillionPhotos.com Image from BigStockPhoto.com

Economic Forecast for 2018

by Christeen Skinner

Our economic forecast for 2018 takes into account the positions of all the planets and their interaction with lunar cycles.

It is now a decade since Pluto arrived in Capricorn: an ingress that coincided with what has become known as the "global financial crash" (2007–08). Pluto's transit of Capricorn does not complete until 2024 and before then we should expect echoes of that earlier calamity to be heard. Indeed, these echoes could, at times, be heard as thunder claps. Pressure on bond markets between 2018 and 2021 is likely to be great, with a very real threat of collapse.

As you may know, Pluto is associated with major corporations of all kinds: governments and banks included. Before Pluto completes its journey through Capricorn, we should expect to see these being downsized and restructured. This is unlikely to be an easy passage. Though true, many feel that difficulties have been overcome through either austerity or quantitative easing measures, pressure on these major institutions is not yet over and, as Saturn moves to conjoin Pluto before the end of the decade, the threat of another global collapse should be taken seriously.

In 2010, Neptune moved from Aquarius into Pisces—the sign with which it is said to have greatest affinity. Until 2016, Neptune and Pluto, which align only every 496 years, were just a seventh of a circle apart from one another. This is a special relationship last seen in the late 1930s when the term "creative accountancy" was first coined. Quantitative easing could yet prove to be the "creative accountancy" of the first part of the present decade.

As of late 2016, the two planets moved into a different relationship: a thirteenth of a circle apart from one another. This relationship speaks of the possibility of the threat (Pluto) to bubbles (Neptune) so underlining the possibility of bond market collapse.

To assess the probability of such an event, we turn next to the position of Uranus (planet of the unexpected) in 2018 to discover that it aligns with the Full Moon on October 24th, 2018. If there is to be a major financial debacle in 2018, it is likely to occur around this date. Closer inspection alerts us to areas of the world most likely to be affected as will be seen later.

Solar Activity

Having determined the very real possibility of a global financial crisis in 2018, we now turn attention to the Sun itself. The Sun has various rhythms: internal and external. The most well-known of these is the sunspot cycle of approximately 11.2 years. Twenty-four cycles have now been recorded over the last two centuries, it being noted that they are each very different. Some sunspot cycles are considerably "busier" than others. Cycle 24, which is now drawing to its conclusion, has been a relatively quiet cycle with the maximum number of recorded sunspots being less than

100 (in some cycles as many as 300 have been recorded). There is some apprehension about the potential inactivity of Cycle 25 that should "begin" at the end of the decade (it is not possible to forecast the exact date or even month). This is of some considerable concern as a low number of sunspots has consequent effect on terrestrial weather and growing seasons.

What is known is that stock market indices tend to rise as the number of sunspots increases and reduces as the number of sunspots falls. This being the case, and with the next expected minimum due around 2020, as the number of sunspots declines in 2018, it seems unlikely that stock markets will have much upward momentum. Indeed, as we shall see, there is much to suggest that the later months of 2018 will see marked decline in index values. This concurs with the earlier forecast of difficulties at the end of October that year.

Eclipses and Major Ingress: Cosmic Punctuation Marks

In any year, there will be at least two solar eclipses, and in some years, as many as five. These events are important. It is not necessary for a solar eclipse to be accompanied by a lunar eclipse, though that is often the case—nor is it true that there will be marked financial activity on the days of either a solar or lunar eclipse, though that does sometimes happen. What is true is that the signs in which these events take place offer clues as to which market sectors are likely to experience particular volatility. It is also the case that the position of another (usually fast moving) planet in aspect to the eclipse degree can trigger reaction. For example, if Mars occupies the exact degree of an eclipse—even some weeks on either side of the eclipse itself—there may well be a reaction in the marketplace.

For a solar eclipse to occur, the Moon has to pass between the Earth and Sun and at an angle and position that masks the Sun's light. The nodes of the Moon must be within a few degrees of the Sun's position. Note that not all eclipses are total and that areas of the world in which the eclipse can best be seen are also the areas—and markets—likely to see greatest reaction.

In the 1930s, Louise McWhirter identified links between the business cycle and the Moon's nodal cycle. The observation was that as the lunar node moved from Aquarius through to Leo (note that this cycle moves through the signs in reverse sign order), business activity increased. Once the node moved from Leo to Cancer, then decline was apparent, arriving at a low in business activity as the node returned to Aquarius.

If this cycle continues to operate as it has done in the past— and there is little to suggest any change—then in 2018, with the node making its passage from Leo to Cancer, a slowdown in business activity is to be expected before the end of the year.

There are three solar eclipses in 2018. The first solar eclipse of the year occurs mid-February and is in the sign of Aquarius. This eclipse will only be partly visible from Argentina and Chile. It is more likely that major global indices will be affected by the second solar eclipse on July 13th. This eclipse will be visible in southern Australia. It is likely that the Sydney All Ordinaries index will experience volatility between that date and the accompanying lunar eclipse later in the month.

This second solar eclipse of the year is in the sign of Cancer, drawing attention to the building, home improvement, and food sectors. The chart for this event shows Pluto to exactly oppose the eclipse and may well signal fissures appearing in global bond markets. It is not inconceivable that the potential bankruptcies of some countries will be under discussion. Some South American countries may be affected. While very real difficulties may be faced both there and in Indonesia (another area highlighted by the geodetic chart for this eclipse), the subsequent collapse of related bonds—and perhaps even currencies—might not occur for some weeks. The trigger here could be the arrival of Ceres at this eclipse degree on October 22nd.

The third solar eclipse is on August 11th in Leo. In contrast to the July eclipse, this chart does not contain stressful aspects. The chart for this event contains a positive aspect between Jupiter and Neptune. This partial eclipse will be visible across northern Europe and much of Asia. It may be that rare earth metals from this vast region increase in value as investors seek places to invest.

Decline in business confidence—and subsequently in share values—may not be felt until the mean lunar node moves to Cancer in December: a period of the year that, assuming history repeats, looks fraught with difficulty.

As might be expected, lunar eclipses often coincide with fierce reactions or, perhaps more accurately, overreaction. The lunar eclipse of January 31st is exactly aligned with Ceres, now considered to be a dwarf planet and often apparent at times of great political and economic upheaval. Perhaps as a result of some political statement, traders could overreact at the end of January, prompting sharp moves in many indices, particularly those located near coastal regions (i.e., New York, Tokyo, London, Sydney, and Rio de Janeiro).

The second lunar eclipse of the year, on July 27th, comes exactly between two solar eclipses and could mark a low between two relative highs. At this point in the year the lunar node will still be in Leo. Between the two solar eclipses much effort could be put into "talking the market up," even if some traders respond to the lunar eclipse on July 27th by allowing prices to fall before they recover in the days leading into the August eclipse.

Eclipses offer one type of cosmic punctuation mark, another is an ingress: the entry of a planet into a sign.

Uranus 2018

You may know that Uranus's orbit is approximately 84 years.

2017 © VelourRouge Image from BigStockPhoto.com

Since December 31st, 2013, Uranus has been traveling through Aries. On May 15th, 2018, it enters Taurus for the first time since leaving that sign in 1941 (it entered Taurus in 1934).

Uranus is one of the outer planets whose sign changes mark developments on the social, economic, and political stage. To understand the trends likely to arrive from May 2018, we should consider events in 1934. Taurus is one of the fixed signs of the zodiac, and Uranus is most associated with another of the fixed group: Aquarius. It should come as no surprise to learn that the advent of Uranus into Taurus coincided with inflexible political thinking. Hitler declared himself the ultimate ruler (the Führer) while Mao Tse Tung was advancing communism in China. Meanwhile, Stalin was carrying out massacres, Brazil became a near fascist state, and many countries (including Bolivia) fell under military control. Japan renounced two naval treaties (Washington and London) and was then able to build its naval power. In the United States, the Great Depression drew to its conclusion while money poured into housing and public works. Also in the United States, severe drought resulted in many farm bankruptcies.

Clearly, if history repeats, then Uranus's Taurus ingress will likely not be a happy period. Indeed, Uranus's seven-year sojourn through this sign has seen conflicts escalate: financially beneficial to those investing in armaments but problematic for many other industry sectors.

Yet no year is an exact repeat of another and though there is much to suggest that 2018 will see a turning point in political thinking and, quite probably, the emergence of leaders whose power is later seen to have been autocratic and harmful, it will not be an exact repeat of 1934. The planetary pictures involving Uranus in 2018 are different to those of 1934—even if there are similarities.

Two periods are particularly striking in 2018: On June 29th, Uranus is on the Jupiter-Pluto midpoint. This midpoint is associated with great wealth and great power. Viewed from the military perspective around this date, there could be awesome displays of firepower. In the financial world the effect could be felt in the bond market. The "firepower" displays here could see high stakes and an increased number of bankruptcies

The other critical date is October 24th when the Sun is exactly opposite Uranus, which is at the midpoint of Jupiter and Saturn. The latter pairing is considered to be one of the major business cycles. The presence of Uranus at this midpoint is indicative of serious disruption. Noting that the Sun-Uranus opposition that day is across the Taurus/Scorpio axis (highly sensitive for financial matters), this could prove one of the more volatile financial days of the year.

Note that once again—and using this different perspective—there is much to suggest major (and probably negative) moves in the marketplace at the end of October.

Chiron

Uranus's Taurus ingress is likely to be hugely significant but so too will surely be Chiron's arrival in Aries. Though most often thought of as the "wounded healer," Chiron often features in the planetary pictures surrounding key events in the markets. It could be thought of as an auditor or corrector. As it travels through a sign, sectors associated with that sign usually experience considerable volatility until they settle as Chiron moves on into the next sign. Chiron's transit of Pisces has certainly brought unease in both the oil markets and shipping industries and, at times, to the pharmaceutical sector.

Chiron's move into Aries is unlikely to pass without notice. It arrives here on April 17th, though, as viewed geocentrically, it slips back into Pisces from late September 2018 through to February 2019. Thus Chiron makes more than one Aries ingress. Both are likely to be important with the first especially so. This ingress comes within hours of the Sun's annual conjunction with Uranus. It is not unreasonable to imagine that this will be an explosive period with some people breaking long-held habits. In the marketplace this could lead to considerable volatility.

The first degree of Aries can be thought of as the "human race" point: it marks that special time when the Sun crosses the celestial equator, bringing the start of spring and new beginnings. The arrival of the "auditor" at this point may well signal major and sudden correction. That said, certain sectors should gain as Chiron arrives here:

Aries is the first sign of the zodiac and is associated with raw materials and sharpness—from small paring knives and scissors to military hardware. Metalwork of all kinds comes under this sign. Those born under this sign are usually willing to be front-runners and can be excellent entrepreneurs. Many have business deemed to be "at the cutting edge." This though creates a difficulty: it is not always easy to attract investment. One of the many weaknesses of 2018 may be the lack of easy capital and the consequent delay in many needed products and services coming to market. Those seeking funds would be well advised to take action early in the year prior to Chiron's Aries ingress.

It is salutary to recall Chiron's last Aries ingress. Within days, Martin Luther King had been assassinated. Riots in Baltimore and other major US cities followed. Across the world social orders changed, and for a few months Czechoslovakia broke free from Soviet rule, while in Japan there were student riots. Some have even called 1968 the year of global revolution. The Vietnam War had drained US gold reserves, the London Gold Pool collapsed just days before the ingress, and within the space of a few short weeks, demand for actual gold increased, driving the price up. Repetition could yet occur.

Bright Notes

The position of the so-called "outer planets" and their relationship to one another offers another useful perspective as to the financial pulse of any year. Dominating 2018 is a trine (third of a cycle) aspect between Jupiter and Neptune. The former spends most of the year in Scorpio and continues its long transit of Pisces: the sign in which it is said to be most "at home" and appears to have strongest influence.

These two planets align every 12.5 to 13 years. Tradition suggests that the combination coincides with a surge of interest in magic, idealism, higher intuition, and compassion. This does not always have a positive connotation. Their last conjunction was in 2009 and may well have been a factor in the steps taken to conceal the structural damage to the global financial system. Jupiter and Neptune together speak of wishful thinking and grand dreams.

As with all planet cycles, the Jupiter-Neptune cycles reaches quarter and full moon–type phases. No less important are those years when the two are one-third of a cycle apart: aspects termed "trines." Then, the two planets will share the same element; in 2018, the emphasis is on water signs.

Since Jupiter will be traveling through Scorpio—a sign known for research, intensity, healing, and powerful intuition—as Neptune moves through Pisces—an area of the zodiac linked with both oil and pharmaceuticals—it is reasonable to expect considerable activity in these areas.

This aspect might not favor oil prices. A glut (Jupiter brings excess) of oil could result in falling prices, which in turn could have massive repercussions on the world's political stage. Yet this same aspect suggests increased activity on the high seas. The shipping industry could find this to be a profitable period.

No less important though may be scientific breakthroughs—especially those connected to bioengineering. Though the charts of specific companies would have to be studied with care, it is these stock prices that are most likely to buck any falling trend in equity prices.

Long-term investors might like to mark April 20th. This date marks the Sun's Taurus ingress, but is also the date when Mars is exact on the Jupiter-Neptune midpoint. With Mars acting as a kick-start and the Sun in Taurus indicating a drive to build structure, companies coming to market within 48 hours of this date would be starting under very promising conditions.

The trine aspect between the two planets is exact (geocentrically) on May 25th and again on August 19th. Both dates may be highly significant in both oil and pharmaceutical markets.

The Jupiter-Saturn Business Cycle

These two planets form a conjunction every twenty years. In 2018 they conclude a cycle that began in May 2000. Their next conjunction coincides with the December solstice in 2019. Many will recall the dot-com drama of 2000 when the value of certain technical stocks had soared. Given the many other factors at work, it seems unlikely that any sector will soar during 2018. It is arguably important that investors recall that earlier time and, if they do invest in young industries, take ample time to review a company prospectus. In particular, it would be wise to give particular attention to those companies coming to market late in the year. These companies might take many years before they realize profit.

Saturn

Saturn will have made Capricorn ingress at the December solstice in 2017, joining Pluto in that sign. Though the two do not make conjunction until 2019, lunar patterns throughout 2018 indicate that the two might act as if they are "working as one."

As the ruler of Capricorn, Saturn's transit through this sign marks an important part of its near thirty-year journey through the zodiac. Often thought of as the cosmic headmaster, Saturn demands attention to rules and regulations and speaks more of contraction than expansion. We should anticipate a slowdown in many businesses during this period and, perhaps, discussions about deglobalization by some companies.

Jupiter

If Saturn brings contraction—or even pessimism, by contrast—Jupiter is said to bring the opposite: expansion and optimism. For the greater part of 2018, Jupiter transits Scorpio. The link between Scorpio and Capricorn is constructive so that those businesses on secure foundations should at least hold steady even as global financial winds start to chill. It is interesting that Jupiter arrives in one of the signs it rules, Sagittarius, on November 8th. This ingress occurs just two days after Uranus returns to Aries. The presence of the two in fire signs could signal a last hurrah before markets take a more definite downward turn.

2017 © Flynt Image from BigStockPhoto.com

Mars

The "red planet" Mars plays crucial role in economic activities. This is the energizing planet. On its twenty-seven month journey through the various signs, it excites each business sector in turn. You might expect that Mars would spend an equal amount of time in each sign. Like the other planets though its orbit is elliptical causing it to appear to move through some areas at faster pace than others. Mars also has retrograde periods resulting in it spending many weeks in a particular area of the zodiac.

Mars does not have a retrograde period in every year, but in 2018, it is retrograde between June 26 and August 27. The planet begins the year in Sagittarius where it makes a conjunction with Vesta (the trading asteroid). This could boost the travel sector though perhaps not for long. Just before Mars makes Capricorn ingress (March 17) it forms a right angle to Chiron. This could signal disruption to travel services: perhaps as a result of concerns about the spread of disease (as happened with the SARS virus).

Mars has prominent position at the Full Moon on March 31. The chart for this lunation contains both a mystic rectangle and a cardinal T-square where Mars is at the midpoint of the Sun and Moon. This suggests a major turning point: perhaps a minor high in the markets. The next New Moon is on April 16 when Mars is on the midpoint of Saturn-Pluto.

An obvious interpretation is that military action will take place. A variation on this in the economic sense would be a tightening in lending and, perhaps, foreign exchange restrictions.

Mars conjoins Pluto on April 26 and this too points to a singular and potentially dramatic event that impacts the financial scene. Note that this is within days of the Uranus and Chiron ingresses mentioned above. This is an unsettling planetary picture. As mentioned earlier, this has all the hallmarks of tightened controls and dictatorship, and it could present enormously challenging trading conditions.

Thanks to its long retrograde period, Mars does not pass through many signs in 2018. It starts the year in Sagittarius and concludes it in Pisces, thus only traveling through approximately a quarter of the zodiac. Its retrograde period takes it from Aquarius back into Capricorn, putting further emphasis on this sign (also ready accented through the presence of both Saturn and Pluto).

From the economic perspective this highlights major agencies and businesses with some forced to downsize or at least to consider downsizing exercises mid-year. Arguably the only businesses immune to this pressure will be those that provide essential services: food and its distribution.

Venus

Venus does not have retrograde periods every year, but in those years where Venus has retrograded, shifts of the market to the downside have been observed. It is worth noting that every year between 2008 and 2016 there was immediate decline in market value when Venus made Libra ingress. The situation in 2018 is complex in that Venus makes Libra ingress in August, moves on into the next sign, Scorpio, before returning to Libra for the entire month of November. It is, of course, entirely possible that there will be two declines: one in August and again in November. A key date however may well be October 5: Venus's retrograde station.

The last time that Venus retrograded over similar degrees was in 1767—long before many of the present indices were in operation. The fact that we do not have comparable data is unfortunate. Even so, and taking Mercury's movements in the last quarter of 2018 into account, we may well conclude that the end of 2018 will not see hoped-for market returns.

Venus also ventures "out of bounds" in 2018. Venus does not venture out of bounds every year, but in May 2018 it reaches over 25 degrees of declination. This comes into the category of "unusual." Unsurprisingly, when there is unusual activity in the cosmos, there is often unusual activity in the marketplace.

Again, we look back and find that Venus was out of bounds in May 2015, a period that saw significant rise in many indices. So, though the general picture is negative in the last quarter of 2018, gains could be realized earlier in the year.

Viewed from Earth, Venus passes through all twelve signs every year, forming conjunctions with each of the slower planets along the way. These alignments are viewed as part of the lexicon of cosmic punctuation marks.

Mercury

We move next to consider Mercury's role in 2018. In any year Mercury will retrograde three times. There is a pattern to these retrogrades which, in 2018, will all be in fire signs. The first occurs at 16 Aries on March 23 (within days of the Equinox). It stations direct on April 15—again accenting mid-April dates already mentioned in connection with Uranus and Chiron. We first look back to 2005 when Mercury last retrograded from mid-Aries again making its retrograde station within hours of the March Equinox. The SPX index began a decline at the retrograde station, a situation that was not reversed for almost two months.

The Full Moon of March 31—with Mercury retrograde—is important in that Mercury will then appear at an apparent right angle to Saturn while the Sun opposes Chiron. This configuration in a Full Moon chart implies considerable stress, which, in the world of finances, could prompt loss in confidence.

Those whose financial year-end is March 31 should note this difficult planetary picture too. As explained, this is not the easiest of planetary pictures and in many cases could indicate very real financial difficulties.

The next Mercury retrograde station in 2018 is at 23 Leo—again reflecting 2005. That year the SPX rose for some days after the retrograde but then turned negative. Recovery began only after Mercury returned to its retrograde station degree (20 Leo) on August 30 that year. If history repeats then the SPX might rise for a few days after the retrograde station on July 26 but then decline in August before beginning a recovery as Mercury reaches 23 Leo once more.

The final retrograde of the year is at 13 Sagittarius on November 17th. Of the three Mercury retrograde stations in 2018, this one should pique the interest of astro-traders. Mercury will have turned direct at exactly this degree on December 23, 2017, and was stationary retrograde at precisely 13 Gemini (opposite this degree) in May 2005. Such accent on a particular axis implies the probability of marked volatility in sectors associated with these signs: principally communications, publishing, and transport. It is quite possible that November 18th will mark a downturn in market indices led by businesses operating in these sectors.

Of course, before making a forecast and determining an appropriate trading strategy the astro-trader must consider all the various planetary pictures at work in the given time frame and determine which might either cancel or exaggerate any effect.

In November 2018, Jupiter crosses 18 Pisces in the week prior to Mercury's retrograde station. Jupiter (the exaggerator) will have opposed Mars's position in the NYSE chart. Again checking with the past we might reasonably draw the conclusion that trading as Jupiter crosses this degree tends to be upward. Mercury's retrograde station might well mark the turning point after which indices decline.

There are however two further signals suggesting that this particular Mercury retrograde period will indeed bring a short-term downturn: firstly the Sun at 28 Scorpio is in 150 degree geocentric aspect to Saturn and secondly that Mars will be at right angles to the Galactic Center.

If technical analysis supports this thinking, then our trader might choose to sell a day before the retrograde with a view to buying back in at lower prices mid-December.

2018 Quarterly Forecast

First Quarter

The first key date is January 24th when alignment of Mercury, Vesta, and Pluto coincides with the first quarter Moon. Investors should look back to trading conditions at the March 2017 New Moon. Decisions taken then could return to haunt markets. Specifically there may be large moves in foreign exchange. A week later, the lunar eclipse of January 31st may see further trading pressures with some losses across major indices.

The solar eclipse mid-February may well herald a bumpy ride for technology stocks. This may be particularly apparent at the Full Moon on March 1st. Indeed, it is possible that around this date a delayed eclipse effect may be seen. This could be one of the more volatile periods of this quarter.

Those stocks that do not recover before March 10th could suffer further loss around March 17th. The period of March 17th through to just after the March Equinox should be seen as treacherous. Inexperienced traders should be ultra-careful between 17th and 22nd.

Second Quarter

With both Chiron and Uranus making ingress this should prove a highly eventful quarter. Mercury is stationary direct within hours of a New Moon on April 16th. Indices could then start to rise, recouping earlier losses. Yet war cycles suggest momentum with significant effect on markets. This may be most apparent as Uranus moves from Aries to Taurus on May 15th coinciding with the May New Moon. A day later Mars makes Aquarius ingress forming a right angle (square) aspect with Uranus. This is an explosive combination and indicative of major confrontation. Market volatility is to be expected.

The New York Stock Exchange (NYSE) came into being on May 17th. The NYSE solar return (birthday chart) has the Moon (in Cancer) opposing Saturn. This and other factors suggest at the very least a gloomy year and, more likely, one of serious losses though those may not be so apparent until after the September Equinox.

As we saw earlier, Venus is out of bounds through much of this quarter. This may well result in indices staying high despite the fact that there are so many signals that they should be in decline. That, though, may come in the next quarter.

Third Quarter

The chart for the solar eclipse of July 13th suggests difficulties to be faced in the banking sector, bond markets, and mortgage sectors. Home prices may be affected. Mercury joins an already retrograde Mars at the lunar eclipse on July 27th, which could yet prove a turning point. Technical analysis closer to the time will indicate the probable direction. Whether this is the downside or upside, the next significant date is the first Full Moon after the solar eclipse on August 11th. This Full Moon on August 26th could prove a recovery date. The chart contains a grand trine involving the Sun, Saturn, and Uranus, suggesting stabilization. Mars then turns direct and recovery could then continue for some weeks.

Fourth Quarter

As has been mentioned many times in this chapter, October 2018 looks set to be a most difficult month with the high probability of indices falling markedly in the last days of October especially. The Full Moon on October 24th shows the Sun and Venus opposing the Moon and Uranus with all in square to the lunar nodes. Sectors that have been struggling through the earlier part of the year could suffer suddenly and dramatically. Businesses may find that offers of capital underpinning (loans) are withdrawn resulting in many business failures before the end of the year.

If indices decline on October 24th, they could fall further on October 31st as Venus, then retrograde, returns to Libra. Recovery is unlikely until mid-November.

Even then there may be difficulties ahead. Those who have waited to exit the market-place might consider doing so before early December when a negative trend could take hold once more.

In Summary

2018 is likely to be a challenging year for both investors and traders. The latter would be well advised to consult with those who worked through the dot-com debacle at the start of the millennium and learn from their experience. Though it seems unlikely that investors will make much gain (with the exception perhaps of those invested in military hardware or food distribution), they could make small gains through crowd-funding type projects that will surely gather momentum between 2018 and 2024.

About the Author

Christeen Skinner *is author of* The Financial Universe *(2004 and 2009), in which she forecast the banking crisis of 2008,* Exploring the Financial Universe *(2016), and* The Beginner's Guide to the Financial Universe *(2017). She works in London and has a broad clientele—city traders, entrepreneurs, and private investors. She taught for the Faculty of Astrological Studies for a decade, was Chair of the Astrological Association of Great Britain, and is now Director of Cityscopes London Ltd, Chair of the Advisory Board of the National Council for Geocosmic Research, and a Director of the Alexandria I-base Project.*

2017 © BackyardProductions Image from BigStockPhoto.com

New and Full Moon Forecasts for 2018

by Sally Cragin

No matter how many lights we keep on at night, the Moon will always be the brightest object in the night sky. For millennia, our species has gazed upon it and endeavored to interpret its movements—and those of the planets beyond—to provide guidance. I do presentations on astrology, tarot, and the phases of the moon all over New England, and I have yet to find an audience who doesn't agree that the moon is beautiful, mesmerizing, and mysterious. What should you do when the moon is full? What should you do when the moon is new? Are there greater risks when you take action during a waxing versus a waning moon?

If you are curious about astrology, learning about the phases, stages, and activity of the moon is a great way to begin. The moon takes just 29.5 days to move around the earth. This is lightning-fast when compared to the movement of the planets, which range from months to many years. In just one month, the moon goes from new, to second quarter, to full, to fourth quarter, to new. Each of these intervals takes a little more than a week, and learning about your energy levels in conjunction with the moon can be useful for your relationships and occupation.

The New Moon to Second Quarter

The moon is new when you see a thin silver crescent in the shape of a capital letter "D," which then increases in size. Generally the Full Moon gets the most conversation in terms of being the "action-packed" lunar phase, but look no further than scripture to see that the New Moon traditionally brought feasting, worship, and celebration: "Blow the trumpet at the new moon, at the full moon, on our feast day"—Psalm 81:3.

Start projects during the period from the New Moon to the second quarter. Make opportunities to meet new people, and stay open to new experiences. What is "new" in your life—and where can you get information or guidance? This is the time to review a database and see where you need to expand (clients, job prospects, territories). The second quarter can be a helpful turning point (this is when there are equal parts light and shadow on the moon). It can also be a reminder that if you have been slacking off, the moon is only getting larger, and the tension is building. Overall, the New Moon to second quarter is helpful for planning, and it is also a time when the shy may feel more encouraged.

Key words: Build, emerge, grow.
Useful phrase: "I'll think about that. Tell me more."

The Second Quarter to Full Moon

You'll see the Moon go from halfway visible to the glorious orb that ornaments the night skies. Many cultures have stories about what the Mariae represent, and Chinese legend says a brilliant archer named Houyi shot down nine of the ten moons and was given an elixir of immortality to drink. He did not want to drink this without sharing with his wife, Chang'e, and when his treacherous apprentice, Fengmeng, tried to steal the elixir, Chang'e drank it all, and then was banished to the lone remaining moon. There she lives with her companion, a giant rabbit. Parts of this tale resemble the Adam and Eve story, but with more drama. And drama is the story of the Full Moon.

Friends in health care, education, and those who work with geriatrics and the developmentally disabled report higher levels of agitation during this lunar phase. And if you have an indoor pet, like a cat, the Full Moon might be when they are literally climbing the walls. This is the time of the month when Type A personalities go into hyperdrive, making commitments left, right, and center. If you are someone who enjoys a lot of action, or functions well when life is chaotic, this is your time, along with the four to five days that follow the Full Moon.

Keywords: Accelerate, expand, enlarge.

Useful phrase: "Do we have all the information to make a decision? I wouldn't want to rush into things."

The Full Moon to the Last Quarter

Here you'll see the beautiful sphere slowly diminish as the shadow of the earth creeps across her face from right to left, reducing the moon to half her size. ("Quarter" refers to the time, not the proportions of Luna!) Some folks find the time of the Full Moon hectic and difficult. Others thrive on the energy and excitement that comes with a Full Moon (particularly when the Full Moon is on a weekend).

Yes, the Full Moon can make you feel exposed and singled out. But if you are looking for a kick in the pants—this is your time of the month. We have all heard the stories about how "lunatics" are in their glory when the moon is full. But consider how this lunar period can help you. Full moons can bring surprising and unexpected personalities into your life. The time of the Full Moon can also be when a plan that was just eking along turns out to have problems.

Jettisoning one course of action and looking for another is a state of affairs I've heard a lot about during the Full Moon. Think of the "Full Moon" as not just a day, but the day or so before and after. If you try to develop your imagination and improvisational skills during this period, you may enlarge on your scope of talents.

Keywords: Focusing, narrowing, consolidating.

Useful phrase: "If things continue moving in this direction, it will become obvious what needs to happen next."

The Last Quarter to the New Moon

After the last quarter, you might have to work to find the moon in the night sky. She diminishes to a slice, and then a sliver, and then disappears completely. So this quarter phrase can be a fragile period. When I speak to clients during this phase, they don't know what they're thinking. They have a general idea: they should move or should seek another position, but can't quite commit to the transition these actions would take. This is when the time of the last quarter to the New Moon is very helpful. Letting go, leaving behind, reducing, refining, and relinquishing will do you good. And for those who live in a sea of papers and assorted clutter, the last quarter to New Moon is super for being able to sift through flotsam and jetsam and toss what's not useful. The waning moon is a time to let things go, and if plans are stalling, don't panic. Sometimes one (or one's boss) commits to a course of action that will not be successful, and rather than panic, this final week of the lunar cycle is a time to be quiet, versus speaking up.

Keywords: Simplifying, removing, refining.

Useful phrase: "Is a rush really necessary, or does it make more sense to reflect on where we are before moving forward?

Full Moon in Cancer, January 1

This moon is in the sign of its ruler, and Cancer is adept at the sideways-strut. With Venus at odds with the moon, you'll need to be more than usually determined to make those New Year's resolutions about improved diet and exercise come true. However, this Full Wolf Moon is a fine time for frankness with a loved one or sharing an activity such as baking or massage. In tune with the moon and willing to listen to all include Cancer, Leo, Scorpio, and Pisces. Looking to be annoyed might be Capricorn, Aquarius, Libra, and Aries. Tempted to indolence: Gemini, Taurus, Sagittarius, and Virgo.

New Moon in Capricorn, January 16

Super day for banking, or going over accounts. Interior design or architecture is favored. If you've been unhappy with your configuration of furniture, now is the time to shove that couch against another wall. This New Moon is in sync with Saturn, which is about limitations and long-term growth. Efficient (if plodding): Capricorn, Taurus, Virgo, and Cancer. Aries, Libra, Leo, and Gemini: fatalism comes easily, but does not become you. Aquarius, Sagittarius, Pisces, and Scorpio take on projects that take a long time to complete.

Full Moon in Leo, January 31

The first Blue Moon of the year. With Mars harmonizing with the moon (in Sagittarius), go-Go-GO is the theme. This Leo moon brings out everyone's fondness for children (or childlike behavior) and is a fine time for publicizing a special project. You may find the crustiest person in your circle projects a "may I have a hug?" vibe. Leo, Sagittarius, Aries, Gemini, and Libra: being generous to others, or defending an underdog will give you enormous satisfaction. Taurus, Scorpio, Aquarius, and Capricorn: Fizzy high spirits could fizzle, or find you frustrated, particularly if others promise and don't deliver. Cancer, Virgo, and Pisces: your typical caution serves you ill. Live a little!

New Moon in Aquarius, February 15

Thoughtful and innovative Aquarius finds us desirous of new ideas and new company. Are you feeling like you want to follow a trend? Or that you need apparel in the hottest new color and pattern? A touch of "attention-deficit" will accompany this New Moon for some, so if you are feeling scattered, you are in tune with the moon. However, Jupiter is at odds with Luna, so "over-doing it" comes easily for Taurus, Leo, Scorpio, and Virgo. Libra, Aquarius, Gemini, and Pisces: innovation is healing; routine will stifle you. Capricorn, Aries, Sagittarius, and Cancer: listen to that little voice that says you need to speak up for others.

Full Moon in Virgo, March 1

The Worm Moon. "Spring cleaning" is a process, and this Virgo moon will be helpful for reviewing a collection (of items to be discarded) as well as a health overhaul. However, with Mars at odds with this moon, some folks may be "looking for a fight," such as Aries, Leo, Sagittarius, Gemini, and Pisces. Taking the initiative will be rewarding for Taurus, Virgo, Libra, Scorpio, and Capricorn. And Aries and Aquarius may find "plotting and planning" enormously rewarding, particularly as far as the next step on your career is concerned.

New Moon in Pisces, March 17

As the spring equinox nears, a desire for renewal captivates, particularly for people in their late 20s and late 50s (those having a Saturn return). This Pisces moon is in sync with Jupiter, the planet of expansion, as it moves through Scorpio. Caring for others is key, particularly for those who may have emotional or mental difficulties. Compassion will come easily for Pisces, Aries,

2017 © Denis Rozhnovsky Image from BigStockPhoto.com

Scorpio, and Cancer. Gemini, Virgo, and Sagittarius may not "get" what people are saying to them—particularly loved ones who may rely on shorthand to send a message. Libra, Aquarius, Leo, Taurus, and Capricorn: stick to your guns and don't be persuaded otherwise.

Full Moon in Libra, March 31

The second Blue Moon in the year. Now that Mercury is retrograde (since March 23 and until April 14), meetings and communication will be compromised. What you're hearing isn't the whole story, but Libra can help people find a common ground because the lunar emphasis is on partnership and harmony. However, with Venus in Aries, at odds with Saturn in Capricorn, finding the limits of love could follow. Capricorn, Aries, Cancer, and Taurus could be emotional, or needlessly stubborn, while Libra, Aquarius, Scorpio, and Gemini look for alternatives (changing direction at the Full Moon is A-OK!).

New Moon in Aries, April 15

Bring on new people, methods, and ways of thinking, because the old ways of conducting business don't cut it. If you perceive stagnation in your worklife, seek out those who innovate (except where taxes are concerned in the US—consistency is your key to filing correctly and on time!). Mars and Saturn (taking action and restrictions) are conjunct in Capricorn, which slows forward momentum, particularly for Libra, Capricorn, Scorpio, and Cancer. Aries, Leo, Sagittarius, Gemini, and Taurus are willing to build something new, while Virgo, Aquarius, and Pisces could be surprised if others find fault with them.

Full Moon in Scorpio, April 29

The Pink Moon may seem to be a time of clarity, but the Scorpio moon brews complexity, particularly in situations involving sexual relationships and identity. Emotions run high, thanks to Jupiter shadowing the moon in Scorpio. And creditors could be on the hunt, so if you've been robbing Peter to pay Paul (so to speak), the buck might stop here. However, this Full Moon is fantastic for sensual excess, deep healing, and intrigue.

Anything hidden emerges with a flourish, which may be welcomed by Aries, Leo, Sagittarius, Libra, Aquarius, and Gemini. Scorpio, Cancer, and Pisces will assume situations are more complicated than they appear, while Taurus, Virgo, and Capricorn may be surprised by others' emotionality.

New Moon in Taurus, May 15

The garden beckons—as does friendship among mentors and students. This Taurus moon is all about improving your immediate environment, which could mean new curtains and decorating accents. And with Saturn in Capricorn accenting the moon, home investments will pay off. But don't overlook amusement. Do you have a favorite band or singer? Buy tickets to a concert if you can. Putting exciting events on the calendar keeps you looking forward, regardless of what roving planets have in store. Taurus, Virgo, Capricorn, and Gemini: take financial matters seriously. Leo, Aquarius, Scorpio, and Sagittarius: stubbornness doesn't become you. If others set limits, respect them. Libra, Aries, Pisces, and Cancer: don't skimp on luxury.

Full Moon in Sagittarius, May 29

The Flower Moon, which sounds more delicate and decorative than Sagittarius themes usually are—such as taking risks and speaking up for the underdog. If you ride a bike or like to hike, get your tools ready to hit the road if you didn't during Memorial Day weekend. Mars in Aquarius could make you curious to upgrade your running shoes or gym membership. This moon may also bring out the rush-rush-rush impulse of us all. Ask yourself—if you hurry, will it make a difference? Sagittarius, Leo, Aries, and Aquarius have no patience for details (which may matter less than you think). Virgo, Pisces, Gemini, Taurus, and Cancer: your accommodating side resists if others try to control you. Libra, Scorpio, and Capricorn: righteousness comes easily.

New Moon in Gemini, June 13

The Twins—like the Scales—encourage us to see "both sides now," and hold seemingly contradictory thoughts simultaneously. This means that if you're considering changing your home, you may not be able to arrive at a clear decision regarding aesthetics. With Mars in curious Aquarius, syncing up with the moon, everyone's maternal (or nurturing) instinct comes to the fore. Novelty is a solace for Gemini, Aquarius, Libra, and Cancer. Virgo, Pisces, Sagittarius, Scorpio, and Capricorn could be indecisive and made very uncomfortable about being pressed to commit. Aries, Taurus, and Leo could surprise themselves by being fierce about a situation that hadn't mattered just a few days before.

Full Moon in Capricorn, June 28

The sweet Strawberry Moon brings us back to the practical things of life. Capricorn encourages us to move slowly and steadily—no matter what deadlines are looming. Make time for folks who are more difficult, or who don't have the "friend-making" personality in full gear. With Saturn also in Capricorn, a feeling of constraint or disappointment could be present in the form of altered status. If this is your story, stick with Capricorn, Taurus, Virgo, and Aquarius, who can see the big picture. Libra, Aries, Cancer, and Leo: don't poke the bear. Sagittarius, Gemini, Scorpio, and Pisces: commitment isn't a bad move right now. Think about settling in rather than bailing out.

New Moon in Cancer, July 12

Water, water everywhere, and this moon brings out everyone's desire to immerse themselves in a warm bath, whether it be fresh or salt water. Fishing and planting are recommended. Look for opportunities to build something in or around your home to make you feel more secure. (And Mars in innovative Aquarius will support your desire for new technology.) Remember that Cancer moons can bring out a defensive side, so if folks around you are grumpy, try to give them space (Cancer favors the "sideways shuffle" so people aren't moving in a direct line). Aries, Libra, Capricorn, Sagittarius, and Aquarius: you could be impatient with others moving more slowly than you. Cancer, Scorpio, Pisces, and Leo: emotions run high, but so do insights. Taurus, Virgo and Gemini: comfort triumphs over style

Full Moon in Aquarius, July 27

The Buck Moon references deer, but Aquarius is all about "bucking" tradition and the status quo, a trend that's amplified since Mars in Aquarius is adding fuel to the fire. This Full Moon draws out everyone's desire for freedom. If you haven't scheduled a getaway, the urge to escape will be overwhelming. With Mars harmonizing with the moon in Aquarius, crazy new ideas will bubble over for some, and tolerance for eccentricity will mark you as someone to listen to. Aquarius, Libra, Gemini, and Pisces: honesty counts, particularly if you've been on the fence with some matter. Taurus, Leo, Scorpio, and Virgo: are you feeling contrary? You're in tune with the moon. Aries, Sagittarius, Capricorn, and Gemini: don't hesitate to chase a trend right now.

New Moon in Leo, August 11

This moon will encourage childlike wonder in some—tantrums in others. With Mars moving through couple-crazy Libra, this moon will favor fresh starts in romance. However, Mercury retrograde means that intent may be obscured for some. Since Leo's energy can bring out the egomaniac hidden in us all, you may find you have more to say about situations than you thought you did. Leo, Sagittarius, Aries, and Virgo could be affectionate, or desirous of non-human company. Taurus, Scorpio, Aquarius, and Pisces: others may be pulling your tail. No need to give the satisfaction of a good yelp. Gemini, Cancer, Libra, and Capricorn: let others sing your praises (yes, you can rehearse them).

Full Moon in Pisces, August 26

The Sturgeon moon means we'll all swim deep, or have feelings that were buried come bubbling to the surface. Thanks to generous Jupiter moving through harmonious Scorpio, the lunar energy could come with a desire to over-indulge (in food, consumerism, or romance). Looking at photographs, or wallowing in nostalgia, particularly since autumn is looming, is a fine occupation for Pisces, Scorpio, Cancer, and Taurus, and even emotionally detached Aquarians and Aries may want to muse on the past. Gemini, Virgo, Leo, and Sagittarius will have difficulty seeing clearly, while Libra and Capricorn could be the repositories of others' confidences.

New Moon in Virgo, September 9

Taking the initiative may not be appealing—Virgo's perfectionist aspects delay all but the most impetuous from quick and decisive action. Emotions may not run high during this lunar phase, but logic will be a refuge for many. Assessing, or analyzing, your current situation (finances, health, dwelling) is a favored activity for all. Cleaning and tidying could be a ritualistic solace for some, particularly Virgo, Capricorn, Taurus, Libra, and Cancer. But with Mars about to move into innovative Aquarius, any curiosity you have about "healthy habits" should be indulged. Leo, Aries, Sagittarius, Pisces, Aquarius, and Gemini will need their voices heard by all.

Full Moon in Aries, September 24

Shine on, Harvest Moon. Everything accelerates, including the hot tempers of those inclined to be a touch rumbustious. Aries moons are excellent for fresh starts. If you began a project around the September 9 New Moon (or even around the summer solstice), you'll be able to take your ideas to the next level. Streamlining a project or a method of communication can also come easily, particularly for Aries, Leo, Sagittarius, Aquarius, and Gemini. Capricorn, Virgo, Scorpio, Libra, and Cancer: beware of getting irritated by trifles, or careless comments. Taurus and Pisces: use this period to get out of your own way!

New Moon in Libra, October 8

Authority figures could rankle for some this New Moon, and solace might be found in the pursuit of self-improvement (beauty treatments, delicacies on china plates). Mars in Aquarius does a do-si-do with the moon, and helps some of the shyer folks to speak up for themselves. Libra, Aquarius, and Gemini: your sociable side is in full gear, as is your sense of purpose. Be decisive and don't look back. Capricorn, Cancer, Aries, Taurus, and Pisces: you may be influenced by others whom you wouldn't usu-

2017 © rasica Image from BigStockPhoto.com

ally heed. Why is that? Leo, Virgo, Scorpio, and Sagittarius: keep your head down as mavericks may be punished.

Full Moon in Taurus, October 24

Tradition calls this the Hunter's Moon, but since only a small percentage of folks are stocking their larders by felling their meals, you may be more inspired to indulge in situational shopaholism. Taurus moons bring out the urge to acquire, and with Jupiter in Taurus waltzing with the moon, a spirit of generosity pervades all. Patience is a virtue for Taurus, Virgo, and Capricorn, but could frustrate Leo, Libra, Sagittarius, Scorpio, and Aquarius (who will be leaps ahead of others during this phase). Gemini, Pisces, Cancer, and Aries: have faith that wheels are turning in your favor.

New Moon in Scorpio, November 7

This moon brings deep feelings, dark secrets, and romantic fantasy. Which all have their positive points, but with Mars in freedom-loving Aquarius, it's a combustible situation for couples in the "opposites attract" category. Scorpio moons stir up drama, particularly for Taurus, Leo, Gemini, and Aquarius (who may be attracted to The Wrong Person today). Scorpio, Cancer, Pisces, and Sagittarius: as much as you rely on a team, look at yourself as the team leader who may need to go it alone. Libra, Gemini, Leo, and Aries: you'll have strong and passionate insights about others. Trust your instincts.

Full Moon in Gemini, November 23

The Beavers Moon is actually a time when people can talk more than usual—which could be a gut-response to nervousness. Jupiter, the planet of expansion and taking chances, is opposing the moon, so it's not a "lucky" time for folks who usually rely on chance as much as planning. However, for those who want to take the time for precision, measurement, and analysis, now is the time to take action. Gemini, Aquarius, Libra, Leo, Sagittarius, and Aries: you may find you're moving faster than you intended, and the multitasking that came so easily accelerates during this Full Moon. Taurus, Virgo, Capricorn, Cancer, Scorpio, and Pisces: you may be craving emotional depth and resonance that others don't have.

New Moon in Sagittarius, December 7

The sign of the archer favors those in the military, so take a moment to honor our fallen soldiers at Pearl Harbor. And if you have the urge to get away (like I do!) you should pat yourself on the back for being absolutely in the lunar groove. Reassessing an education project is also smart, particularly for Sagittarius, Capricorn, Leo, and Aries. Pisces, Gemini, Virgo, and Cancer: if others seem skittish, don't take it personally. Libra, Aquarius, Taurus, and Scorpio: finding the humor in a situation will salvage your self-esteem, and the wise ones among you will not take yourselves too seriously.

Full Moon in Cancer, December 22

Traditionally, this is the Cold Moon, but Cancer can bring out the warm and protective side of everyone. However, this moon might also make you feel exposed and behaving uncharacteristically. (Suddenly the most outgoing extrovert at the party turns into a wallflower.) Domestic wizards make miracles happen and if you've been waiting for the mood to bake for the holiday to strike, today's the day. Venus in Scorpio, Mars in Pisces makes a trifecta in super sensitive water signs with the moon (this is called a "grand trine," and means "no holds barred" in terms of true feelings). Scorpio, Pisces, and Cancer: your insights and affection for others will fill your heart with joy—if you allow. Capricorn, Libra, Aries, Aquarius, and Sagittarius: be aware of your defenses being higher than you think. Leo, Gemini, and Taurus: is someone you love needy? Be alert and respond.

About the Author
Sally Cragin is the author of The Astrological Elements *and* Astrology on the Cusp *(both Llewellyn Worldwide). These books have been translated and sold in a number of countries overseas. She does readings (astrological and tarot). Visit "Sally Cragin Astrology" on Facebook or email sallycragin@verizon.net*

2018
Moon Sign Book
Articles

2017 © Darios Image from BigStockPhoto.com

What's the Buzz? Honey and the Use of Backyard Apiaries

by Mireille Blacke, MA, RD, CD-N

For some, the topic of honeybees provokes lighthearted memories of Winnie the Pooh and his beloved honey pot. For others, the mere suggestion conjures images of nightmarish swarms worthy of assembling the Avengers.

In general, honeybees don't cross my mind often. In my career as a registered dietitian I may educate and counsel patients about honey on occasion, particularly when it comes to weight management and certain medical conditions (like diabetes). But recently an unexpected opportunity to manage my own backyard beehive presented itself.

Arborists I'd hired to prune my sky-high white oaks asked me to house an established beehive from a beekeeper friend of theirs in my backyard. This was a curious prospect to me. Why would someone offer me a beehive? Because I had no idea what would be involved in backyard beekeeping, I decided to investigate further. Would there be any benefit to maintaining a backyard beehive, an apiary? What are the challenges of creating and managing an apiary of your own? Why would you want to do such a thing? Isn't it easier just to buy a plastic honey bear at the local supermarket like most people?

Bees are pollinators, and without them most of the foods you enjoy from your garden or grocery store would vanish. In fact, bees are directly or indirectly involved in producing approximately ninety commercial crops in North America and over a third of foods produced globally. Bees pollinate fruits, vegetables, seeds, and nuts, including almonds, apples, blueberries, broccoli, grapes, olives, peaches, pumpkins, strawberries, sunflowers, and watermelon. Milk-producing cows graze on plants pollinated by bees and dairy products are the result; other by-products of pollination include lemonade, tofu (made from soybeans), and guacamole. In addition, it is clear that pollinators like bees greatly impact our economy and produce supply; in the United States alone, honeybees pollinate an estimated $15 billion in crops annually.

Since 2006, a drastic decline in bee colonies has been observed, posing a threat to our economy, produce supply, and global agriculture. This threat to the bee population has been named colony collapse disorder, which results in the disappearance of adult honeybees from the hive and the abandoning of the queen and immature bees. Specific causes of colony collapse disorder have not been determined, but contributing stressors appear to be lack of habitat, use of pesticides, parasites (such as varroa mites), and viruses.

One attempt to recover from colony losses is for beekeepers to split their hives. This is one reason to take an established beehive from another beekeeper's property. Other potential reasons to split beehives include increased hive production, decreased risk of swarming, and reduced risk of mites.

After consulting with local beekeepers and researching the topic of backyard beekeeping online, it seemed that the consensus was:

1. Backyard beekeeping takes about as much time as traditional gardening. If a person was capable of regular gardening, he or she was capable of maintaining a backyard apiary.

2. Backyard beekeeping benefits your other plants, vegetables, and flowers: crops up to four miles away may be pollinated by one hive.

3. This effort would help the pollinator crisis and the local ecology.

4. I could learn a new skill or hobby.

5. Depending on your efforts, you might expect three to four gallons of honey after the second year of beekeeping. In some cases, a backyard beekeeper might see fifty pounds of honey per hive.

Given this information, the effort to become a backyard beekeeper seemed worth considering. I was informed that an experienced apiarist (beekeeper) would handle the beehive for me, manage the bees, and collect the honey for me. Being somewhat cynical, I wanted to research the subject even further and learn the specifics of what was involved in maintaining a backyard apiary in the event that this beekeeper changed his mind, didn't show up, or fell off the face of the earth and these responsibilities became mine. What then? Could I still handle the challenges as well as reap the rewards?

Apiarists, Assemble!

There are a number of basic issues to address when first considering if backyard beekeeping is appropriate for you. Assess the size of your backyard; a tenth of an acre is usually enough to accommodate one bee colony. However, if you have no access to a nearby open water source, you must provide the bees with water (a tub or birdbath will do) within forty feet of the hive in order to prevent them from seeking water from your neighbors. Ideally, the hives will be placed in a location where they will be mostly undisturbed, with warmth from the morning sun and an open flight path. Check your zoning regulations and local ordinances as some towns and cities prohibit backyard beekeeping or impose strict regulations (for example, distance from a neighbor's dwelling) and uphold generalized nuisance laws.

Are you or anyone you live with allergic to bee stings? If you are uncertain, consult a physician. Consider your pets as well. Also assess how your family, children, or those who live with you might feel about having a beehive in such close proximity.

Neighbors represent another challenge. Will your hives be out in the open? Depending on the color and style of the hive, this might be an eyesore to some neighbors or a lure to mischievous neighborhood children. Installing a sight-barrier (tall screen, hedge of plants, evergreens) or placing the hive behind a garage or out of sight may solve this problem. Bribing the neighbor with honey might not hurt either.

Gear

Recommendations vary on the basic beekeeping equipment you'll need to get started. All-inclusive prebuilt kits for new apiarists are available. Precut hive and frame components are also available for easy assembly with glue and nails, or you can build your own hive boxes inexpensively using directions found in books or online (see References). Regardless of how you choose to acquire them, you will need boxes (the hives) and frames with beeswax foundations. In addition, you will need a bee suit or other protective clothing, the bees, and a stainless steel smoker. Additional supplies may include a hive tool, 2 × 4 cement blocks, exterior latex paint or natural stain, or outdoor wood glue. I will expand upon each of these.

Note: Though you may find deals on used equipment, never buy secondhand hive and frame components, as you risk disease or mite infestation.

Safety First

When working with bees, particularly at first, you will need to purchase protective gear. Most beekeepers recommend at minimum a combination of a simple hat and veil. Depending on comfort level, a full bee suit may be more appropriate, especially for beginning beekeepers who feel uncomfortable working with bees. The full protective outfit usually includes a zipper veil bee suit and helmet, gloves, and boot bands. If you're more comfortable and confident, a lightweight jacket with an attached veil and gloves is another option.

When assembling the boxes that will house your bees, keep in mind how bees naturally form a hive. Those of us new to beekeeping may not be familiar with the construction of the natural nests of honeybees. Generally, within the beehive the honey will be stored near the top and the outside, acting as a layer of protection; pollen is stored below the honey to nourish the hive's inhabitants; eggs are laid and young are raised in the lowest, most protected area of the nest. All of this may occur within two to three cubic feet. Your backyard apiary should fit the needs of the honeybees in a similar fashion.

I refer you to Kim Flottum's *The Backyard Beekeeper* for greater detail on the natural nests and specific inner layouts of backyard apiaries, as there are numerous possibilities. In general, your

2017 © Kzenon Image from BigStockPhoto.com

bees will be living on beeswax sheets that hang vertically inside the boxes you select as their home. Each sheet of beeswax is surrounded by a wooden (or plastic) frame; the outside of each frame provides a small "bee space" that allows bees to move around inside the hive. Boxes may be deep, medium, or shallow, and vary accordingly in terms of number of frames of beeswax (and therefore bees and honey) they hold. Beekeepers often select box size based on weight; choose an amount that you can lift when working with your honeybees. (For example, a medium box when full may hold forty pounds, while a deep box may hold ninety pounds.)

It's wise to use a hive stand to keep your hive off the ground, to act as a deterrent to skunks, other animals, hive beetles, or fire ants. A hive stand can be constructed easily and inexpensively with 2 × 4 cement blocks to sit approximately 18 inches off the ground.

Boxes are traditionally painted white because lighter colors prevent overheating in summer months. However, keeping in mind that white might not fit your aesthetic or that of your neighborhood, know that backyard beekeepers also use natural, brown, green, and other colors for their apiaries. Just be sure not to use an old lead-based paint.

A necessity for the backyard beekeeper is the smoker, which is a cylinder with a bellows attached. The smoker is often stainless steel and sends smoke wafting into the hive. The smoker's purpose is to disrupt the communication of the bees, which results in you (as the beekeeper) being left alone to work.

I will quickly mention the "hive tool" here, because I have seen it referenced as an instrument used for a variety of purposes, from scraping to opening. Since hive tools vary by price, use, and size, it is difficult to recommend one to fit everyone's needs. Furthermore, since common household tools (like a screwdriver) may suffice for the beginning beekeeper, I will not add this item to the expenses for those readers who are still undecided about back-

2017 © Darios Image from BigStockPhoto.com

yard apiaries. It is (seemingly) possible to have a backyard apiary without a hive tool.

The same cannot be said about your bees. You will (obviously) need bees for your hive, and there is no way around that. But it's not like you can make a quick trip to Walmart to acquire them. When it comes to bees that are appropriate and readily available for beginning beekeepers, there are primarily three types from which to choose and several ways to obtain them. The Italian type is the most common; if you like your bees yellow, these are for you. This type is productive and considered easy to manage. By contrast, the Carniolan type is more demanding to manage and darker, but they handle harsh winters better than Italians. The Russian type is regarded as complicated to manage, but resistant to parasitic varroa mites; they appear in yellow and dark colors.

For one hive, you will need three pounds of bees, including an egg-laying queen; this translates to roughly 12,000 bees! The cost for this amount of bees runs from $55 to $80, plus shipping charges, which may be substantial. Though the concept of receiving a "package" of bees in the mail may seem strange, acquiring bees via a mail order supplier is common. Check your local beekeeping association and beekeeping journals because they will have information about local suppliers of equipment and bees. Using a local or regional supplier should save you some money on shipping charges.

Experienced apiarists may add new bees by taking in swarms (groups of worker bees that leave an existing colony with their queen to create a new one). People interested in collecting swarms may alert the local police, exterminators, and fire departments to have their names added to the appropriate lists of beekeepers.

As you might expect, seasonal timing is important with backyard beekeeping. The ideal time to set up a new hive is after the last hard freeze of spring; therefore you'll want to have your honeybees delivered by then. No matter the season, continue to do your research: there are many informative books, journals, and online resources available on backyard beekeeping to increase your working knowledge of honeybee behavior and hive organization. In addition, you might find a local beekeeper to mentor and guide you through your first season; check with your local beekeeping association for suggestions, a beekeeping course recommendation, or find a beekeeping club at "Bee Culture."

In my case, an experienced apiarist planned on handling my hive and honey extraction. For specifics on how to collect honey from an active hive, I again refer you to Kim Flottum's *The Backyard Beekeeper* or "Bee Culture" online. It will be necessary to check your hive to monitor progress, feed the bees, and harvest honey in late summer. This process may be initially intimidating, which is why having a local beekeeper mentor is a common practice for many beginning beekeepers. Wearing the full bee suit and using the smoker to calm the bees' alarm response is particularly helpful in the beginning stages of this beekeeping process.

Effort is required to keep the beehive healthy and flourishing. Some experienced beekeepers note that you should make an effort to "bond" with your bees from the beginning. In the hive's first year, the majority of the honey is left for the bees, so you should not expect to harvest a significant amount of honey until the second year of beekeeping. Some beekeepers recommend replacing the queen every August to increase productivity.

Experienced beekeepers will generally explain that the behavior of honeybees is extremely organized and fascinating. If you have the opportunity to watch worker bees in a hive, intensely guarding their queen and laboring diligently over the honeycomb, several things become obvious. The honey-making process from floral nectar to shimmering elixir is an arduous one, where the lifelong effort of one bee results in a mere 1/12 teaspoon of honey. Teamwork is clearly the status quo of the hive, and honey is only one precious result. You may come away with an unexpected appreciation for these tiny creatures that perform so intently and industriously.

Ultimately, you may have decided that your beekeeping confidence level is lacking (even with a full suit), that you don't have the money required to invest in such an endeavor (though you find it worthy), or you just don't have the time to care for and maintain a beehive. You can still help the bees and improve pollinator health!

Here are some possibilities:

1. Grow more bee-friendly flowers to attract more bees. Popular choices include apple (including crab apple) trees, butterfly bush (one of my favorites), foxglove, globe thistle, heather, hollyhock, iris, lavender, marjoram, mint, snapdragon, sunflower, and wisteria.

2. Consider native bees to help pollinate your plants. While they won't generate honey, they also don't require hive care and are hardy and found in most locations.

3. Install a Mason bee house (available on Amazon). Mason bees are excellent pollinators; they are also efficient and cold-hardy. Add this bee house to a shady area of your garden or backyard and these native bees are sure to find it.

4. If you already have a birdbath on your property, add a rock or stone to it to create a landing to encourage bees to take a drink.

5. Hate to mow the lawn? Great! Let the wildflowers and weeds (clover, dandelions, etc.) flourish and attract pollinators.

In my case, I was familiar with the importance of bees as pollinators after researching the needs of my finicky stone fruit trees (as noted in the *2017 Moon Sign Book*). In general, I am happy to have learned a new, practical skill and increase efforts to help the environment. Also, I'm certainly not against adding a mini-honey factory to my own backyard. However, my own inexperience with bee-wrangling as well as lack of time to potentially maintain the hive and gather the honey if necessary made this endeavor unrealistic for me and unfair to the bees. Still, I was able to increase the number of native bees to my yard using many of the tips listed above. I remain grateful for the lush, tall hedge of butterfly bushes that spring up every summer to attract various pollinators; this year I was watching for them even more closely.

It's encouraging that all of us can contribute to increasing the dropping numbers of pollinators, even if we're allergic to bees or unable to don a full beekeeper suit and maintain our own backyard apiary. It's not like our combined efforts will create swarms of unstoppable bees or anything.

If so, it can't be that tough to assemble the Avengers.

Additional Resources:

American Bee Journal: http://americanbeejournal.com/

American Beekeeping Federation: www.abfnet.org/

"Bee Culture"—the Magazine of American Beekeeping: www.beeculture.com/category/beekeeping/

Beethinking—Beekeeping Simplified: www.beethinking.com

Local Beekeepers: www.beeculture.com/find-local-beekeeper/

The Honey Board: www.honey.com

Refrences

Blacke, Mireille. "Stirring the Pot." *OKRA Magazine*. October 1, 2013. http://okramagazine.org/2013/10/01/stirring-the-pot-honey-and-health/.

"The Best Garden Flowers for Bees." University of Sussex. www.sussex.ac.uk/lifesci/goulsonlab/resources/flowers.

Yoest, Helen. *Plants with Benefits*. Pittsburgh: St. Lynn's Press, 2014.

Cargel RA, and Rinderer TE. "USDA Honey Bee Breeding, Genetics and Physiology Laboratory." www.ars.usda.gov/SP2UserFiles

/Place/64133000/PDFFiles/401-500/462-Cargel--Effects%20 of%20Varroa.pdf. Published February 2009.

"Colony Loss 2014–2105." *Bee Informed website.* May 13, 2015. http:// beeinformed.org/2015/05/colony-loss-2014-2015-preliminary -results/.

"Fact Sheet: The Economic Challenge Posed by Declining Pollinator Populations." June 20, 2014. www.whitehouse.gov/the-press-office /2014/06/20/fact-sheet-economic-challenge-posed-declining -pollinator-populations.

Flottum, Kim. *The Backyard Beekeeper,* 3rd edition. Beverly, MA: Quarry Books, 2014.

Goulson D, Nicholls E, Botías C, Rotheray EL. "Bee Declines Driven by Combined Stress from Parasites, Pesticides, and Lack of Flowers." *Science.* 2015; 347 (6229): 1255957.

"Honey Bee Health and Colony Collapse Disorder." *United States Department of Agriculture.* www.ars.usda.gov/News/docs.htm?docid =15572.

Jones, Richard and Sweeney-Lynch, Sharon. *The Beekeeper's Bible.* New York: Abrams Publishing, 2011.

A picnic without bees. Earthjustice website. http://earthjustice.org/fea-tures/infographic-bees-toxic-problem

Proceedings of the American Bee Research Council 2010. August 13, 2013. www.extension.org/pages/30792/abrc2010-effects-of -varroa-mites-and-bee-diseases-on-pollination-efficacy-of-honey -bees#.VX89HPlViko.

Sammataro, Diana and Avitabile, Alphonse. *The Beekeeper's Handbook.* 4th ed. New York: Comstock Publishing, 2011.

"Report on the National Stakeholders Conference on Honey Bee Health" *United States Department of Agriculture.* May 2, 2013. www.usda.gov/documents/ReportHoneyBeeHealth.pdf.

"Vanishing Bees." *Natural Resources Defense Council.* July 25, 2008. www.nrdc.org/wildlife/animals/bees.asp.

Yeager, David. "Protecting Bee Populations." *Today's Dietitian.* 2015 August; 17 (8): 44–47.

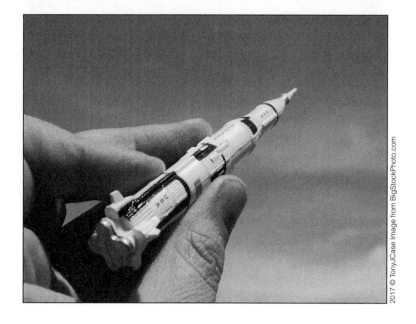

2017 © TonyJCase Image from BigStockPhoto.com

Man on the Moon:
Discovery and Politics

by Bruce Scofield

With all land masses on Earth now occupied, that relentlessly expansive and most clever animal *Homo sapiens* has nowhere to go except up into space—and the first stop on that challenging journey is the Moon. Centuries of speculation about getting to the Moon ended in 1959 when rockets reached Earth's lone but massive satellite. The Soviet Union got there first in January with a flyby, and two months later the United States did the same thing. Later that year a Soviet Union rocket impacted the lunar surface and then a real probe, Luna 3, took pictures of the far side of the Moon, the side that no human had ever seen before.

The space race, which began with the launching of satellites, became focused on the Moon. In the following years many more flyby and impact missions were launched by Soviet Union and the United States, but it wasn't until 1966 that a real soft landing took place. Again, the Soviet Union was there first, followed a few months later by the US.

The Space Race

The Soviet Union's Luna 9 spacecraft landed on the Moon on the last day of January 1966. It was thought that the lunar surface was a very fine dust and that a probe would sink—but it didn't. Luna 9 was small, basically two feet across and weighing about 200 pounds, with a camera and radio for transmission that ran on batteries. It looked a lot like Sputnik, the Soviet Union's first satellite. Before the batteries died a week later, it had sent back to Earth the first panoramic pictures of the lunar surface. Close on Luna 9's heels was Surveyor I sent by the United States. It was the first of several like it that tested the technology for lunar landings, which included reverse thrust rockets and communication technology. Surveyor I was weird looking—a tripod of tubes with a stem holding solar panels that reached up almost ten feet. It sent back thousands of photos for more than a month before something went wrong with the electronics and it shut down. These two landers kept Soviet Union and the US in a tight competition in space race, with no other country in sight.

More and more shots at the Moon were taken by Soviet Union and the United States in the next couple years—but then in December of 1968 the United States sent a manned mission, Apollo 8, into lunar orbit. This wasn't a scientific mission, per se, it was a test of rocket and communications systems and a bold attempt to take the lead in the space race. During the 10 orbits around the Moon, astronauts Borman, Lovell, and Anders took photos of the lunar surface, including one showing the distant blue Earth rising over barren surface of the Moon in the fore-ground. This photo, taken by Anders and named "Earthrise," has turned out to be probably the most iconic of the many photos taken on the Apollo missions, one of the most popular space photos of all time, and a rallying symbol for the new environmental movement.

Man on the Moon

In July 1969, Apollo 11, with crew Armstrong, Collins, and Aldrin, landed on the Moon. For all intents and purposes, this was the event that won the space race for the United States. Boots on the ground is as good as it gets and, as if to rub it in, six more Apollo crews went to the Moon, all landing except the aborted mission of Apollo 13, which only flew around the Moon. The last mission, Apollo 17, was in December of 1972 and with it the era of manned trips to the Moon was over.

There is no question that a lot was learned about the Moon on these missions. Astronauts drove lunar vehicles around the sur-

2017 © kjwarden Image from BigStockPhoto.com

face, hit golf balls, made all kinds of scientific measurements, and studied the lunar surface. The missions, one of which included a geologist, also brought 842 pounds of lunar rocks and surface material back to Earth which are still being studied. Why the Apollo missions ended was in part due to funding—the Nixon administration was at the time cutting spending—and part due to NASA's own questions about the value of the program and conflicts with other things the agency wanted to do. Another factor was that once the public got over the first landing, the others, which were mostly scientific expeditions, became less and less interesting. For many Americans, the reason for the landing in the first place was to beat the Soviet Union. It was part of the Cold War. And we won. And with weakening public support for more Moon missions came weakening political support. The vast majority of politicians don't understand science, but they do understand public sentiments, and so there was little incentive to keep the Apollo program going.

No human has gone to the Moon since 1972, and since then human space activity has shifted to space stations in low Earth orbit. Beginning in 1971, the Soviet Union put up a series of single section Salyut space stations and then the modular multipiece Mir space station in 1986. The United States put up Skylab, a large single piece station, and used it between 1973 and 1979. With the Cold War over in 1991, Russia (no longer the Soviet Union) and the United States, the two countries that had the know-how and the rockets, were joined by other countries that contributed funds, engineers, and scientists to jointly build a modular orbiting habitation to serve as a testing ground for life in space and a laboratory for all kinds of scientific research. The project got going in 1998 when the first pieces of the International Space Station (ISS) were launched to an orbit 250 miles or so above the Earth's atmosphere, just one thousandth the distance to the Moon. The ISS has been spectacularly successful and makes news regularly with its international cast of astronauts making space walks, doing experiments, and managing the payloads coming and going that now include those launched by private corporations, not just national space agencies. The 2013 Hollywood film *Gravity* is a tale of a bad day in the lives of ISS astronauts. So it seems like humanity has achieved peace in space through international cooperation on a space station while the Moon as a goal has faded and attention becomes focused on a manned mission to Mars.

Lunar Real Estate

But meanwhile some people haven't forgotten about the Moon. In spite of the fact that an Outer Space Treaty, sponsored by the United Nations in 1967, declared space and everything in to be an international commons and the province of all of humanity, and the International Moon Treaty of 1984 prohibited private ownership of real estate on the Moon, a number of individuals have made outlandish claims of lunar ownership. At least one has gone as far as to sell lunar lots to people willing to pay. Possibly inspired by science fiction writer Robert A. Heinlein's book *The Man Who Sold the Moon*, or maybe just the unstoppable cleverness and greed of some members of our species, lots on the Moon are for sale. You can buy one acre for about $50, or a VIP special of about $125 for 10 acres. And if you don't want to buy lunar lots, you can also buy land on Venus or Mars. What? This is the business of Dennis Hope, who claims to have signed a deal with the United Nations, the United States, and the Soviet Union in 1980 that gave him the rights to sell lunar land. He runs the Lunar Embassy Commission, claims to have sold millions of acres, and claims that he sold two US presidents—Reagan and Carter—lunar real estate. He has at least two websites selling extraterrestrial real estate—Moonestates.com and Lunarembassy.com—both well worth perusing.

2017 © ArchMan Image from BigStockPhoto.com

Modern Politics

While real estate on the Moon was being sold to suckers and people with money to burn for a novelty, the US Space Shuttle program moved astronauts back and forth to orbiting space stations from 1981 to 2011. As the program was winding down and with the Space Shuttle *Columbia* disaster having just happened, President George W. Bush, born under Cancer, the sign of the Moon, proposed in 2004 a return there to establish a base for space missions—basically a plan for an extended human presence. The base would allow people to live and work there and mine raw materials that might be used as fuel or to produce oxygen. Bush's new National Space Policy, which was a bit more territorial and stated the right of the United States to deny access to space to those hostile to US interests, also promoted American preeminence in space and commercial interests. Some thought this policy violated the Outer Space Treaty. At the center of Bush's agenda was the Constellation Program, a human spaceflight program that had the goal of a manned mission to the Moon in 2020. After review by the Obama administration, most of the Constellation Program was declared to be over budget and behind schedule, and so it was canceled during a time of extreme budget cuts. So the Moon was on US radar for a few years, but then it was turned off again.

And meanwhile the China National Space Administration, which got off the ground decades after all the Russian and US missions, was turning its attention to the Moon. The Chinese Lunar Explorer Program launched a lunar orbiter in 2007 and then another in 2010. By 2013 the Chinese had made a soft landing on the Moon. The spacecraft, named Chang'e 3 for the Moon goddess, landed and deployed a lunar rover named Yutu (Jade Rabbit) after the pet rabbit of the Moon goddess. (Interestingly, both the Chinese and the Mesoamericans saw the shape of a rabbit, not a man, etched out by the darker Mare regions of the Moon.) During this successful mission, Chang'e 3 took pictures and Yutu drove around and made some discoveries with its ground-penetrating radar. China has entered space on its own terms and has a powerful booster rocket, the Long March space launch vehicle, which puts it in the same league as Russia. (The United States has been without its own booster for some time and has been relying on the Russian Soyuz rockets to get back and forth to the ISS.) China has also had successful manned orbital missions, has begun its own space station, and has plans for a manned mission to the Moon, probably collaborating with Russia, by 2036. China, which doesn't participate in the ISS, is now a contender for whatever is up for grabs on the Moon.

Private Interests on the Moon

Meanwhile a lot is happening in regard to commercial activities in space. Google has a Lunar XPRIZE in which privately funded teams compete to land a robot on the Moon that travels at least

500 meters on the surface and sends back quality images. As of this writing in 2016 there are 16 teams in competition for the $20 million prize. Another future commercial prospect is lunar tourism, but that awaits reliable transport and a permanent base on the Moon.

There have been a few efforts made for funding private exploration and mining of the Moon, but nothing has come of these so far. The mining of titanium is an incentive, which is apparently abundant on the Moon. The Moon is also rich in rare earth elements (REE), which are today mined in and marketed by China, and this monopoly also motivates private interests to set up lunar mining operations—so it's just a matter of time and money. All of this business is uncharted legal territory, though in some ways similar to Antarctica, which has claims by eight nations but was finally declared a scientific preserve by the Antarctic Treaty of 1959. Another possible motivating element for mining the Moon is helium-3, an isotope of helium that could be used in nuclear fusion reactions. The 2009 sci-fi film *Moon* is about a corporation mining helium-3 on the far side of the Moon and its inhumane cost-cutting procedures.

Clearly the Moon with its minerals could be a big prize. When nations and corporations begin competing for whatever turns out to be worth taking from it, the necessary engineering and technology for a permanent base will become well-funded and progress will accelerate. We're almost there now and it's anybody's guess if international cooperation or commercial greed will become the new normal on the Moon.

About the Author

Bruce Scofield, Ph.D., is an author of numerous books and articles and teaches evolution at the University of Massachusetts and astronomy and astrology for Kepler College. He has an international practice as a consulting astrologer. His interest in Mesoamerican astrology, mythology, and astronomy has a web presence at www .onereed.com.

2017 © TomMisch Image from BigStockPhoto.com

Simple Meditation for Daily Life

by Robin Ivy Payton

Find a quiet place free of distractions and take a comfortable seat or lie down on your back. Close your eyes and see if you can tune in to the rhythm of your heart. If the sound or sensation of your heart is elusive, that's okay. As you reach for the beat of your heart, you're tuning inward. Bring your lips together and draw in air through your nose with this fresh breath. Open your mouth and breathe out until all the air seems to be released. With a closed mouth, breathe in through the nose and exhale through the mouth like this a few more times. Your energy has already shifted. Let your breath grow into long, slow inhales and equally full exhales through the nose, counting to four, five, or six. Feel the chest, rib cage, and stomach naturally expand and contract. As you breathe consciously, continue to search for your heart. Whether you feel the heartbeat or not, scan your body from hands to feet, including the head, neck, legs, arms, and front and back body. Breathing like this, notice any sensations or positions of the body; for example, your hands may be folded or resting on your lap, your feet may be touching the ground, or your heels may be turned in and toes out if you're lying on your back. Aim to relax the body a little bit more with each exhale. See if you can find 5 or 10 percent more ease throughout the body as you move through your mind's eye. Think of nothing other than body and breath. To help you do that, choose a word that's pleasant and free of anything negative. Repeat that word over and over as you breathe beyond your initial body scan. You are meditating.

The practice of meditation is shrouded in mystery, sometimes misunderstood, and often considered unachievable. In modern Western culture, the idea of clearing the mind of thoughts, plans, pressures, and control is foreign and may be daunting. During days and nights consumed by cell phones, texting, emails, and other media and technology of all sorts, it's rare to unplug. Yet, because of constant contact with each other, with news and information, and with work that's now easier to access from home, meditation is more valuable and necessary than ever. The ability to focus inward and find your center on a regular basis is like pressing restart or returning to factory settings. Returning to your routine with a clear mind and relaxed body, you can better solve problems, communicate calmly and clearly, and think creatively. A meditation practice is likely to improve and maintain your mental and physical health as your blood pressure, heart rate, and the tissues, muscles, and organs of your body respond and return to their natural state.

Beginning

Designate spaces and times for meditation and you'll be more inclined to follow through with a regular practice. Rather than deciding meditation is just another thing to add to your to-do list, make it a pleasurable experience free of expectations. You might even think of this as your little secret escape every day. If you're lucky enough to live in a natural environment where there's peace and green space or water, a morning, noon, or late afternoon walk is one way to begin. Choose a time of day when there's a natural break, wake up a bit earlier, or find time before going home or out for the evening. Build in time where you can be alone for half an hour or even less. Bring a cushion or shawl for comfort, and have a seat where you are not likely to be disturbed. If you feel you should keep your eyes open, find a focal point and set your gaze there. This gaze is your drishti, and it can be as simple as the petal of a flower, a knot in the wall, or a mark on the ground in front of you. Choose something unmoving, and

2017 © fizkes Image from BigStockPhoto.com

imagine you can see only that one point in space. Begin breathing in through the nose, with your first few exhales through the mouth to release surface tension. Then settle into a pattern of nostril breathing, matching the length and quality of each inhale and exhale. In this way, you create a steady, full breath and the mind naturally begins to still.

Like anything else, meditative breath can take some practice. Be patient with yourself if extraneous thoughts are hard to avoid at first. Notice what floats into your mind or floods your emotions, say hello and then let it go like a helium balloon on a string. If you prefer, send each thought away on a cloud or the wings of a bird. Rather than attaching to ideas or images that come in during meditation, acknowledge them with a nod and send them on their way. Bring attention to each part of the physical body at first, concentrating on only yourself, the sound of your breath, and the beat of your heart. Choose a word to repeat again and again. With eyes open or closed, seated or on your back, keep a long spine from tailbone to the back of the head. In fact, you could visualize the inhale moving up the spine and the exhale back down. Make your meditation simple and as free from distraction as possible.

Environment

When meditating in an indoor environment, clear any clutter and surround yourself with only items you love. Ideally, your space is for meditation specifically. However, if that's not realistic, do something special to set the intention. For example, light a candle or add pleasing aromatherapy with organic oils or sprays. Peppermint is one of many scents you can incorporate for refreshing energy and centering the mind. Consider including natural crystals, stones, flowers or plants, a bubbling fountain, music or other soothing sounds. Explore what helps you settle into a calm state, and with repetition you'll train yourself to respond to a certain set of circumstances; the setting, the scent, the time of day, and the breath, for example. Meditation, like all things, becomes more familiar and routine over time.

Outdoor meditation is wonderful because you get the additional benefit of connecting with nature. A garden spot, your own or public, provides a variety of focal points for your drishti (gaze). Tune into one flower or tree, and as you breathe, draw in the energy of the plant. Sit with your back against a tree for seated meditation and allow the trunk to absorb any emotional energy you need to dispel. Each exhale represents letting go, and the trees send any negative or useless energy down through the roots and back into the earth. When meditating in the natural world, hear without listening, see without seeking, and feel without trying. Let your senses be receptive rather than active. As your mind and body become quiet, you may notice things you would otherwise overlook. Animals' habits, cycles of life, dormancy and restoration, and patterns of light and dark hold information that's relevant to us as humans too. With your mind in a relaxed state, you can receive signs, solutions or insights without pressure or expectation. Let the earth take care of any judgments, residue from challenging confrontations, and pointless thoughts or impressions from excessive consumption of media. Anything toxic you release in meditation can be transmuted by the elements and returned to a neutral state.

Walking meditation is another alternative to a seated practice. What makes walking a meditation is your attention, completely in the present moment. Begin by focusing on your connection to the earth, the soles of your feet. Breathe conscious breaths as you feel your heels followed by your entire foot touch the ground with each step. As in other meditations, center on your breath and avoid any tendency to attach to emotions or thoughts. Let them come and go without fixating and letting them take you down a different path. Feel and hear your footsteps, the sensations of just walking and breathing. Be present with the wind, sun, rain-

2017 © f9photos Image from BigStockPhoto.com

drops or other elements touching your skin, and be grateful for your senses with each step. This is a simple version of meditation in motion. To add to your walking meditation, practice loving kindness in which you extend positive intention to everything you come in contact with. Send well wishes to passersby, the front door of each home or business, and all beings of the natural environment. You can practice breathing and walking with just one focal point in mind, such as collecting sea glass, shells, or feathers. Walking meditation, though it may seem easy, can be quite challenging because of the many potential disruptions to inner stillness. The mind can stray to daydreams according to the locations, people, or scenes you pass through. People may engage you in conversation. Observe your own tendencies during walking meditation, and refocus as needed. While in a relaxed state of mind, you are more aware and open for wisdom or lessons unexpected encounters bring.

Breathing Techniques

Meditation is withdrawing from other sensory input and thought by centering on breath. Diaphragmatic breath, in and out the nose to expand the belly, rib cage, and chest, is just one of many breathing techniques to explore. Alternate nostril breath, also known as nadi shodhana, is practiced to clear blocked energy and balance the mind. Begin or end meditation with about nine cycles of nadi shodhana, and as it comes more easily you can use this to help you fall asleep or neutralize emotion during stressful circumstances. This breathwork can be done seated or lying down.

Start by taking your right index and middle finger to the space between your eyebrows. Your thumb will land at your right nostril and your ring finger at your left. Inhale through the nose, close the right nostril by pressing your thumb to it, and exhale a slightly longer breath through only the left side. Follow up with an inhale through the left, then close the left nostril with the ring finger and exhale slowly through the right nostril. Keeping the left side closed off, inhale through the right nostril, then close it with the thumb press and exhale through the left. Continue with long exhales followed by an inhale on the same side, close that nostril, and exhale and inhale on the other side. Take smooth, steady breaths with no forcefulness and without using the mouth.

Nadi shodhana is reputed to be safe for most people, even during pregnancy. With practice, you will be able to move the breath from left to right without using your fingers at all. As you sit at your work station or relax at home, no one will know you're finding your center with conscious breath.

Candle breath also encourages relaxation. Simply inhale through the nose and softly part the lips to exhale slowly, like a whistle, or as if you were blowing out candles on a birthday cake. There's no need to push the breath out, though. Instead let it come softly. In spring or summer you can practice candle breath with dandelions, feathers, or flowers. Let your smooth exhale blow against the length of a feather or at each petal of a flower. With the gray dandelions, your breath may blow the seeds away. A second variation of candle breath is to let the exhale out so softly that you wouldn't disturb a burning candle flame. For either version, sit tall from the tailbone to the crown of the head to keep energy freely flowing through your breathing channels and the chakras, power centers located from root to crown in the physical and energetic body.

Your body breathes 24/7: while you sleep, when you're irritated, and when you feel joy. Meditation requires no special ability other than willingness to breathe consciously, releasing attachment to thoughts, words, or ideas that cause you pain, anxiety, or concern. By breathing with attention centered, you open more easily to peace, calm, and bliss. As you train yourself to let thoughts pass by without judgment or strain, you decrease the domino effect that stressful thinking causes. Meditation helps you reset, release old patterns of thought, and tune into all that you are blessed with and grateful for. Meditate, and create space for more intuition, pleasure, and ease in your daily life.

About the Author

Robin Ivy Payton teaches yoga and meditation in the Portland, Maine, area and beyond. She blends astrology and yoga with RoZoYo®, tuning the subtle and physical body with the energy of Moon, Sun, and planets. Robin offers horoscopes, yoga, and other insights across various media. She began writing for Llewellyn Publications in 2003. Follow her schedule of events and weekly astrology forecasts at Robin's Zodiac Zone blog, Facebook, Instagram, and www.RoZoYo.com.

2017 © kdshutterman Image from BigStockPhoto.com

Once in a Blue Moon

by Charlie Rainbow Wolf

Once in a Blue Moon." You've probably heard the saying. You may even understand that it means something rare, something that doesn't happen frequently. This phrase was intriguing enough that respected composers Rodgers and Hart wrote a song about it in 1934, which has been covered many times over the years and is still a classic. "Once in a Very Blue Moon" is the title track of Nanci Griffith's third album, released in 1984, and it has also been covered by Dolly Parton, Mary Black, and other noteworthy singers. The mystery around these moons has captivated musicians, poets, writers, and artists over many years. But just what is a Blue Moon? Why is it rare—and does it really change color?

A Blue Moon is an astronomical event, and even though it's quite unusual, it can be roughly predicted. It's all a matter of math. It takes the Moon just over 29 days to go from new to full and back to new again. However, there are more than 29 days in a calendar month—in fact, the word "month" has its origins in the word "Moon." There are exceptions to every rule, and in this instance, the anomaly is February, which usually has only 28 days. The numbers alone mean that sooner or later we're going to get two Full Moons in the same month, although it will never be in February—even taking into account a leap year. The last time the Moon was full on February 29th occurred in 1972—but it was still the only Full Moon that month.

Modern Versus Traditional

There are three types of Blue Moons—and there's a lot of disagreement as to which one is the "true" Blue Moon. The first is a calendar Blue Moon as mentioned above, where there are two Full Moons in the same month. The second of these moons is called the Blue Moon. This is largely based on a misconception printed in the *1947 Maine Farmer's Almanac*. In this article, James H. Pruett talked about the second Full Moon of the month being the Blue Moon, and for some reason, this seemed to gain popularity. As a result, many people today call the second of two Full Moons in a calendar month a blue one.

Looking at it this way, then it's February—being the shortest month of the year—that gets skipped if there are going to be two Full Moons in another month. That also makes it more probable that January or March will catch the extra Moon. The calendar Blue Moon can happen in any month, and the math makes this event more common in the longer, rather than the shorter, months. Calendar Blue Moons occur approximately every two and a half years, but this still doesn't guarantee that the second Full Moon in that month is going to be what is traditionally believed to be a Blue Moon.

These moons aren't always counted as being blue, because the calendar as we know it is a manmade concept. Even if they are noted, the difference in time zones means that one area of the globe might have a Blue Moon, while another one does not. Some people think that these inconsistencies make observing the seasonal Blue Moons a more viable idea.

Seasonal Blue Moons

Prior to 1947, most of the recognized Blue Moons were the seasonal ones. This happens when there are four Full Moons in the same season, and calculating when that occurs is both complicated and confusing. Not every culture or tradition keeps track of time in the same way, so determining exactly when the seasons start and end might be a bit subjective. Even now there are those who believe that the Moon cycle starts when it is full, while others mark the start of the period when the Moon is new.

When observing the seasonal Blue Moons, it's the third Moon

2017 © diomedes66 Image from BigStockPhoto.com

in the quarter that is considered to be blue, not the last one. Many cultures referenced each Moon of the year by a unique name—like "harvest moon," "wolf moon," or "blood moon." To have the last Moon of the period be the Blue Moon throws that cycle out of harmony, so the first Moon keeps its customary name, as does the second and the last. It's the rogue third Moon that is considered to be blue. These deviations in the annual cycle caused problems for Catholicism, too, as their holy calendar was interrupted if this extra Moon happened during their festival of Lent.

Astrological Blue Moons

The third type of Blue Moon is astrological, and this is when there are two Full Moons occurring in one sign of the zodiac. At first this might seem to be complicated, but once you start to work with lunar astrology, you might find that it makes the most sense—particularly if you plant your garden and do other things in sync with the phases and signs of the Moon. These calculations are not based on any man-made calendar; they're established instead by the sun's movement. It is the sun's reflected light that makes the Moon shine full. These Blue Moons only occur every three years or so—quite possibly making them the rarest of the Blue Moons we've discussed.

For those who follow lunar astrology, then this Blue Moon is thought to bring the most intensity. It's believed that the characteristics of that sign of the zodiac will get a "double dose" of the available lunar energy, with the second Moon having more clout than the first one. That goes for mundane tasks such as trimming a hedge to encourage growth, as well as for personal exploration.

Is It Really Blue?

Does the Moon really appear blue during these times? Not usually. The association between the Moon and the color blue seems to have been first recorded by King Henry VIII's advisor, Cardinal Wolsey, who wrote that his enemies would have him believe that

2017 © Allexxandar Image from BigStockPhoto.com

the Moon was the color blue. The phrase is believed to have lost popularity until somewhere around the mid-1800s. It's quite probable that most people at that time didn't really understand what a Blue Moon was, they just knew it to mean something that happened infrequently, and was an exception to the norm.

Sometimes a misty aura will appear around the Moon, but that doesn't mean that it's blue. This is a weather phenomenon, happening when the cirrus clouds are high. Those thin clouds contain ice crystals, and when the frozen particles catch the Moon's light, they shine around it like a halo. Weather lore says that when you see this phenomenon, storms aren't far away—and it's usually right!

Upcoming

The Moon's phases have great influence on the planet. Our oceans ebb and flow because of the pull of the Moon; without it, we'd have less dramatic tides, although they'd still be there due to the Sun's gravitational force. Although the Sun is larger than the

Moon, it's also farther away, so in this instance, the Moon is master of the tidal rhythms. The Moon also controls the Earth's natural wobble. Without the gravity of the Moon, the Earth would be much more unsteady on its axis. This would greatly affect the days and seasons, making their length and temperature completely unpredictable, which would have an impact on the planet's lifeforms. The Moon is more than just a pretty light in the sky.

While folks may disagree on just when a Blue Moon falls, it is accepted that the Moon has four main phases: new, first quarter, full, and last quarter. There are secondary phases halfway between those points, too. These are called waxing crescent, waxing gibbous, full, waning gibbous (or disseminating), and waning crescent (or balsamic). The Moon makes it easy to mark time, for on clear nights the different phases are easily visible to the naked eye.

Full moons are times of gathering together, of things coming to fruition and ideas coming into fulfillment. They are a time of action, when emotions can be fierce, and where enthusiasm can outweigh logic and reason. Intuitive or sensitive people often feel at their most powerful or vulnerable during this Moon phase. Full Moons help us to understand our shadow self, because the light of the Moon brings an awareness and allows us to see what still needs to be done. The Moon doesn't realize that it's blue—it's just going through its orbit and doing its thing; it's the importance that we put onto it that gives it the extra oomph in our lives, ceremonies, and practices.

Whether you choose to honor Blue Moons by calendar, season, or astrological sign is a matter of personal choice. Both January and March of 2018 have calendar Blue Moons on the 31st of each month. There is no Full Moon in February this year. The second Full Moon in January is in a different sign of the zodiac than the first, so it's not an astrological Blue Moon. The second March Full Moon is not in the same season or astrological sign as the others, so it also is just a calendar Blue Moon. The next astrological Blue Moon doesn't occur until May 2019, with the following one being August 2021. As infrequently as they happen, you could say they only come around once in a Blue Moon!

About the Author

Charlie Rainbow Wolf is happiest when she is creating something, especially if it can be made from items that others have cast aside. Pottery, writing, knitting, astrology, and tarot are her deepest interests, but she happily confesses that she's easily distracted, because life offers so many wonderful things to explore. A recorded singer-songwriter and a published author, she is an advocate of organic gardening and cooking and lives in the Midwest with her husband and special-needs Great Danes. www.charlierainbow.com.

2017 © lilkar Image from BigStockPhoto.com

The Moon as Autopilot

by Amy Herring

Stress is a word that has many applications, but the applications tend to center on the idea of pressure. We often say we are stressed out or feeling stressed when the pressure of life's demands threatens to overwhelm us. Not all stress is bad; experienced temporarily, stress can motivate us to accomplish great things or find the strength and endurance we need to see something through. Conversely, chronic stress can take its toll on us physically, mentally, and emotionally, weakening our ability to respond and manage life. Outside of these extreme examples, we all experience stress on a daily basis from sources such as navigating traffic, fending off rude people, hurrying to get somewhere on time, or getting all the errands done before the day is over.

No matter how we handle everyday stress, we all have a breaking point: a level of saturation where we simply can't take any more setbacks, criticisms, failures, or demands. When life becomes overwhelming, something in us says "enough is enough!" We may cry, scream, withdraw, or laugh maniacally, but the energy that builds up from relentless pressure must be released, and it may sometimes happen despite our best intentions to keep it together.

Ideally, we find a way to release that pressure before it reaches critical levels, but we don't always take the opportunity to turn our attention to our behaviors, thoughts, and actions to assess our inner needs. Nevertheless, the symptoms of that pressure in our inner state will show up somehow, and our Moon sign—our heart—can reveal not only how those symptoms manifest but also what's needed to regain our emotional equilibrium.

The Moon and Stress

Your Moon sign is not just about straightforward emotional responses, such as what makes you happy, sad, scared, or mad. Your Moon sign can also reveal your instinctual behaviors, those things you do automatically to comfort or protect yourself. Some of these behaviors and preferences are meant to help you relax at the end of a long day, and some of the symptoms of stress can reveal what happens when you go too long without doing that one thing that you really love.

Our instincts are, well, instinctual—we don't have to think about what we are doing or how we are behaving because it happens automatically. We may not even realize some of our automatic coping behaviors, and if we do, we may not know why we do some of those things except that we know it makes us feel better. Your Moon sign reveals the nature of this inner autopilot behavior and what it's designed to do when you've reached emotional overload.

Like defense mechanisms serve to keep us safe, our inner

autopilot can keep us going, but these automatic systems can also steer us off course if we don't set some parameters. Doing what feels good and instinctual may create additional problems for us if we let instinct take over indefinitely without guidance. Understanding your particular signs of stress overload can help you work mindfully with your natural instinct and get your needs met more efficiently.

Signs of Stress

Aries

Aries has a reputation for having a bad temper, but much of the time this is not because you are an angry person but a direct person who doesn't hide how you feel. Therefore, when you are beginning to feel emotionally overloaded, it will usually be apparent to those around you. Patience is not your strong suit, but when you find yourself snapping at family members or coworkers and everything seems to be an irritant, you are probably close to emotional overload. You may also tend toward careless or reckless behaviors when you are on edge. Suppressing your fiery nature rarely works, so let it rip if you won't be afraid you'll hurt others or yourself, and you'll soon burn off all that pent-up energy.

Taurus

You have a steady heart and even moods overall, so you don't easily get to an emotional breaking point. When you've almost had enough, you will start to dig your heels in, resisting whatever you feel is pushing you. Your autopilot's instinct is to put the brakes on until you can get hold of yourself, so the harder you are pushed, the more you naturally resist. When you reach a level where you are feeling generally uncooperative and stubborn, put yourself in a time out! No one can make you do anything you don't want to when you get into this state, not even you. Allowing yourself to come to a full stop will help your heart take that deep breath it needs to carry on.

Gemini

The first thing to go is your concentration when you reach emotional overload. You may find yourself unfocused, losing your train of thought, or absentmindedly talking in circles. True, sometimes you have just been so busy that you forget to eat and may simply need a snack. But when life pushes you over the edge, you tend to mentally short-circuit. Your inner autopilot may try to analyze the situation and brainstorm solutions, but your hunger for information can be a double-edged sword in cases like this. Seeking out answers to questions can help you to calm down in some cases—information is empowering in that sense. Talking it out can also help burn off the nervous energy. But if information overload is the culprit to begin with, your autopilot may steer you off course. In these cases, change the input. Redirect yourself by busying your hands or mind with something entertaining and

2017 © Kasia Bialasiewicz Image from BigStockPhoto.com

inconsequential. Knitting, a crossword puzzle, or idle conversation can help you calm down without agitating your mental state.

Cancer

You contain a vast inner ocean of emotions, but you are not always keen to wear your heart on your sleeve. When you start to become emotionally overwhelmed, that ocean may start leaking out of your eyeballs! This is a healing instinct, but it can make you feel even more vulnerable if you can't let your guard down. In response to this heightened sense of vulnerability, you may instinctively try to close that Cancer shell and retreat into it like a cocoon, but you'll drown if you don't open it again and bail yourself out. Getting yourself to a place where it feels safe to let it out is key. Your caring nature makes it easier to take care of others' needs, but letting others take care of you, or at least engaging in self-care, will restore your equilibrium.

Leo

Your best defense is a good offense, and for you, that means never letting them see you sweat. You have a great need to maintain your dignity so pride may keep you from admitting when you are feeling overwhelmed or defeated. When you do reach that breaking point, your inner diva may come out. You may find yourself behaving in a demanding or impatient manner with those around you. Your instinct may be to retreat to have a private temper tantrum if you are angry, but if you are sad or just emotionally exhausted, pampering your inner royal can also be just the thing.

Virgo

Virgo is often labeled as too critical, but a general sense of fussiness is usually the first sign that you have had enough. Virgos are great at spotting the problems that need to be fixed, but when everything looks like a problem, your anxious Virgo heart defaults into damage-control mode, and your inner micromanager may come out to take care of business (yours and everyone else's!). You are built to solve problems, so let yourself do it. Putting something in order, getting something cleaned up or taken care of, even if it's just one small task to cross off your list, will help you regain your calm. Virgo is a practical earth sign, so the more straightforward and hands-on the task, the better!

Libra

As the sign of the scales, your heart is very sensitive to tension, and a rise in your inner tension is the first thing you will notice when you start to reach an emotional breaking point. Your tendency toward indecision comes from a desire to be fair-minded, but when you are emotionally overwhelmed, you may feel so hesitant and uncertain about making any move that your indecisive nature goes into overdrive. Your instinct may be to simply retreat into yourself and let others take the lead. You don't like to succumb to emotional outbursts or feeling like you are out of control. Seeking out reassurance from others who you feel will be able to validate your feelings can get you on even ground again.

Scorpio

When you get emotionally overwhelmed, others around you may suffer your classic scorpion sting. Anger and moodiness may start bubbling up as you feel less likely to filter or tame your responses to whatever or whoever is triggering you. Your breaking point can seem more like a point of no return, in some cases, and you may tend to want to break away from whatever or whomever is stepping on your last nerve, permanently. Often times, your best way out is through. Don't burn bridges you may want to cross again later, but do follow your instinct toward catharsis by seeking out intense experiences that can fulfill your need to let the inner phoenix burn.

Sagittarius

Your flexibility allows you to take things as they come and let most things roll off your back, so it can take a lot of pressure in a

2017 © djedzura Image from BigStockPhoto.com

short amount of time for you to reach maximum overload. When you get emotionally overwhelmed, your instinct may be to play it down or shrug it off, not only to fool others but yourself as well—the more "just fine" you try to tell yourself you are, the closer you may be to losing it. Your spontaneity may reveal itself with impulsive and surprising outbursts of anger, but your instinct is often to avoid confrontations altogether and just move on. Your instinct to shrug it off and go out to play is not always the best method for problem-solving or conflict resolution, but it can be a great way to help you settle your mood and bounce back.

Capricorn

Your composure is often the envy of other signs. You keep your cool longer than most, but when you do lose it, it gets colder, not hotter. As a Capricorn Moon, you are not one to avoid your responsibilities, but when they start to seem pointless or unending, your breaking point may cause you to check out, emotionally speaking, yet still keep going through the motions. The cold or robotic stereotype you often get labeled as isn't always a fair assessment of you, but it may be a method you instinctively employ when you've had enough but can't or won't step away. Solitude often gives you a chance to gather your wits and focus on your own goals without the needs of others or the endless demand of your problem-solving capacities weighing on your sense of duty. Follow your instincts to check out when you've hit your limit, but take your mind and body with you!

Aquarius

Your mood shifts can seem abrupt or unexpected, even to you, so you may not easily be aware of your inner emotional state or that anything is wrong until you have already redlined. Testiness, impatience, and general agitation may be the first signs that you're reaching maximum overload. You may find you get especially fervent and stubborn in arguing your point, turning conversations into debates or arguments seemingly unintentionally. Your autopilot may be trying to get you a little more breathing room by pushing everything away—give yourself the room you need.

Pisces

Although tears may not be infrequent in the ups and downs of your life, when you hit your emotional saturation point it may seem like a circuit breaker trips somewhere inside of you and something in you withdraws or shuts down. Escapism can be a necessary defense for you in the moment as too much coming in may simply cripple your ability to deal with whatever is overwhelming you. Down time often does the trick for you, but prolonged escapism will tend to create emotional numbness rather than replenish you.

About the Author

Amy Herring is a graduate of Steven Forrest's Evolutionary Astrology program and has been a professional astrologer for over 20 years. She has written two books on astrology: Astrology of the Moon *and* Essential Astrology. *She especially enjoys teaching and writing about astrology. Visit HeavenlyTruth.com for readings, classes, and educational videos.*

2017 © kegfire Image from BigStockPhoto.com

The Nodes of the Moon

by Dallas Jennifer Cobb

The nodes of the Moon hold deep meaning to our life's purpose and provide insight and understanding of our growth and stagnation points. Astrologically they are indicators of where we need to weed, and feed, in our lives.

Knowing which sign the nodes of the Moon sit in can provide specific information on past life experiences and present life learning goals. We can use this information to guide us in our conscious evolution.

What Is a Lunar Node?

While the Earth circles the Sun, the Moon orbits the Earth. At times the Moon appears to be in front or on top of the Earth, and at times it appears to be behind or under it. The front node is the north node, and the back node is the south node. Technically mathematical points, they sit opposite one another on a chart with a 180-degree separation and describe the relationship of the Moon relative to the Earth and the Sun, at the time of birth.

Astronomically, the north node is ahead of the Earth, charting new territory and leading the way. The south node lies in our wake in the past, territory that has already been explored.

Astrologically, the nodes are associated with spiritual evolution. The south node represents "where we've come from"—our strengths, abilities, skills, and propensities from previous lives. The north node represents "where we need to go"—the cutting edge or learning curve we need to engage in to evolve in this life.

Together, the north and south nodes signify our personal karmic imbalance. Knowledge of natal nodal placement can enable consciousness of life lessons that, when tackled, will eventually cultivate our shift to karmic balance. The nodes represent over-developed and underdeveloped parts of us that we need to consciously weed and feed, respectively, to create balance.

The south node represents areas that tend to be well developed and that we fall back on in times of stress. This is our comfort zone, and includes things we are good at and feel confident doing. But, like our parental home, the south node is a safe place we need to leave in order to grow, learn, and have adventures.

The north node represents what we need to explore in order to evolve, grow, and develop. It's where we're going and what we are growing into. It is our learning curve, what we came to accomplish, and what will help us evolve. If you believe that the meaning of life is to evolve spiritually, then the north node speaks to the meaning or purpose of life. Its sign placement indicates where we need to grow and expand in order to accomplish what we have come here to learn.

It's not necessary to deny our karmic past represented by the south node, but to consciously evolve into the divine intention of the north node placement. When we make choices honoring the north node, we consciously aid our evolution. The north node is our life's mission, and the sooner one consciously chooses to master what is required, the sooner life will become more "higher-purpose-driven."

Alternately, if we rely on our south node skills, abilities, and ways, we'll be mired in the past and fail to evolve. If we see someone has been "stuck" their whole life, it is worthwhile looking at their south node placement. Often they stay stuck because they're choosing to repeat the same lessons from their karmic past over and over again.

Nodal Placement

To determine where the lunar nodes are in a natal chart, use one of the many free online resources, such as Astrodienst, Astro Lab, or CafeAstrology. (Links at end of article.)

Enter birth data (date, time, and location of birth) and a natal chart will be generated, showing the lunar nodes and what signs they sit in. Then consult below for the meaning of each astrological sign pair.

Zodiac Pairs

Because north and south node always sit 180 degrees apart, they can be discussed in pairs. In gardening terms, they identify what to weed out (old energy—south node placement) and what to seed, water, and cultivate so that it may bear fruit (new energy—north node placement).

Aries and Libra

Aries south node—weed out the "me first" attitude and let go of self-centered thinking, aggression, conflict, and oppositional energy. Perhaps you were previously self-reliant, pushy, and hotheaded. Your acquired skills may include independence, self-sufficiency, and the ability to take on conflict. It is time to let these go.

2017 © dolgachov Image from BigStockPhoto.com

Libra north node—cultivate balance and the power of partnerships. Learn to compromise and commit, collaborate, and cooperate. Coming to a win-win agreement benefits everyone. Learn how to ask for help, rely on others, compromise, find balance and cultivate peace.

Libra south node—weed out peacekeeping and continual compromise. In your past life you maintained peace and were gentle, loving, and conciliatory. You have strengths in collaboration and partnership and coming to agreements. You are being asked to let these go. Release the need to put others first and let go of unhealthy relationships and passive-aggressive behavior.

Aries north node—cultivate leadership skills. Learn to stand alone and take care of yourself. Be self-sufficient and cultivate autonomy. Develop your inner warrior and fight for your rights; lead campaigns, resist conformity, and stand on your own two feet and express your anger clearly.

Taurus and Scorpio

Scorpio south node—weed out the need to "use" other people. Let go of manipulation, seduction, and relying on others to support you. Stop using sex to hold power over someone or secrets to manipulate.

Taurus north node—practice being grounded physically. Cultivate habits and routines that support you and enable you to be more fully connected to the people around you. Make your own money, and engage in sex as an honest expression of attraction and care. Be honest, tell it like it is, don't fabricate. Be fully present to who and what is in front of you.

Taurus south node—weed out over-indulgence. Let go of excessive appetites, binge eating or drinking, excessive sweets, and overly fatty foods. Release attachment to luxury items and the idea that you should have something better. Let go of always providing for others.

Scorpio north node—feed your divine self through prayer, meditation, and simple living. Cultivate a connection to the divine and life's mysteries. Welcome gifts and financial support from others, benefit from joint financial ventures, and cultivate sources of passive income.

Gemini and Sagittarius

Sagittarius south node—weed out intellectual superiority, shooting your mouth off without accurate facts, being too theoretical or philosophical, or acting arrogantly. Release close-mindedness, zealotry, and feelings of being better than, and let go of greed, pickiness, and being pompous.

Gemini north node—focus on being present, cultivating mindfulness and awareness, and connection to what's happening around you. Engage deeply with others in partnerships, clubs, teams, and community, and stay deeply focused on one thing at a time. Have reverence for people and listen deeply to them.

Gemini south node—weed out two-faced lying, false pretense, and deception. Avoid gossip, saying mean things, or making up stories. Root out your desire to be more important socially, and fixating on small (insignificant) details. Release busyness and multitasking. Let go of being spread too thin.

Sagittarius north node—cultivate big-picture thinking, lofty ideas, higher education, international allies, and friends from various cultures. Seek to learn new things, and sow the seeds for adventure, travel, and long-distance exploration.

Cancer and Capricorn

Capricorn south node—weed out materialism and status seeking, consumption, consumerism, and defining yourself by your possessions. Let go of competition, social climbing, a hunger for power, and workaholism. Root out sexism and patriarchy. Don't value thoughts over feelings, or head over heart.

Cancer north node—nurture your emotional self and relationships, soften and develop compassion, self-care, self-esteem, and

2017 © Rido81 Image from BigStockPhoto.com

deep love for others. Connect emotionally with people and let your heart rule, and allow yourself to express care through gentle nurturing and compassionate acts. Create a safe home environment that nurtures your need for safety and belonging.

Cancer south node—weed out a fear of abandonment, let go of being overly emotional, and release meekness. Release the need to hide in relationships and resist being overly feminine.

Capricorn north node—cultivate your public life, be strong, dynamic and forceful, and speak with authority. Grow your leadership and professional skills to excel in the business realm, and learn to manage others, empowering them to succeed under your leadership. Cultivate the masculine traits of public confidence and strong self image.

Leo and Aquarius

Aquarius south node—weed out trying to make people like you. Let go of hiding your feelings. Release being rootless, unattached, and alone. Release your lack of emotion.

Leo north node—cultivate creativity and shining public performances. Collaborate and bring great things to light. Grow your ability to follow your heart, treat yourself and others to good things, and display your affection openly. Treat yourself well, and develop deep and abiding self-esteem.

Leo south node—let go of making everything all about you. Stop performing to win approval. Release your focus on external approval and attention seeking. Give up needing to be at the center of everything, so let go of drama and taking everything personally. Release your need to control people, and stop overreacting.

Aquarius north node—seek out opportunities to collaborate and develop a deep sense of community with other individualistic people. Find ways to live sustainably, detached from drama, chaos, and manipulation, and become very practical and rational in your approach to living.

Virgo and Pisces

Pisces south node—release your need to be a victim. Let go of self-pity and making excuses, and stop allowing others to bully you. You have made too many sacrifices and now you can let go of denial and deception.

Virgo north node—embrace fact finding, data, and research. Let results guide your decisions. Seed routines and rituals to accomplish the tasks of daily living easily, and use structures to support your creative output. Being personally responsible enables you to set clear boundaries, stand up for yourself, and get lots done.

Virgo south node—let go of the need to control everything. Let go of rote, monotonous routine, and the need to be perfect. No one is. Release the need to self-medicate or escape reality through drug or alcohol use. Release your reliance on facts and data. Stop asking for proof.

Pisces north node—trust your instincts, use your imagination and intuition, and believe in the divine. Develop your psychic powers, your relationship with a higher power, and connect to the wide-reaching divine energy. Cultivate the ability to process your emotions, using therapy and creativity to heal yourself and recover from addiction.

Armed now with the knowledge of the nodes of the Moon, consciously tend to your garden, carefully weeding and feeding.

Resources:

Astrodienst: *http://www.astro.com.*
Astrolabe: *https://alabe.com/freechart/.*
Cafe Astrology: *http://astro.cafeastrology.com/natal.php.*

About the Author

Dallas Jennifer Cobb practices gratitude magic, giving thanks for personal happiness, health, and prosperity; meaningful, flexible, and rewarding work; and a deliciously joyful life. She is accomplishing her deepest desires. She lives in paradise with her daughter, in a waterfront village in rural Ontario, where she regularly swims and runs, chanting, "Thank you, thank you, thank you." Contact her at jennifer.cobb@live.com or visit www.magicalliving.ca.

Weekly Tips Provided by:

Penny Kelly *is a writer, teacher, author, publisher, consultant, and naturopathic physician. After purchasing Lily Hill Farm in southwest Michigan in 1987, she raised grapes for Welch Foods for a dozen years and established Lily Hill Learning Center, where she teaches courses in Developing Intuition and the Gift of Consciousness, Getting Well Again Naturally, and Organic Gardening. She is the mother of four children, has cowritten or edited twenty-three books with others, and has written seven books of her own. Penny lives, gardens, and writes in Lawton, Michigan.*

Robin Ivy Payton *teaches yoga and meditation in the Portland, Maine area and beyond. She blends astrology and yoga with RoZoYo®, tuning the subtle and physical body with the energy of Moon, Sun and planets. Robin offers horoscopes, yoga, and other insights across various media. She began writing for Llewellyn Publications in 2003.Follow her schedule of events and weekly astrology forecasts at Robin's Zodiac Zone blog, facebook, instagram and www.RoZoYo.com.*

Charlie Rainbow Wolf *is happiest when she is creating something, especially if it can be made from items that others have cast aside. Pottery, writing, knitting, astrology, and tarot are her deepest interests, but she happily confesses that she's easily distracted, because life offers so many wonderful things to explore. She is an advocate of organic gardening and cooking, and she lives in the Midwest with her husband and special-needs Great Danes. Follow her at www.charlierainbow.com.*

Mireille Blacke, MA, RD, CD-N, *is a registered dietitian, certified dietitian-nutritionist, and addiction specialist residing in Connecticut. Mireille worked in rock radio for over two decades before shifting her career focus to psychology, nutrition, and addiction counseling. She has been published in Llewellyn's 2016 Moon Sign Book, Today's Dietitian, and OKRA Magazine. Follow Mireille on Twitter @RockGumboRD and read her irreverent blog posts at rockgumbo. blogspot.com and radiowitch.com.*

GET MORE AT LLEWELLYN.COM

Visit us online to browse hundreds of our books and decks, plus sign up to receive our e-newsletters and exclusive online offers.

- • Free tarot readings • Spell-a-Day • Moon phases
- • Recipes, spells, and tips • Blogs • Encyclopedia
- • Author interviews, articles, and upcoming events

GET SOCIAL WITH LLEWELLYN

 Find us on
Facebook

Follow us on

www.Facebook.com/LlewellynBooks

www.Twitter.com/Llewellynbooks

GET BOOKS AT LLEWELLYN

LLEWELLYN ORDERING INFORMATION

 Order online: Visit our website at www.llewellyn.com to select your books and place an order on our secure server.

 Order by phone:
- • Call toll free within the U.S. at 1-877-NEW-WRLD (1-877-639-9753)
- • Call toll free within Canada at 1-866-NEW-WRLD (1-866-639-9753)
- • We accept VISA, MasterCard, American Express, and Discover

Order by mail:
Send the full price of your order (MN residents add 6.875% sales tax) in U.S. funds, plus postage and handling to: Llewellyn Worldwide, 2143 Wooddale Drive, Woodbury, MN 55125-2989

POSTAGE AND HANDLING:

STANDARD: (U.S. & Canada)
(Please allow 12 business days)
$30.00 and under, add $4.00.
$30.01 and over, FREE SHIPPING.

INTERNATIONAL ORDERS:
$16.00 for one book, plus $3.00 for each additional book.

Visit us online for more shipping options. Prices subject to change.

FREE CATALOG!

To order, call
1-877-
NEW-WRLD
ext. 8236
or visit our
website

New for 2018!

Llewellyn's 2018 Moon Sign Datebook

Weekly Planning by the Cycles of the Moon

New for 2018, *Llewellyn's 2018 Moon Sign Datebook* is a perfect companion to the bestselling *Moon Sign Book*. This weekly planner features Full-Moon lore, tips for gardening by the Moon, Mercury retrogrades, void-of-course, equinoxes, and solstices—everything you need to plan a successful future.

The *Datebook* has been designed to be used in conjunction with *Llewellyn's Moon Sign Book*, so combining the strengths of these books increases the practical effectiveness of each. With this planner, you will be able to determine the best day for an appointment or special event, and you will be able to make a note of it in the book. Plan your important gardening, career, and personal milestones far in advance or even within days or weeks for optimal outcomes using the power of the Moon.

978-0-7387-5259-4, 192 pp., 5¼ x 8 $12.99

To order, call 1-877-NEW-WRLD
Prices subject to change without notice
Order at Llewellyn.com 24 hours a day, 7 days a week

Notes